Table of Contents

Top 20 Test Taking Tips

1. Carefully follow all the test registration procedures.
2. Know the test directions, duration, topics, question types, how many questions.
3. Setup a flexible study schedule at least 3-4 weeks before test day.
4. Study during the time of day you are most alert, relaxed, and stress free.
5. Maximize your learning style; visual learner use visual study aids, auditory learner use auditory study aids.
6. Focus on your weakest knowledge base.
7. Find a study partner to review with and help clarify questions.
8. Practice, practice, practice!
9. Get a good night's sleep; don't try to cram the night before the test.
10. Eat a well-balanced meal.
11. Know the exact physical location of the testing site; drive the route to the site prior to test day.
12. Bring a set of earplugs; the testing center could be noisy.
13. Wear comfortable, loose fitting, layered clothing to the testing center; prepare for it to be either cold or hot during the test.
14. Bring at least 2 current forms of ID to the testing center.
15. Arrive to the test early; be prepared to wait and be patient.
16. Eliminate the obviously wrong answer choices, and then guess the first remaining choice.
17. Pace yourself; don't rush, but keep working and move on if you get stuck.
18. Maintain a positive attitude even if the test is going poorly.
19. Keep your first answer unless you are positive it is wrong.
20. Check your work, don't make a careless mistake.

Counseling and Guidance

Concerns addressed in counseling

Through addressing such issues as relationship issues, anger or stress management, family dynamics, sexual topics and academic goals, the counselor acts as a guide and mentor for students in their academic and personal lives, as well as in the process of choosing a career. Since students may be referred by school officials, family members or other students, the counselor should anticipate varying levels of openness by the student and/or the family. It is vitally important for counselors to be trained in the strategies and techniques necessary to recognize and address issues in a manner that will capitalize on the counseling session to the maximum benefit of the student. The first step in this process is recognition of the key issue or issues, which may take more than one session to determine. Beyond that, counselors can use various strategies focusing on the particular situation as well as the individualities of the student.

Techniques and Interventions

Human development

Childhood development
Infancy is typically considered to extend from birth until the age of 2. During this period, the individual develops social attachments, basic motor skills, and an idea of cause and effect. Toddlerhood is thought to extend from age 2 until age 4, and is marked by the development of language, the exploration of life through fantasy and play, and an improvement in self-control. Between the ages of 5 and 12, sometimes called early and middle school age, the individual learns the value of cooperation, basic morals, gender roles, and some basic skills. This is also the period in which individuals typically are able to begin honestly appraising themselves and considering their place in the world.

Piaget
According to Piaget, students in early childhood the years between 2 and 6 spanning preschool to kindergarten generally are incapable of grasping abstract concepts such as those dealing with time and space. They are developing motor skills, usually through play, as well as language skills and the ability to imitate events. These skills will grow and develop during these years, which will be reflected in their use of language, increased motor skills, and the appearance of more concreteness in their drawings. During this time, they are egocentric; however, they are also developing social skills relating to their peers as well as the ability to regulate some of their own emotional responses. Counselors will be well served to use a child's imaginative skills in the session, as well as some of the theoretical concepts of childhood experts such as Piaget.

Jean Piaget noted four stages of cognitive development in children. Sensorimotor stage is the period from birth until approximately age 2, during which the infant develops his or her sense organs and learns that objects still exist even when they are out of the visual field. The preoperational stage typically lasts from age 2 to age 7 and is marked by the child's increasing ability to imagine the mental lives of others: in other words, to develop sympathy. The concrete operational stage generally lasts from age 7 until age 12, as the child develops a number of cognitive structures, including the rule of conservation (the understanding that an object's volume does not decrease if its shape is changed). The final stage is known as the formal operational stage and takes place after age 12. In this stage, which not every human goes through, the capacity for abstract thought (the ability to theorize rather than to rely on direct observation for knowledge) is developed.

Erik Erikson
In this theoretical paradigm, these key years

of development are defined by a series of crises, resulting in positive or maladaptive behaviors. Each developmental stage is preceded by a crisis that ideally is resolved through positive development of skills and behaviors. For instance, ego development may be prompted by the crisis of self-promotion being perceived as counter to obligation to others, i.e. the drive to grow and develop being possibly tempered by a sense of guilt. Refining the balance between these two directives, incorporating self-worth, imagination and sometimes gender, contributes to the child's self-discovery. Counselors should encourage students to explore positive behaviors or actions that may be out of the student's normal realm, toward development of new skills. Further, increase in language and motor skills tends to encourage this action toward self-promotion and self-discovery. Opportunities for developing these skills are beneficial in the counseling setting.

<u>Play-time setting</u>
For the child between the years of 2 and 6, play is an integral part of their development. Children often express emotions, describe events, and project their desires in a play setting. In the counseling session, a good strategy is for the counselor to interact with the child in play-time settings, using such manipulatives as dolls, other toys, puppets, art projects, or other favorites. The play-time setting can be a wonderful opportunity for children to explore not only their environment, but also their own capabilities and skills. The counseling session will be best served if the child is allowed sufficient and reasonable latitude for exploring the boundaries of self-discovery, self-confidence and emotional self-regulation. The play setting provides an environmental medium for developing and regulating skills and behaviors. Counselors can provide such media as dolls, animals, art supplies and animals through which children can express and explore their self-discovery.

Middle childhood

<u>Development</u>
Middle childhood, generally associated with the ages between 7 and 11, is most easily distinguished by the ability to think logically, increased literacy skills, and the ability to mentally reverse actions. While they are still unable to grasp many abstract ideas, students in this age group are nonetheless increasingly able to manipulate concrete information. They are able to generalize about their actions or their environment based on this information. The development of logical thinking allows children in this age group to interact more cooperatively, partly because they are more able to recognize intentionality and are becoming less egocentric. Counselors working with this age group can use such strategies as exploration, manipulation of information, and action. Sessions are best served if the counselor remains aware that students in this age group are generally able to reason logically, based on concrete information, often called the concrete operational stage.

<u>Positive feedback</u>
Middle childhood is distinguished by a developing, and often fragile sense of competency. This sense of competency is particularly dependent on external feedback, from friends, family and authority figures. A sense of competency is also encouraged by the student's own success in accomplishing increasingly challenging tasks, or conversely discouraged by failure. Counselors working with this age group need to be sensitive to this fragility, and respond by providing tasks that are manageable and more likely to be successful for the student. Positive, encouraging feedback is also very valuable to students in this age group. Both positive feedback and opportunities for success provide valuable buffers against the development of feelings of inadequacy in students in middle childhood, including self-fulfilling behaviors that validate a sense of incompetence and failure.

Peer relationships

During this time of competency development, peer interaction is particularly important for the student in middle childhood, for a number of reasons. Not only is peer feedback important, but also peer interaction provides an opportunity for students to observe the same fragility and balance of successes and failures that they experience, thus validating and endorsing their own vicissitudes of self-confidence. Likewise, students in this age group develop a sense of understanding and tolerance for differing appearances and behaviors through healthy peer interaction. A counselor can provide opportunities for peer interaction by holding group counseling sessions, as well as encouraging healthy friendships for students in this age group. Often, friendships are formed that become significant, such as that of a best friend. These friendships can be pivotal to the development of a student's sense of self-competency and significance among their peers.

Adolescence and early adulthood

Adolescence is generally thought to extend between the ages of 13 and 22. During this period, individuals undergo a rapid physical maturation. They will typically begin to have sexual relationships, will seek to develop a personal identity, and may emphasize a peer group more than the family. During this period, individuals should begin to consider possible careers, and should be establishing an internal set of moral values. Early adulthood is thought to extend from age 23 to 30, and to involve a movement towards marriage or longer-lasting romantic relationships. Early adulthood often is focused on the establishment of a career, though individuals will often have children of their own during this period.

Characteristics

Adolescence is a time of breakthrough transition between childhood and adulthood, and is generally divided into three sub-stages. Although the stages are very individualized, the years between the ages of 11 and 14 usually frame adolescence, between 15 and 18 middle adolescence, and 18 and above late adolescence. The accomplishments realized during these three stages affect physical appearance, social interaction, and thinking processes. Physical changes are those defined as puberty, resulting in physical maturation. Students in this age group develop a more comprehensive understanding of social roles and relationships. Further, thinking processes evolve from concrete to formal, resulting in an increased ability for abstract thinking. Counselors working with this age group need to be mindful of both the stage at which a student is operating and the next phase of development, and provide opportunities for that development.

Therapeutic strategies

Adolescent students are increasingly able to apply abstract thinking to possible solutions and scenarios of situations. Counselors working with this age group can take advantage of this abstract thinking by soliciting the student's collaboration in generating and implementing solutions to dilemmas or problems. The beginning of this process can be asking a student to view a situation differently, allowing for a larger spectrum of options for its solution. These students are able also to participate in reflective thinking, allowing for ownership and responsibility for actions. Students in this age period are also increasingly egocentric, and less dependent on external feedback, sometimes resulting in reckless behavior. They are also more self-conscious, particularly with students of their age group. Counselors are best served by facilitating the student's ability to balance these feelings with increased social awareness and abstract thinking skills. Counselors can also provide students in this age group with opportunities for development and implementation of alternate approaches to problem solution.

Puberty

The onset and evolvement of puberty complements and often perpetuates role confusion for the adolescent student.

Adolescence is a pivotal time in which students refine self-concepts of worth, value in the larger society, and life goals. This self-definition is often validated by peer interaction. The counselor should work with students in this age group by encouraging them to develop goals and values of their own, not necessarily those of their peer group. Counselors can assist students in developing their own sense of identity and worth, separate from social cliques or idolized hero symbols. Students in this age group begin to understand that their actions and beliefs form an integral part of their role and their value system. Counselors can positively facilitate this connection when working with adolescents. It is important that counselors endorse the idea of worth and significance of every individual.

Counseling
Counseling approaches and intervention strategies need to all be determined and assessed within the context of developmental theory. In other words, counselors should be trained in and cognizant of the different stages of development in adolescents, including the appropriate behaviors for a particular age group. Counselors may dismiss behaviors that would be unacceptable for an adult, but perfectly normal for a child in a particular age group. Conversely, if a child is exhibiting behavior that is not typical of his/her age group, this may be a symptom or behavior that needs to be addressed in the counseling session. Further, counselors developing intervention strategies should be mindful of the range of reasonable expectations within an age group. It is important that counselors enter each session with an understanding of the age group of the student, referring to outside resources for that information if necessary.

Middle and later adulthood

Middle adulthood is generally though to extend from about the age 31 until the age of 50. During this period, individuals are usually occupied with the maintenance of their household, and the rearing of children. Many individuals will also devote a great deal of their middle adulthood to advancing their professional interests. Later adulthood begins at 51 and last until death. It is inaccurate to suggest that all personal growth has been accomplished by this point. On the contrary, most individuals in later adulthood will gradually accept the events of their life, will develop a healthy perspective on life and death, and will begin to redirect their personal energies to new roles and responsibilities.

Gender
At the onset of puberty, the pituitary gland begins to release the hormones that further differentiate between the sexes. Specifically, the pituitary gland releases gonadotropins, which stimulate the gonads to generate the appropriate sex hormones. As these gonadotropins do their work, the secondary sex characteristics are developed. In females, larger amounts of estrogen cause the breasts to enlarge, the hips to widen, and for fat to be deposited on the hips and buttocks. It also causes her external genitals to enlarge, and initiates the processes of ovulation and menstruation. For males, large amounts of testosterone cause the voice to deepen, the penis to become thicker and longer, muscles to grow stronger, and hair to develop in new places.

It is well documented by science that men and women not only have differences in appearance, but actually think and sense in different ways. In most cases, women have stronger senses of hearing, smell, and taste, while men tend to have better vision. Males tend to be stronger, though females often have better fine motor skills. Brain scans have displayed significant differences in the areas of the brain that are more active in males and females. Of course, there is no telling whether these differences are entirely physiological, or whether upbringing and environment contribute. Most scientists believe that a combination of nature and nurture create the differences between the sexes.

There are only a few basic physiological differences between males and females. Males have the ability to make sperm and to contribute the y-chromosome that enables a female to give birth to a male. Only females are born with sex cells, menstruate, give birth, and are capable of breast-feeding. In the embryonic stage, males and females have similar sex organs. After a few weeks of development, though, the gonads differentiate into either testes or ovaries. This differentiation depends on the genetic instructions given by the sex chromosomes. If a y-chromosome is present in the embryo, it will develop into a male; if there is no y-chromosome, the embryo will develop as a female. All future differentiation will be motivated by the gonads, not the chromosomes.

Puberty and hormones

Hormones are the chemicals that motivate the body to do certain things. They are produced in the organs that make up the endocrine system. With the exception of the sex organs, males and females have identical endocrine systems. The actions of the hormones are determined by the hypothalamus, an area of the brain about the size of a pea. The hypothalamus sends messages to the pituitary gland, which is directly beneath it. The pituitary gland turns on and off the various glands that produce hormones. Hormones, once released, are carried to their targets by the blood stream, at which point they motivate cells and organs to action. Hormones can influence the way a person looks, feels, behaves, or matures.

The sex hormones that are most important to women are called estrogen and progesterone and are produced in the ovaries. In males, the primary sex hormone is testosterone, which is produced by the adrenal glands and testes. Both men and women do, however, have small amounts of the opposite hormone. Indeed, men need estrogen to have effective sperm. Sex hormones are at work very early in the development of the embryo. When testes are formed, they begin releasing testosterone, which causes the formation of the other male reproductive parts, like the penis. If no testosterone is present, the embryo will develop female genitals. This is true of both natural females and males with malfunctioning testes.

It seems odd and even perverse to refer to sexuality in childhood, but many of the foundations for later sexual experience are laid in the early years of an individual's life. For infants, the mouth is the main area for sensual pleasure. By the age of 3 or 4, most children become interested in the differences between males and females, and may start to develop vaguely romantic feelings towards another person. It is very important for parents to discuss these topics with their children, so that the children will have a framework of understanding for these complex and often confusing emotions. Children are likely to have lots of questions, some of them perhaps uncomfortable; parents should do their best to answer honestly and with a minimum of embarrassment.

As boys and girls enter adolescence, their interest in sex typically intensifies and seeks expression. This makes it essential that health providers give adolescents the necessary knowledge and skills to enter this time in their lives. For teenage boys, it is typical to experience frequent erections, and to begin having nocturnal emissions, or wet dreams. Masturbation is the most common form of sexual expression for adolescents, especially males. Adolescents may also experiment with kissing and petting, oral sex, and even sexual intercourse. At this point, as many as a quarter of all people will experience a same-sex attraction, though this does not predict any future homosexuality. Though American teens are not known to be any more sexually active than teens elsewhere in the world, they do have a higher rate of pregnancy, indicating that adequate birth control information and supplies are not being provided.

Decision making

Part of the job of a counselor is equipping students with the skills they will need to lead healthy, safe sexual lives. The first thing they must have in order to make good decisions is accurate and comprehensive information on the subject. Health textbooks are a good place to start, but students should also be directed to whatever books and authorities are qualified to give them well-researched and thoughtful information. Students should be especially well informed about birth control, pregnancy, and sexually transmitted diseases before they have any sexual contact. Part of keeping students informed is making sure that they feel comfortable asking questions and discussing their feelings. This can be with a teacher, parent, or other community leader.

Abstinence
Abstinence can either mean totally refraining from sexual intercourse, or refraining from exchanging bodily fluids altogether. Those who make a point of remaining abstinent throughout their lives are said to be celibate. Abstinence is the only way to avoid the risks of sexual activity, and so many high school students have begun making the commitment to refrain from sex until they are older or in a more committed relationship. Before deciding to engage in sexual activity, students should ask themselves whether it would be in line with their values and moral beliefs. Many people will rush into sex without fully considering the physical, mental, and emotional consequences.

Sexual attraction
Sexual attraction is just one of the many factors that contribute to the formation and maintenance of long-term relationships. In most studies, individuals are found to be most sexually attracted to people who share their age, race, ethnicity, and socioeconomic background. Many sociologists speculate that this is because individuals have more access to people that are similar to themselves, and because they intuitively understand that they are more likely to be approved by similar people. In general, men put more emphasis on looks in determining sexual partners, whereas women may value other qualities like dependability and affluence. This may be due in part to the historical need for men to find women who can reproduce easily, while women have sought a man who can provide for them during their period of pregnancy and child rearing.

Dating

Though the word dating has come to assume a romantic connotation in American society, dating is any time that is set aside to spend exclusively with another person. Friends are dating if they make a point to see one another. Unfortunately, the tendency to confuse dating with casual sex and drinking has led to a decrease in the amount of casual dating in the United States. Many people assume that dating is strictly for finding a mate, whereas dating has a host of other benefits, from teaching one to make good conversation to introducing them to various kinds of people and ways of life. Dating, in its ideal form, is a great way to explore oneself by getting to know a wide variety of people.

Mature love relationships
Scientists have marked a difference between passionate love, in which the partners are sexually charged and ecstatic, and companionate love, in which partners are friendly and deeply affectionate. In many cases, relationships that begin with passionate love eventually evolve into companionate love. On the other hand, everyone has experienced or heard of cases in which a long-term friendship suddenly becomes a passionate affair. A healthy and mature love is one in which each partner breaks down the barriers between themselves and the other, while retaining their individuality. Mature partners respect one another's differences, are not threatened by each other's independence, and constantly communicate with one another.

Breakups

Although people traditionally assume that being abandoned by a romantic partner is worse than leaving a partner, many studies have discovered that the partner who ends a relationship is often more subject to psychological traumas like guilt, uncertainty, and awkwardness. The only real help for the pain of a breakup is time, but the process can be eased if both parties treat one another with respect and kindness. During a breakup, it is important to remind oneself of one's own value as an individual, and not to take the other person's decision as a definitive statement about oneself. It is also important to remain engaged with other people despite any feelings of fear you may experience; it is easy to allow feelings of insecurity caused by a breakup to contaminate all the other relationships in your life.

Marriage

Despite claims that the institution of marriage is eroding in recent years, over 90% of Americans will marry in their lifetime. In the past, marriage was as much a business deal as a romantic union; parents often arranged the marriages of their children to advance in society. Though this is still common in some countries, in the United States people are more likely to wed because of a romantic affection for one another. People are increasingly likely to marry someone with whom they share a background and have similar values. Even today, many couples marry because the woman is pregnant, or as a way to escape the authority of their parents. Typically, males are slightly older than females at the age of marriage.

For the most part, people marry someone from the same geographical area and culture as themselves. However, interracial and intercultural marriages are becoming more common and socially accepted. Most studies have revealed that individuals desire a partner with whom they share values and can communicate effectively, and for whom they are willing to make adjustments and tolerate

flaws. Many couples undergo premarital assessments to determine if they are truly right for one another. These assessments typically try to measure how compatible the interests, values, and behavior of the two people are. In any case, most couples benefit from some form of counseling before marriage.

According to sociologists, there are two kinds of marriages: traditional and companion-oriented. In a traditional marriage, the two people conform to the prescribed marital roles of their society; for instance, the man becomes the provider and the woman the child rearer. In a companion-oriented marriage, the partnership and the rewards of romantic love are more important than the marital roles. Some sociologists add to this distinction different categories for romantic marriages, in which the sexual passion that originally sparked the union remains present for an abnormally long time, and rescue marriages, in which one partner sees marriage as a way to escape some traumatic event in his or her past.

However ideal the beginning of a marriage may be, eventually there will be some conflict. One of the major causes of marital discord is the harboring of unrealistic expectation by one or more of the parties. Sometimes, people assume that their partner will always be just the same, physically and mentally, as they were during the period of courtship. Sometimes they assume that to be truly meant for one another, they should always automatically agree on every subject. Of course, both of these assumptions are dangerous for a relationship. In a truly healthy relationship, both parties have room to grow and change without alienating the other, and both feel empowered to speak their minds and to disagree without endangering the union.

Many marriages or committed relationships go askew because the individuals disagree about money. Interestingly, fights about money are rarely about how much money the

- 11 -

couple has; instead, couples tend to fight about how the money will be spent, and who will keep track of their collective finances. Another subject about which partners often fight is sex. As a relationship matures, one party may lose interest in sex, to the consternation of the other. Marries couples often fight if one party feels they always initiate sex, or if one party feels hurt by the other's indifference. The sex life of a couple will likely change many times throughout the course of a long relationship; the best way to ensure mutual satisfaction is to always be compassionate and communicative.

Extra-marital affairs are about the most devastating thing that can happen to a marriage. If one partner is discovered to be cheating, the other partner is likely to feel abandoned, inadequate, unloved, and angry. When extra-marital affairs are a problem, the parties need to ask themselves whether they really love one another and feel any commitment. In a different sort of way, marriages in which both members work can be difficult. It may be necessary for one party to move for work, or for one to stay home and raise children. When one person's career seems to be more important than the other's, conflicts can often develop. In order to avoid the problems caused by dual-career marriages, individuals should understand their partner's ambitions before deciding whether that person is right for them.
Special situations

Children of divorce
In the event that a divorce becomes necessary, there are a few things that parents can do to minimize the damage to their children. First, even though it may be tempting, it is inappropriate to indulge children because you feel sorry for them. Spoiling a child so that he will prefer you is not good for the child. It is important to be honest with your children, but without divulging any unnecessarily painful information. Parents should never fight in front of their children. Parents undergoing a divorce should make sure their children

know that it is all right for them to love both parents, and that they do not have to choose sides. If parents spend quality time with their kids, and constantly reaffirm their love, their transition through divorce can be eased.

One-parent families and blended families
More and more families are composed of children and one parent. Though one-parent families are stereotyped as poor and uneducated, many are headed by wealthy and highly educated professionals. Studies have shown that single parents typically spend about as much time with their children as do parents in a two-parent family. Some of these single parents will eventually remarry, creating what is known as a blended family. Extensive studies have been performed on these complicated and often problematic relationships. One recommendation that many doctors make is that children from single parent or blended families spend time with members of the extended family or community, so that they can acquire other models for behavior.

Dating violence
The definition and parameters of dating violence vary between studies. However, the overall incidences of dating violence have been steadily increasing in recent years. The figures of violence occurring in a dating environ range from a few incidences to a significant portion of the student body. As indicated by the term dating violence, the general parameters define an individual victimizing another individual in a dating environment. This can occur with middle school, high school or college students. Most of the victims are women. The impact of this dating violence is felt at the individual level, often throughout the students' school, family and community network. The victim often is left with feelings of helplessness, which can expand into depression, substance abuse, and risky sexual behavior. Counselors need to be aware of the possibility of dating violence in a student who is presenting at-risk behavior.

Sexual violence

Although sexual violence must ultimately be blamed on the offending individual, there are a few social factors that contribute to its prevalence. First, there is an unhealthy tendency for individuals to accept male aggression as natural, and to suggest that women should be receptive to all male advances. It is also a myth that the male sex drive is somehow unstoppable. Too often, our society seems to blame the victims of violence as if they had somehow provoked others to act out against them. Similarly, many aggressive tendencies of feelings are condoned if they are part of a "joke" or "prank." This only serves to trivialize behavior that can be very painful to the victim. Finally, the prevalence of media in which sexual violence is condoned or even glorified sends the wrong message to would-be offenders.

Learning theories

Behaviorism

The theory of behaviorism states that if a new behavior pattern is repeated so many times it will become automatic. This theory is associated with the Russian physiologist, Pavlov. He performed an experiment on a dog. The dog would salivate when it saw food, so Pavlov would ring the bell seconds before he showed the dog his food; therefore, he trained the dog to salivate after hearing the ringing of the bell. Another famous psychologist associated with this theory is an American, John B. Watson. He performed an experiment on a young boy named Albert. Albert was initially not afraid of a white rat, but when the rat was shown to Albert along with a loud noise, he soon became afraid of the rat. Skinner is also associated with behaviorism except he studied operant behavior. According to his studies, the learner behaves a certain way according to the environment.

Cognitivism

This theory states that learning involves using certain information that has been stored in the brain. One of the most famous psychologists associated with this theory is Jean Piaget. A key concept of the cognitive theory is schema, existing internal knowledge that has been stored in the brain and compared to new knowledge. There is also the three-stage information processing model, which means information is inputted through a sensory register, then is made into short-term memory and last is made into long-term memory and used for storage and retrieval. Other key concepts are a meaningful effect, which means information that has meaning is easier to remember and learn. Serial position effects mean that a person can remember items on a list if they start from the beginning or end. Some other effects that are associated with this theory are; practice, transfer, interference, organization, levels of processing, state dependent, mnemonic, schema, and advance organizers.

Constructivism

The theory of constructivism states that a person develops their own knowledge based on their experiences. This theory states that each learner is unique because every learner comes from a different background and experiences. Social constructivism encourages the unique traits in each individual learner. The learner should become involved in the learning process; therefore, the responsibility of learning does not solely rest on the instructor. The learner will take and active role rather than be passive. This theory also states that the learning environment should be set up in order to challenge the learner to their full potential. The instructor's role is not to just give the information and answers according to a curriculum, but rather to encourage the learner the find conclusions and answers on their own. The goal for the instructor is to help the learners become effective thinkers and challenge themselves.

Motivation

Behavioral views

There many behavioral learning theorists that have created techniques of behavior modification based on the idea that students are motivated to complete an assignment because they have been promised a reward. This reward can be praise, a grade, a ticket that can be traded in for something else or it can be a privilege of selecting an activity of their choice. There are also operant conditioning interpretations that explain why some students like a certain subject while others have a strong dislike for it. For example, math, some students love it and others hate it. The students have love math, may have been brought up to love it. Their past experiences may have shaped them this way because they have all been positive. On the other hand, the students who hate math may have had negative experiences.

Cognitive views

Cognitive theorists believe people are motivated because their behavior is influenced by the way some think about themselves and the environment around them. This view of motivation is heavily influenced by Jean Piaget who developed the principles of equilibration, assimilation, accommodation and schema formation. He stated that children naturally want equilibrium, which means a sense of organization and balance in their world. The cognitive theorists also believe that motivation comes from one's expectations for successfully completing a task. John Atkinson proposed that motivation could also come from a person's desire for achievement. Some are high-need achievers and will seek out more challenging tasks, while others are low-need and will avoid challenging tasks. Those who avoid them do so because they have a fear of failure and that alone outweighs the expectation of success. William Glasser stated that for someone to be motivated to achieve success, he or she must first experience success in some part of his or her lives.

Humanistic view

The humanistic view of motivation is heavily influenced by Abraham Maslow, most famous for Maslow's five-level hierarchy of needs. He proposed that everyone has five levels of needs and each level needs to be fulfilled first before moving on the next level. The bottom level is physiological needs, needs people need to survive, food, water, air and shelter. If this level is satisfied then people will be motivated to meet the needs of the next level, which is safety. After this level comes belongingness and love, and after this level is esteem. These first four levels motivate people to act only when they are unmet to a certain point. The highest and last level is self-actualization, which is also called a growth need. Self-actualization is often referred to as a need for self-fulfillment. People come to this level because they have desire to fulfill their potential and capabilities.

Group counseling

Benefits of group counseling

Adolescents, as a rule, tend to learn better and respond more when interacting with peers. Therefore, group counseling that augments individual counseling can be beneficial for several reasons. In group counseling, students have the opportunity to both experience and contribute support for positive behaviors. Likewise, group counseling provides immediate feedback for negative behaviors and thought patterns, allowing the student to reflect on his or her choices. The format of a group counseling session can also serve as a microcosm of larger society, providing a venue for students to experiment with behaviors in a controlled environment, and to experience the feedback of peers with whom they have developed a trust relationship.

The group counseling, in tandem with the more remedial individual counseling, provides a comprehensive therapeutic environment for the student. Counselors who utilize both formats reap the benefits of opportunities for preventative therapy, as well as a richer school counseling program.

Types of group counseling
Group counseling sessions are generally categorized by their focus and purpose. Task groups focus on an activity, bringing the members together for a common purpose or activity. Some typical tasks for this kind of group may include peer assistance groups, crisis response teams, etc. Other students who need to focus more on specific issues related to life management may be better served in either a psycho-educational group or a counseling group, both of which usually take place in a classroom setting. Some of the issues to be addressed can include skill development, major life changes, or working on personal values. More severely affected students will likely be in a psychotherapy group, which addresses chronic or severe issues of maladjustment. These sessions generally take place in the setting of a mental health institution rather than a school.

To appreciate the distinctions between psycho-educational and counseling groups, it is a good idea to first identify the similarities. Either group can function to address life management issues such as loss, stress issues, academic success, etc. Either group can be categorized into developmental, remedial or school environments. Where they differ lies in the focus within the groups and group sessions. Counseling groups tend to address matters of managing crisis in their focus areas, targeting issues of process more so than specific content issues. Psycho-educational groups, conversely, apply a more concentrated focus on particular content. Counseling groups tend to be less structured than psycho-educational groups. The effect and impact on students of the two groups is often perceived as distinctively different, although counselors tend to view them as similar in format and purpose.

Psycho-educational groups
Psycho-educational groups serve to address and develop personal growth factors within an academic or educational setting. The academic setting provides a framework for targeting common adolescent issues such as emotional development, self-image, identity definition, and interpersonal social skills. The student in the psycho-educational group develops socially and emotionally in tandem with addressing academic skills. The counselor in the psycho-educational setting can take advantage of the opportunity to provide students with increasingly developmental tasks toward optimum benefit for the student. An important added benefit of this model is that it provides students with an array of resources, contributing to an increased feeling of self-worth and self-confidence. An effective psycho-educational counseling group can contribute positively to the futures of the students involved, by both mitigating future problem occurrences, as well as providing a cache of resources that will be useful in career planning.

The initial consideration for choosing topics for psycho-educational groups should be the age and developmental levels of the students involved. While adolescent and pre-adolescent groups will respond better to groups focusing on social and interpersonal skills, groups of younger students would find more to connect with in a friendship or playgroup, or one focused on problem solving. These topics or themes can provide a framework for students to address peripheral issues. It might be advantageous to refer to the school's agenda for academic and social skill development, in order to glean topics or a series of topics for psycho-educational groups. Some typical topics, particularly for adolescents, could include stress management, romantic relationships, time management or career planning. It is also a good idea to ask the school if there are any survey instruments that they have utilized in identifying topics of interest among their students.

The first step in creating a psycho-educational group is to define the following:

- Purpose of the group
- Anticipated membership
- Focus of the group
- Interventions and expected outcomes

Secondly, the counselor should clearly identify both long-term objectives and measured short-term steps toward those objectives, applicable to each session. It is important to delineate the steps necessary toward achieving objectives. The counselor should then develop content and exercises that use an experiential framework that will incorporate and address the following:

- The demographics and targeted needs of the group
- Educational content that fits within the students' academic agendas.
- Opportunities for students to learn from experience
- A format that allows students to make connections between tasks and skills addressed
- Exercises that generate group discussion and response

Lastly, evaluation of the success of the group should include evaluation of each session and process involved in achieving the long-term objectives.

Counseling groups

Counseling groups are generally formed to address personal issues that hinder or prohibit academic success. The groups can target behavioral problems such as outbursts of temper, disruption of class, social maladjustment, etc.; or they can target specific life-altering events such as a death, a pregnancy or other event precipitating a personal crisis. The groups are formed to work specifically on the personal issues aside from any academic issues that have resulted from the personal situation. Students referred to counseling groups have demonstrated an inability or significantly lessened ability, particularly in the case of a personal crisis, to manage and positively respond to their

academic responsibilities. Within the counseling groups, facilitators can provide an environment for students to benefit from peer support, including buffeting a sense of isolation. Benefits include a stronger sense of self-worth as well as healthy strategies to handle emotions.

The counseling group provides a venue for students to express and process overwhelming emotions in a controlled environment. The overall tone of the group should be one of caring, compassion, and empathy. Many of its members will have experienced, or will be experiencing, similar events and emotions. The format of the group should be one of support, trust, and understanding. Members of the group should feel a sense of camaraderie with the other members. Acting as facilitator, group counselors can encourage peers within the group to provide support and suggestions for emotional healing to the other members, contributing to the general benefit of all its members. Counselors should also be cognizant of each student's need to address both actions and thought patterns in the process of working through their issues or trauma with the group.

Crisis-centered groups

A crisis-centered group is formed in response to a traumatic precipitating event. The event could involve a few individuals, or could be school-wide, such as a shooting or other crisis involving a population. The overarching purpose of a crisis-centered group is that of providing a controlled venue where students can express their feelings. In the case of an issue involving a few students, such as a disruptive conflict between students, an additional goal of the crisis-centered group is to facilitate resolution of the conflict. In this case, the group will form for the purpose of resolution, and at least until the matter is resolved. In the case of a large population trauma, the group will form to assist the students in coping with the trauma and/or loss. In both of these instances, additional meetings could be held to work on personal development issues for the student members.

Problem-centered groups

Problem-centered groups are often an outgrowth of crisis-centered groups, formed after the crisis has passed or been resolved, for addressing issues that could erupt in future problems or crises, and may have been one of the precipitating factors. The students in these groups come together to focus on specific issues that may be hindering their academic progress, or their general well-being. Some of the issues that are addressed in problem-centered groups include such issues as managing stress, conflict resolution strategies, academic or career goals, and possibly substance abuse. The effectiveness of the groups depends on the receptivity of its members to resolution. Participation in problem-centered groups is usually an option chosen by the students involved. The members of these groups, which are usually smaller than crisis-centered groups, benefit from the support and input from other members in resolving an issue that may feel overwhelming when faced alone.

Growth-centered groups

Similar to problem-centered groups, growth-centered groups often form as an outgrowth of another group. While a preceding group, such as a crisis-centered group, might be formed to address a shared crisis or situation such as anger management, the growth-centered groups instead address each individual student's issues and concerns, which may be peripheral or contributory to the group topic. Under the umbrella topic of a common issue such as anger management, students may be dealing with low self-esteem, stress as a result of poor time management, conflicting value paradigms, etc. The tone of the group is supportive, and empathetic, allowing students to develop healthy responses to their situation in a controlled environment. The group as a whole works on positive behavior dynamics, as a group and addressing each individual in the group. Growth-centered groups allow counselors to identify and address students on an

individual basis.

Advocacy

It is important for individuals advocating the creation of counseling groups to emphasize first the comprehensive nature of a counseling program within the school setting, pointing out that an effective counseling program works collaboratively with parents and school groups. It should also be stressed that counseling groups serve to address personal issues that can hinder academic performance. Developing a counseling program also should include vehicles for input from school personnel and parents in particular. It might be advisable to hold meetings in tandem with PTA or other parent groups, providing a forum for open communication about the need for and implementation of a counseling program. It is recommended that these presentations be held early in the academic year, to allow for the process of discussion and consensus. It is also important for these meetings to be facilitated by professional counselors who can appropriately address questions and concerns.

Regular communication with parents and school personnel provides continued interface regarding both future and existing counseling groups. Some of the channels for keeping this communication open include:

- Regular, informative meetings with school counselors discussing current counseling groups, future plans, and any peripheral activities occurring.
- Distribution of surveys assessing specific needs for groups, or for topics to be addressed.
- Share information about groups needed as well as groups being formed, as appropriate, to parents and school personnel.

- Be available on a regular basis to hear from school personnel regarding student issues or concerns that may precipitate the need for a counseling group.
- Speak with students in their classrooms about the availability of counseling groups, and provide a clear and confidential process by which they can bring concerns forward.
- Develop and communicate clear procedures for group formation, group participation, and parental and school permission.

Group forming

Once a counselor perceives a need to form a group, based on input from teachers, parents, and/or students, the following parameters need to be explored and established:

- Topic and purpose of the group
- Group meeting schedules and time allotted for sessions
- Proposed members of the group, including group size
- Established process and rubric for recruiting and screening potential members

The focus and purpose of these groups should be primarily for the benefit of the students, within the context of the therapeutic paradigm. Counselors should discuss the group's formation with teachers and other school personnel as appropriate before launching the group. Issues of confidentiality should be clearly and firmly established and communicated clearly to students, parents, and school personnel. Although the groups are generally established for the benefit and well-being of the students, the issue of confidentiality and other counseling ethics continue to apply.

Demographics
While it is not always indicated for counselors to specifically focus on demographics when

choosing group participants, it is nonetheless a good idea to be aware of the demographics vis-à-vis the topics being addressed. Sometimes the referral process might result in a default group of students that is primarily one gender or one ethnicity. Although there are no definitive rules about this, it is often a good idea to include a spectrum of cultures and mix of genders in a group setting, when working with all age groups, but more so with adolescent students. This often allows students to address personal and social skills in a mixed group, within the controlled environment of the counseling session. Younger children may be more comfortable in a group of their own gender. Of course, if the topic relates to culturally- or gender-specific topics, then the group would be comprised of student falling within the specified category.

Topics
Selecting group members based on topic can be approached somewhat holistically, in that some topics may be interrelated, however the group members will want to experience similarities and empathy among themselves. For instance, if the topic being addressed is dealing with authority, which may include students who stay out after curfew, as well as students who are perpetually late to class. Students whose parents are divorced may relate with students who recently moved from their home town, both of them dealing with separation issues and disenfranchisement. Nonetheless, if students are in fact dealing with the same issue, there may be enough diversity in personality in coping skills to comprise a dynamic group. In terms of age similarities, it is a good idea to have students in a group who are within the same age group or developmental level, although a small spectrum of emotional maturity can provide the interactive component that is valuable in a group setting.

Recruitment and screening
The primary considerations for selecting and screening students for group counseling are the willingness and capability of the student to participate in a therapeutic group setting.

Students may be referred by parents, teachers, other students or self-referred. While the self-referred students may intrinsically be indicating their willingness to participate, the other types of referrals indicate the need for counselors to screen students to see if they are amenable to group counseling. All students should be screened for capability to participate in a group setting, and if a group counseling format would be beneficial for them. In general, the counselor should consider the parameters of the group setting, which include both speaking and listening, respecting confidentialities and differences among its members, as well as other components of the group format, when screening potential group members. Some counselors prefer to have individual meetings with potential members before the first meeting; others devote the first meeting to information and screening.

A good way to begin the screening process is for the counselor to give the student an overview of the group counseling format. This overview should include the purpose of the group, the role and expectations of the members, and the role and expectations of the counselor. The counselor should provide an opportunity for the student to ask questions, and express any concerns or anxieties s/he has about the group format. In the context of this conversation, the counselor should look for indications that the student is either likely or unlikely to be able to participate in a group setting. Some of these indications relate to the student's ability to follow the rules of the group, his or her ability to commit to attend, participate and contribute in the group setting, his or her emotional capability to participate, and lastly his or her willingness to participate.

Soliciting participation

Finding appropriate members for a counseling group can be a combined endeavor of advertising and referrals. Of course, counselors should have a profile of the types of groups that would be relevant and beneficial for a particular student body,

which would arise out of conversations and other input from students and school staff. Often, this input will include referral of specific students and the need for group sessions focusing on particular topics. Counselors may otherwise know of students who would benefit from certain types of groups. Once the need for a group has been indicated, counselors can interest others in the group with notices in newsletters, flyers, word of mouth, or talking with students, groups of parents or school personnel. The counselor should specify the topic to be addressed, the philosophy and general format of group counseling, and the proposed times for the sessions.

Unsuitable students

Students who are indicated as not suitable for the group counseling format may be referred to individual counseling. Although some students referred to individual counseling may never participate in group counseling, others may transition from individual to group counseling. For these students, the counselors will want to make a determination of readiness based on specific criteria. S/he then should communicate to parents the recommendation, and the criteria met specifically improvements or maturity in particular areas that indicate the student's readiness for group counseling. The intent, format, and expectations of the group setting distinguished from individual counseling should be included. Counselors should refer to school policy regarding additional procedures to follow when transitioning a student in this manner. Also, students referred into group counseling from individual counseling should sign a consent form indicating his/her understanding, readiness and commitment to the group setting.

Group size and session length

Both group size and session length are primarily determined by age and developmental level of the participants. One of the key deciding factors is the ability for certain age groups to focus on a topic for a specific period of time. Since younger elementary children have shorter attention spans, a rule of thumb for them is to have group sessions lasting about 20 minutes, with about 5 members. Older elementary students, roughly grades 4 through 6, can meet for periods spanning from 30 to 45 minutes, in groups of 7 or so. High school students will benefit from an expanded length of session, but still fare better with smaller numbers. The ideal group size for high school students is 6 to 8, meeting for 40 to 50 minutes. If a counselor feels that a particular group could extend the recommended time or group size, s/he should refer to research regarding both the topic and the group size.

Group dynamics can be very much impacted by the size of the group. There need to be enough participants to provide for peer feedback and support as appropriate, but not such a large group that individuals are eclipsed by it, or that focus becomes dissipated. In addition to consulting published standards regarding ideal group sizes for age group, counselors can determine effective group sizes by considering the age or developmental level of the group, for instance the short attention spans of the participants. The topic being addressed is also a factor. If the strategies indicated for a particular topic, for instance individual exercises versus group exercises, that will affect the choice of group size, of course smaller group sizes allowing for more individual participation. Further, counselors can consider the individual participants in the group, including their modes and likelihood of participation, when determining group size.

Topics

Choice of topics for counseling groups should be representative of the needs of the school community and/or student body. Many topics to be addressed will arise out of regular meetings between counselors and the school staff, or from meetings with parents. Others may be revealed through the surveys that are

distributed to parents, students and school staff. Students themselves can also be a source of potential topics, particularly if they are provided with a clear and confidential process for bringing these concerns forward. Counselors can be proactive in the process of choosing topics, and ask groups to suggest topics, or to choose from a series of topics that might be of interest. Once the counselor has established him/herself as a responsive conduit for topic suggestions, there should be a body of recommendations available from which to determine best topics to be addressed in counseling groups.

Another resource for assessing the need for counseling groups and topics is that of school records. These records can produce profiles that may reveal patterns of low retention, poor attendance, low test scores, or other identifiable areas of need. Counselors can also research commonalties of specific age groups to determine which topics would most likely be appropriate and well received. These topics can range from healthy social behavior to career planning. Some of these general areas can be addressed through specific focus on life experiences, such as beginning a college prep program in high school. It is important that development of groups and group topics be well researched in terms of not only common topics for a particular age group, but the applicability of these topics to the particular student body, as documented by school records and the input of school personnel.

As a part of a comprehensive counseling program that includes addressing specified needs, counselors can also include topics that are generally relevant to particular age groups. Some of these age-specific topics include:

- For elementary students–Students in this age group are dealing with issues relating to such topics as friendships, family roles, problem solving, social behaviors, success in school, expressing emotions, and self-esteem.

- For middle school students–Middle school students are particularly embroiled in issues relating to body image, interpersonal relationships, social skills, conflict management, social roles, diversity issues, self-esteem, transitioning to a new school, and academic development.
- For high school students–As students are preparing to transition to adulthood, topics that are most relevant include career exploration and planning, dating protocol, intimate relationships, self-identity, assertiveness training, stress management and time management.

Although many of these topics overlap between age groups, counselors need to be cognizant of the level of development present in the particular student group or population in the counseling group.

Although no one can, or would want to, experience every difficult situation, it is nonetheless important for anyone in a therapeutic relationship to feel a sense of empathy and recognition from the counselor. This allows students to feel safe, understood, and not isolated in his or her situation. Therefore, it is important for counselors to have a basic knowledge of topics that will be addressed in group counseling. They should be able to discuss the processes and effects of such situations as divorce, teen parenting, stress management, poor academic performance, and peer pressure. It is also valuable to develop a cache of information and resources about particular topics that can be shared with students. Counselors can also recommend activities or anecdotes that relate to the student's situation. Combined, these not only provide the empathy of knowledge, but also can serve to assist and empower students toward resolution.

Scheduling

It is important to remember that the responsibility of the school counselor is simultaneously for the student as well as the school community. Because of that, the counselor should work with school personnel and school schedules when developing group counseling schedules. This is particularly pivotal in high school and middle school because counseling sessions that are scheduled at the same time every day, or every week, will necessarily affect that same school subject because of the way classes are scheduled. Collaboration with teachers and other school personnel is probably the first best approach, soliciting their input about best and worst times to schedule counseling sessions, such as avoiding sessions on days when standardized tests are administered. Beyond that, it is always a good idea to stagger group counseling sessions, especially in the middle or high school setting, although this may be the case in an elementary school also, if indicated by the teachers.

Ground rules

Once the members of a group are selected and brought together, at either the first meeting or a pre-meeting, the counselor should give an overview of the guidelines and expectations of group counseling. This first meeting or pre-meeting will define the individual members as a group brought together for a purpose. As a collaborative group, students can be given a presentation of the ground rules in group counseling, and then individually sign forms of understanding and consent. These ground rules can include the importance of commitment, issues of conduct, and the importance of respect and confidentiality. It is significant that they agree to these ground rules as a group, since they will be implementing them as a group, with the counselor as facilitator. The counselor can also talk about group expectations, and allow members to voice their concerns and expectations.

Ground rules in a group counseling setting serve to cohere its members in unity of conduct and purpose. When reviewing ground rules, it is helpful to solicit input from the members, allowing them to participate in the establishment of the ground rules. Rules also contribute to a healthy and productive dynamic in a group setting. Lastly, rules can provide and ensure a sense of safety and trust in the counseling environment. Some typical rules that address these issues include, but are not limited to:

- Give respect to the counselor and other members by listening attentively and without interruption.
- Be willing to participate and contribute by sharing feelings and experiences.
- Respect the experiences, perspectives and backgrounds of the other members.
- Maintain confidentiality.

Although confidentiality cannot be legally mandated for group members as it is for counselors, it is nonetheless effective to have members include a commitment to confidentiality in their overall consent to the ground rules.

Role of the group counselor

The counselor in a group setting has the overall role of balancing and maintaining healthy and productive group dynamics. This includes attending to both the group as a whole and to the individual members. The counselor needs to be sensitive to the levels of participation within the group, observing fairness and contribution from all members. S/he should be available for consultation regarding any concerns, and act as the overseer and reminder of the ground rules. Counselors should facilitate the interaction of the members toward the benefit of each of the members. This may involve working with a resistant student, or intervening when there is negative, unproductive behavior. The counselor in a group setting can encourage group dynamics, while working with individual vicissitudes of exploration as appropriate. S/he should also strive toward a more integrated and self-regulating group by

encouragement and guidance.

Particularly in a group counseling setting, counselors need to be sensitive to the possibility of the group becoming distracted and losing focus of the topic and goal(s) of the group. Although there will be a modicum of flexibility to incorporate the individual needs of the participants, it is the role of the counselor to maintain the focus and progress of the group. One of the early safeguards against this possibility is clear communication to the members, parents and school staff as appropriate, about the a) purpose and goal(s) of the group, as well as b) an overview of the therapeutic format and c) the process of resolution in a group setting. Defining and reviewing the goals and parameters of the group with participants is also helpful. It is important for counselors to be well-versed of the basic tenets of group dynamics in a therapeutic setting.

Planning and flexibility
It is the counselor's role to maintain focus on the topic, goals, and strategies to employ in each group and session. Therefore, it is important to approach each session with enough preparation beforehand to be able to facilitate the session effectively. This preparation should include discussion topics, planned activities and an informal agenda. Within the grid of this agenda, counselors will often allow time and flexibility for longer group discussion, particular concerns that might arise in the session, or individual responses or behaviors that may require extra time and attention. However, because of the preplanning and the agenda, counselors can redirect the group toward activities, specific discussion topics and the goals of that particular session, to maintain the focus and progress of the group. The activities and discussion topics in each session are understood as part of a larger agenda outlining the long-term goals of the group.

Beginning sessions
Before tackling the topic(s) and goal(s) of a counseling group, facilitators should first establish the environment and tenor of the

group. In the first session or sessions, participants can become acquainted and possibly share a bit about themselves. The counselor's role is to assist in establishing an environment that is understood as safe. It is important that participants experience a sense of camaraderie with the other group members. Throughout the remainder of the sessions, they will be sharing personal insights and experiences as well as addressing possibly difficult topics. Therefore, this initial introductory period is vital in developing a close and collaborative group. During these first sessions, the counselor can review the purpose of the group, ground rules for participation, and the importance of confidentiality, all of which will serve to establish a safe and controlled environment for sharing experiences.

Middle sessions

Although particular activities will vary between groups, and particularly between different age groups, there are similarities that all will share. Counselors should establish a relatively standard routine for the middle sessions during which the group will be most heavily pursuing their goals. A good idea for each session is to include an initial time of greeting the members, to reinforce each member's importance and contributions. Counselors can briefly review the ground rules and guidelines during the early part of the session. A review of the previous session's events, activities and accomplishments is recommended. Counselors can then focus the group's attention on the current topic and direct them to a preplanned activity or discussion designed for that session. As the session draws to a close, counselors can briefly review the session's activities and insights, and establish a regular routine for ending the session.

Closing sessions

Developing a structure for the closing session(s) of group counseling incorporates a different focus than the beginning or middle sessions. The closing sessions are those meetings that review accomplishments as a group and anticipate individual futures. There will necessarily be a refocus and possibly some apprehension. Counselors should announce the upcoming final session at least 3 meetings in advance. An important component in the final session or sessions is a review of the initial goals, and the reminder of the achievement of those goals. Counselors should take this time to empower and encourage participants to remember their newly discovered skills and insights, and to apply them to future situations, as well as to a continuum of changed behavior. Time should be allowed for participants to express feelings and for leaders or other group members to respond to those feelings.

Particularly in the closing session(s), counselors should refer to a defined listing of topics and issues to be addressed, toward a healthy transition. Although the particular modes and media may differ between age groups and topic groups, the following are key components to consider when structuring a closing session:

- Review of the initial goals from the first meeting(s)
- Review of the accomplishment of those goals in subsequent meetings
- Review of strategies, resources and activities experienced in the sessions
- Validation of growth and new insights of the participants throughout the sessions
- Direction for incorporating this growth and insight in future activities and behaviors
- An opportunity to address any unfinished business or lingering concerns
- An opportunity for the group to respond to unfinished business or lingering concerns
- Allow substantial time for personal goodbyes
- Counselors may also want to schedule a post-meeting for evaluation purposes

Group meeting evaluations

In order to assess the effectiveness of the group sessions, counselors should complete an evaluation at the end of each meeting. The format of these evaluations will in large part determine the kind of information that will be returned. If counselors are looking for the group response to particular components of the sessions, such as the scheduling or the structure of the sessions, a multiple choice or graded response format can be used. The results of these surveys will be more quantitative and focused. Another model is that of questions or open-ended sentences that ask participants how they felt about a session, such as "my favorite part of the session was…".These types of survey instruments can provide more qualitative information, as well as provide an ongoing profile of participant satisfaction and involvement. Counselors may also provide pre- and post-surveys to parents and school staff, as wall as post-surveys to participants several weeks after the last session.

Multicultural group counseling

The dynamics of group sessions can be particularly impacted by cultural factors. Counselors who are forming counseling groups should be sensitive to the cultural backgrounds and premises of its members. Understanding how different cultural groups respond to stereotypes, oppression, discrimination, and prejudice can assist the counselor in forming groups. Likewise, student perceptions of the counselor as facilitator or authority can affect the group dynamics. Although the recommendation is not necessarily to limit groups to similar cultures, and in fact in some cases it might be indicated to blend cultures, it is up to the counselor to be sensitive to the ramifications of multicultural dynamics. It is worth noting that culture can include gender, religion and other criteria. Counselors can refer to literature, research and other resources regarding considerations and practices regarding cultural diversity in group counseling.

Although multicultural groups can benefit from a richness of blended cultures, counseling groups comprised of diverse cultures may also be more susceptible to misunderstandings and conflicts as a direct result of the differences in perspectives. The counselor as facilitator can provide valuable leadership by encouraging the interchange of ideas about such topics as self-identity, self-worth, oppression, responsibility to society, etc. Likewise, if there is conflict in the group, the counselor who has been trained in multicultural sensitivity can better recognize if the conflict is culturally based, and take the opportunity to intervene and work with the students to develop strategies for resolution. It may be possible for the group to work as a whole on culturally based conflict resolution, allowing other members to contribute newly learned skills or perspectives. Multicultural counseling groups can provide fertile ground for teaching multicultural sensitivity.

Multisensory stimulation

Students exposed to multisensory stimulation are found to be more engaged, more responsive, and more attentive. This is particularly valuable in a group setting, since one of the inherent weaknesses is the ease with which its members can become distracted. Multisensory stimuli involve the mind and senses of children and adolescents, and target multiple intelligences. This is particularly valuable in a group setting, comprised of unique individuals with unique coping and learning styles. These stimuli provide the group with a comprehensive, experiential mode for addressing issues. Through the use of such creative and multisensory stimuli as puppets, music, drama, and movies, counselors can generate response and participation when broaching difficult topics. An added benefit is that of students forging positive associations between the topic and creative stimuli. Various media such as film, or puppets for younger audiences, can serve to present a problem in a manner that may be more palatable than a lecture format.

Classroom guidance

Counselors as teachers

School counselors in particular can be especially valuable in classroom instruction, in areas of personal and social growth related to academic performance. Although in previous years, guidance counseling was often an added role for teachers, students are now able to benefit from the expertise of trained guidance counselors, both outside and within the classroom environment. One of the benchmark criteria for classroom instruction by school counselors is in the area of empowering students to be productive members of society. Throughout their school years, counselors can assist students in such areas as study skills, time management, social skills and career planning. The American School Counselor Association (ASCA) is a strong proponent of school counselors contributing their expertise to the classroom environment. Counselors can also assist students with preparation for standard-based testing, and other academic goals set by the school.

Benefits

The benefits of classroom guidance are found to be extraordinary and exponential. Results show that students who have experienced classroom guidance are significantly more successful academically as well as socially, and better prepared for future endeavors than those who have not had classroom guidance. This seems to be the case across the board, regardless of school district or even geographic area. In terms of academic success, these students noticeably fare better in attendance, test success, and overall grade point average. Socially, their in-class behaviors improve markedly, and they are better able to cope with personal issues. Finally, students who have had the benefit of classroom guidance are more likely to attend college and to proactively participate in

career planning. Counselors have reported these successes resulting from their interaction with students, including classroom guidance activities.

Assessing effectiveness

As with any counseling strategies, it is important to both qualitatively and quantitatively assess the success of classroom guidance. It is important to establish a rubric that includes such criteria as grades, test scores and graduation rates. Both pre- and post-intervention surveys are recommended. There can also be a qualitative appraisal of the effectiveness of intervention strategies in the classroom, delineating changes in behavior or classroom tenor. Note that demographic information can be valuable in assessing classroom strategies, but that it should not be included in pre- or post-intervention surveys. In other words, data gathering in terms of grades, etc. needs to be free of demographic categories, whereas, as appropriate, information regarding ethnicity, gender, socioeconomic status and other demographics may be included on final evaluative reports. A significant added caution is that all data gathered should be confidential, with little or no reference to identifiable specifics.

Counselors may want to assess student perceptions and student responses to qualitatively evaluate the effectiveness of classroom guidance content. The approach should be informal, gearing the evaluation in a way that is not readily perceived as an assessment. Younger children may respond well to a fill-in-the-blank cartoon; older students may be able to write or complete narratives that allow them to infuse their feelings about academic success, their role in the classroom or society, or other relevant perceptions. Other recommendations include scaled devices to self-report feelings, or other spectrum-like instrument, also user friendly and informal. Counselors will generally want to assess the effect of classroom strategies on behavior, motivation, increased coping skills, and interest in planning their futures. As with quantitative assessments, these more informal qualitative assessments should be administered both pre- and post-intervention strategies, to more effectively assess the effect of the interventions.

Process evaluation is necessarily more focused and more formal, since it is administered to solicit feedback on specific components of the classroom guidance strategies. This type of evaluation is particularly valuable when developing or introducing new strategies, since it provides a kind of rating system to assess the value of the strategy. The format for this type of evaluation should be more formalized and more quantitative than for content. Surveys can be administered with vehicles for rating strategies or activities, using terms like extremely helpful, helpful, not helpful, etc. It is also a good idea to include a comments section that will provide qualifiers for the rated responses. In other words, if a strategy was not particularly well received, what about it could be changed, if anything? This type of evaluation is often administered during the first classroom sessions of a strategy, providing valuable feedback for refining and revising the strategy in subsequent class meetings.

Classroom environment

Seating arrangements
Seating arrangements can be very valuable in establishing tone and expectation, as well as contributing to the efficacy of a guidance lesson in the classroom. Counselors can choose other seating arrangements that are most conducive to the planned activity or lesson. Just the process of rearranging the established seating in a classroom can signal a change in the group dynamic. If students are asked to break into small groups, the expectation is that of discussion within the groups. Counselors can implement this seating arrangement to address interpersonal skills. An added benefit to this kind of seating arrangement is the capability of student groups addressing different topics, which is

best facilitated by the small group seating. Conversely, if the activity is one that requires the group of students to listen to the counselor, which is the more standard seating arrangement, the chairs and desks would all face the front of the classroom. Two key areas impacted by seating arrangements are formality and communication, specifically whether communication is one-sided or open and interactive. The seating arrangement that defines one end of this spectrum is that of all seats facing one direction toward a speaker or screen. This arrangement inherently discourages interaction, and implies one-way communication from the person or event at the front of the room. The other end of the spectrum is occupied by an arrangement of small groups whose participants face each other. This arrangement allows for much interpersonal dialogue, and relegates the counselor to that of facilitator. The gradations in between include U-shaped seating facing the front which encourages discussion with a speaker, seats in a circle which encourages discussion without a speaker, as can seating around a table. Counselors should consider how much participation, if any, would be appropriate for a given session when looking at seating arrangements.

The physical arrangement of a classroom will be best when it suits the style of the teacher. If most classes are going to be lectures, then it makes sense to arrange all the desks in rows facing the front of the room. If students are going to spend a lot of time working in small groups, then it is better to group desks together. Large group discussions are best held in a room in which desks have been arranged so that they face one another. It is also important for a teacher to create a generally welcoming environment in their classroom, by posting picture, laying some rugs, or setting out some plants. The point of arranging your classroom is to make it the place most conducive to meeting your goals, so you should avoid things that will be distracting or unpleasant to some students.

Positive learning environment

In order for teachers to engage the minds of their students at the highest level, they have to make sure that certain lesser needs are taken care of. Lighting, for instance, is important for creating a good classroom environment. Some kids may prefer bright light to dim light, so it is a good idea to include areas that receive different amounts of light. It is not a bad idea for there to be some open space in one section of the classroom, so that kids can move around a bit if they get restless. Many teachers have some softer furniture in their classrooms, so that students can get comfortable and focus on their work. Last, but not least, teachers should try to determine what temperature is most popular in the classroom, and encourage students to bring whatever clothing they will need to be comfortable at that temperature.

Rules of conduct

Just as a business posts its internal rules for employees, so do teachers need to post a set of basic rules for students to follow when they are in class. The most important and all-encompassing of these rules is simply to treat others the way you would like to be treated. Students should also be told to respect the property and personal space of their teacher and fellow students, and to keep their hands off of one another. Students should never laugh at one another. Students should be responsible for their own learning, and work together to create an environment in which they can be successful. This includes being on time for class each day, and handing in all assignments on time.

Managing behavior

Managing classroom tone and behavior is best accomplished with developing appropriate lessons as well as incorporating dynamic content, vocal and body signals in lesson delivery. It is important to develop lesson plans that are challenging yet manageable for the age and developmental level of the students. Added to this,

counselors can incorporate words of encouragement and validation in lessons, giving students a sense of connection to the classroom discussion and activities. Counselors can add a bit of humor, anecdotes, etc., to maintain interest, and to pique students' creativity. In addition, utilizing changes in voice pitch, moving around the room, and making eye contact with different students can add to a counselor's ability to manage the tenor of a classroom. Not only does this contribute to the credibility of counselors in the classroom, but also greatly impacts the efficacy of the lesson.

Giving students not only interesting, but sufficient, classroom content is another pivotal factor in mitigating the occurrences and opportunity for classroom disturbance. Sensitivity to the proverbial problem of idle time, it is important for counselors to provide a consistent flow of content and interaction with students in order to keep the class focused on the lesson at hand as well as away from any possible distractions. This consistent flow also provides a standard backdrop of activity, so that any distractive activities are easily noticed, whereas if a lesson includes lulls or unfocused time, distractions can not only occur more easily, but also can occur relatively unnoticed and pave the way for increased distractive activities. Significant practices for developing sufficient classroom content include good preparation as well as familiarity with the lesson content. During the lesson, no matter how well planned, the counselor should continue to be watchful for any classroom disturbance, and bring students back into focus as appropriate.

If a counselor feels that a classroom disturbance is rooted in a situation or relationship outside of the classroom, whether between two students, or the personal issues of one student, this may present the opportunity to not only restore the learning environment in the classroom, but also provide authority with empathy. In the process of reminding a student or students of the need to not distract from the classroom learning environment, counselors may discover that there are underlying issues feeding the disturbance. It is important to approach each situation from a position of mutual respect and group consideration, as to not be perceived as an unsympathetic, top-down authority, bur rather a knowledgeable person whose concern is for the well-being of all students. A counselor can serve as a sounding board and resource expert for students experiencing problems that interfere with their learning experience.

In keeping with the philosophy of managing with empathy, a counselor can maintain his or her role as authority, while conveying a message of accessibility and expertise. When first approaching a student or students, counselors can establish a kind of partnership, allowing students to participate in addressing issues that are disruptive to his/her learning environment, as well as that of the classroom as a whole. Students who feel they can participate in this resolution are less likely to feel isolated and singled out. However, counselors need to maintain the students' respect for the counselor's role. Not only does this prevent disruptions from becoming more pronounced, it also serves to give students confidence in the counselor's expertise. In the process of working with a disruptive student, counselors can suggest to the student underlying problems that may be fueling the disruption, providing an effectual, holistic response to a classroom disturbance.

Because of the eponymous nature of attention-seeking behavior, it is important that counselors do not reward the behavior with undue attention in the process of disciplining students. Counselors can develop consistent consequences for disruptive, attention-seeking behavior, and make these consequences known to students when first beginning of working with them. Counselors may want to work with teachers and other staff to develop and communicate these consequences to students. Consequences should be directly related and proportional to the behavior. The effect of implementing these consequences should validate a perception that the counselors and teachers are interested in ensuring a calm and productive classroom environment for all students. Disciplinary actions should be free of anger or other emotional volatility. It is also important for counselors to remain objective, and to not infuse personal or moral assessments into their discipline. All of this will serve to downplay and neutralize attention-seeking behaviors in the classroom.

Long-range plans
For teachers, long-range plans are those that stretch out over a grading period, a semester, or a school year. They typically are closely related to state curriculum standards. Usually, a teacher will start a long-range plan by studying a calendar to determine exactly how many instructional hours will be available. Next, the teacher should consider which activities are most appropriate for which time of year. Many teachers use long-range plans to decide how they will try to develop a certain theme throughout the school year. These long-range plans will be frequently referred to when teachers are developing their weekly and daily lesson plans. Long-range plans serve as a sort of point of orientation for the rest of the planning process.

Syllabus
A syllabus is essential for effectively organizing and administrating a class. Preparing a clear and detailed syllabus before the start of the school year allows teachers to be sure that all of the essential areas will be covered, that there will be enough variety among assignments to hold the interest of the class, and to make sure that all the students will understand the program and the expectations. A proper syllabus should include a defined aim for the course, clear assessment objectives, an outline of the assessment structure (that is, how students will be examined), the content of the curriculum, and a grading scale. The grading scale should include a sufficient description of the quality of work that merits each letter

grade. However, there is no one way to order the material of a course, but some ways seem to make more sense than others. For instance, most teachers will want to begin the course with an overview of the general themes of the course, so that students will have an idea of the structure of the course and will be prepared for its various transitions.

An effective syllabus will adequately describe the assessment objectives for the class. The assessment objectives are the skills that the class will be trying to develop in the student. In business education classes, there are four basic assessment objectives. The first is knowledge and understanding, meaning that the student should be able to recall the basic facts and concepts of the course. The second objective is application, the ability of the student to take the facts and concepts he or she has learned and apply them to the appropriate situations. The third objective is analysis, the ability of the student to select, order, and interpret information, whether in the form of text, chart, or number. Finally, students should be assessed on their ability to evaluate material; that is, to develop and justify arguments based on the content of the course.

Teaching plans
A teacher cannot be effective without properly planning every aspect of class. Good plans give a teacher confidence, security, and a definite direction in class. Teachers that are successful planners typically follow four steps when they plan an activity. First, they have a total understanding of the activity: what it will involve, what it is designed to teach, and what potential problems it might have. Next, the teacher imagines its implementation in the classroom, and makes whatever modifications to the environment are necessary. Then, the teacher evaluates the strengths and weaknesses of his or her class, and alters the activity to suit them. Finally, an effective teacher will create a mental image of the finished activity, and imagine exactly how it will be accomplished.

Weekly schedules
Every teacher needs to compose a weekly schedule in order to ensure that progress is maintained. Most teachers use their long-range plans to determine the amount of progress they need to make from week to week. In making weekly plans, teachers should consider which activities are appropriate for classes at the beginning of the day, and which are more appropriate for those after lunch and later. Next, teachers should consider how much direct instructional time will be necessary to give students the abilities to complete any assignments. Many beginning teachers run their weekly plans by more experienced colleagues to make sure that they are viable. The weekly schedule serves as the basic framework for the daily lesson plan.

Lesson plans

Lesson plans are essential to maintaining an organized class and making sure that all of the goals of the syllabus are attained. Just as businesses create detailed budgets to ensure that there is a clear path to their objectives, so must teachers plan every class in advance to ensure success. When drawing up lesson plans, a teacher should consider several things. First, he or she must have a clear idea of what content is to be covered. Second, he or she should know the time and resources available, as well as the ability level of the students. Third, the teacher should have an idea of what teaching method is most appropriate to deliver that particular lesson. Finally, the teacher should make sure that the lesson has a clear introduction, and an end that brings the material together and gives the student an idea of what they need to remember.

Many schools place such a high value on daily plans that they require teachers to show their plans to the principal every week. A good daily lesson plan should include the specific content and activities that will be covered in each class period. It will also detail whatever procedures, assignments, student groupings, and materials will be necessary to meet the day's objectives. The composition of a lesson plan is a good chance for a teacher to consider whether his or her plan has an appropriate balance, and whether they are right for a particular class. In other words, plans should be made with the results of recent assessment in mind.

Components

Generally, regardless of the grade level or the discipline, most successful lesson plans will include three basic steps, or components. The first of these components is the introductory component. In this part of the lesson, students are introduced to the general topic or the particular focus area for that lesson. Secondly, the lesson plan should include activities that will serve to develop the lesson. These activities can be performed by the counselor, a teacher, or can be participatory activities by the students. The third section of the lesson not only concludes the lesson, but also evolves into an application portion, whereby students are able to project the lesson into their daily lives. This portion of the lesson often also includes student discussion. The total effect of this kind of sequenced lesson plan is increased student engagement, and a higher likelihood that students will remember and assimilate the lesson.

*Introductions:*Introducing a lesson topic or area serves several purposes in classroom teaching. Initially, it focuses students' attention on the topic to be addressed. In this sense, delivery of the introduction should be clear and compelling, soliciting student interest and engagement. It can also be valuable to let students know the planned learning goals or areas to be covered. Students can begin to develop a mental blueprint as the lesson progresses, and will be more likely to be receptive to each step of the lesson development, like a concert attendee following a program. It also helps to make connections with previous lessons or knowledge foundations, encouraging student confidence in grasping the lesson and class

participation. Lesson plans that are well introduced are more likely to result in comprehensive student understanding.

Including previous knowledge: Incorporating previous knowledge in a lesson plan imbues students with the self-confidence and orientation to the lesson to be more engaged and more participatory. It also helps to establish a participatory trust between counselor-teacher and students. Students are more likely to feel that they already possess useful information, and the counselor is there to facilitate the expansion of their knowledge base. A useful strategy for incorporating previous knowledge in a lesson plan is to ask questions, to which students can positively respond. Building on this, counselors can introduce next sequences or facets of knowledge, possibly through asking relevant questions, and volunteering the answers. Another valuable strategy is to reiterate previous knowledge, about which students are already familiar, and then to lead the class to the next phase of knowledge or skill development. Students whose previous knowledge is acknowledged are likely to be more receptive and participate more fully.

Developmental activities: Counselors can also incorporate previous knowledge in the developmental activity portion of a lesson plan. Planned activities can address students' existing knowledge about a topic, giving them opportunity to express that knowledge, and then progress to lead the students to a new level of knowledge or expansion on previous knowledge. It is important that counselors develop a clear outline for planned activities, cognizant of the objectives and strategies being utilized to reach those objectives. Additionally, a rubric should be established in order to clearly assess effectiveness of activity strategies. A distinguishing characteristic of developmental activities is that they provide a vehicle for expression through multiple intelligences, further contributing to the collective benefit of the class. Counselors should be sensitive to individual student strengths and needs, and tailor activities accordingly. Developmental activities can provide another vehicle for student confidence and participation.

Different intelligences: Counselors can augment the traditional verbal/text-based classroom lesson plan with activities that engage students' artistic, spatial, logical, kinesthetic and other learning modes. Counselors can present lesson topics through various media including music, pictures, etc. They can also ask students to respond experientially by drawing, writing a poem, use of drums, or possibly composing and performing a song or dance. Multiple media responses are particularly valuable when working with students on qualitative issues such as problem-solving or personal crises. Counselors employing multiple-media and multiple-intelligence approaches to curriculum delivery provide students greater opportunity for engagement and expression. This increases the efficacy of the lesson, and is a more inclusive strategy for students with various learning styles. Counselors should be sensitive to the particular student group in the classroom, and the individual learning styles represented.

Passive and active learning styles: The traditional lecture-based curriculum delivery style is effective in terms of transmitting information, but asks the student to participate in a very limited, passive manner. Students who simply hear the information are not only limited to a particular learning style, but this narrow delivery mode also leaves room for much distraction. Complementing the lecture with videos or handouts can increase students' receptivity by adding visual stimulus. A more effective augmentation would be to include opportunities for students to actively participate and learn. Some examples of active learning include verbal question response, writing on the board, note taking and other activities that require students to be engaged. Also, if students are asked to reiterate information through writing or other activities, they necessarily need to be focused on the information being transmitted. Active learning activities significantly increase the amount of data that students take with them because of their increased receptivity and engagement.

Lesson conclusion: Although the conclusion is generally fewer than five minutes, there are several objectives to be realized in the conclusion of a lesson, which will be reflected in its various components. The conclusion is a time to reiterate what has been learned, and to give students the opportunity to assimilate their new knowledge. Counselors can begin by repeating the previous knowledge that students brought into the classroom, and the increased knowledge that was given during the session. Students should be asked to give a recap or response to the lesson, to indicate that they have understood. Student response increases their receptivity, and gives the counselor an indication of how much the students have understood. This time can also be used to cite examples and applications for the lesson, further increasing students' assimilation of the lesson. Student participation and response is pivotal to this part of the lesson.

Time management

Too many teachers allow time to be wasted in class and cheat their students out of valuable instructional time. There are a few basic ways to remedy this problem. For one thing, teachers can minimize the amount of time students are given to socialize at the beginning or end of class. Next, teachers can try to make transitions between activities as smooth as possible by having the necessary materials ready at the beginning of class. Many teachers try to avoid giving students too much seatwork that could just as easily be completed out of class. In addition, teachers should have a clear policy on restroom breaks, so that their time is not wasted by constant requests to be excused.

Teachers are always being pulled in several different directions, and sometimes they may

- 31 -

feel that the responsibilities they have outside the classroom are making it difficult for them to meet their teaching goals. There are a few good ways to avoid this problem. First, teacher should list and prioritize their responsibilities, so that they do not get caught up in performing insignificant tasks. If necessary, teachers should avoid being drawn into committee and volunteer work organized by the school administration. Teachers should always have quiet space in which they can concentrate. In addition, managing time effectively means abandoning perfectionism and procrastination. Setting firm time limits for open-ended tasks is a good way to avoid spending too much time on things less important than teaching.

Managing paperwork

Most beginning teachers are overwhelmed at first by the amount of record-keeping and procedural paperwork they are required to fill out every day. The barrage of paper coming at a teacher can include attendance reports, lesson plans, lunch counts, report cards, homework, class reports, etc. There are a few good way to avoid being bogged down by paperwork. First, teachers can minimize their grading by having students grade one another for small assignments. Students can even be encouraged to make up their own worksheets. Many teachers try to use a lot of small quizzes to assess their students, so that they do not get caught up in grading large assignments. Teachers can even administer oral exams to their students, and thereby remove the need for paper altogether.

Grading papers can be one of the more time-consuming tasks for any teacher. There are a few ways to alleviate the burden of grading. One method that many teachers use is marking incorrect answers with an "O," so that when the student corrects the answer the teacher can just add a "K" to indicate approval. Most teachers use one chart to keep track of all the student grades so that they can keep them well organized. Students can often be enlisted to grade one another on short or

insignificant assignments, and this may even be an effective learning strategy in some cases. Finally, many teachers use a variety of different ink colors to tell themselves whether a paper is late or on time, or to tell themselves how much of it has been graded.

Effective instruction

There have been times when the principles of effective instruction have been described as art and not something taught to teachers in college. A teacher must possess certain qualities about themselves in order for their instruction to be effective. One quality is the teacher must show an honest interest and enthusiasm for the subject they are teaching. If the teacher is not interested, the students will not be interested either. In the classroom, they must also show respect and interest in each student. The students should be allowed time to ask questions and discuss with others about the subject matter. The objectives should be clear and the students should know what is expected of them. Any class activities, homework or projects should reflect what has been discussed in class and graded appropriately and fairly. The tests and papers should accurately measure what has been accomplished through the course objectives.

Grade-based curriculum

Although counselors teaching at various grade levels are generally responsible for developing and delivering curriculum appropriate to the level, it is recommendable to develop that curriculum as an integral part of a comprehensive K-12 curriculum. For example, counselors who teach at the elementary level, while delivering curriculum appropriate for that grade level, also should be cognizant of the larger curricular goals as well as the next phase of students' studies. It is important that students receive curriculum that builds on previous learning foundations, and continues to develop the foundation as appropriate for the grade level. Student learning within each classroom should not be an isolated experience, nor should it be unnecessarily redundant. Although some schools and districts operate within a paradigm that allows for quasi-isolated curriculum development within broad age groups, it is nonetheless usually recommended that all curriculum development to be designed within a larger K-12 context.

Instructional objectives
Instructional objectives are very specific and describe what the student is expected to do. Therefore, it is important that when deciding what the objectives are going to be, teachers and counselors know exactly what they expect from their students. Instructional objectives are also determined by what the outcome will be. They will state what the student should be able to accomplish after the teacher has finished his or her instruction. It is important to make sure the objectives are used to ensure that learning is clearly focused on a goal and that both students and teacher are on the same track. When determining instructional objectives, it is also important to ensure they line up with the lesson plan. It does not make sense for a teacher to teach a lesson on a certain topic, but the objectives do not follow the same topic.

Learning activities
When choosing learning activities that reflect the instructional objectives, it is important to remember that these activities should encourage students to have meaningful interaction between other students and the instructor. Activities can include anything from writing papers, doing projects, group discussion and hands on activities. It may be difficult for the teacher to decide which activity is best; therefore, after deciding the instructional objectives, a teacher should keep them nearby and use them as a source for deciding which activity to use. There are different levels of objectives and the instructor will want to choose the activity or activities based on that particular level. It is important to remember that whatever activity is chosen, it must support the student in learning the instructional objectives. It

must also align with what the subject of the lesson.

Instructional strategies and priorities
One way to determine instructional strategies and priorities is to examine the assessments of student achievement. Student assessments give counselors and instructors a chance to see on what level the students are achieving or struggling. If students are struggling in a certain area then it is time to decide if a certain teaching method needs to be changed or adjusted in some way. Priorities also need to be set in regards to deciding what teaching methods need to be changed and which ones work best with what student. If the assessments show students are achieving in certain areas, then counselors will know certain methods are successful. Priorities should be set on how to decide continuing with this achievement. The instructors should be asked if they need any additional materials to continue on this road to success.

Student-centered and teacher-centered instruction
An effective class will have a mixture of student-centered and teacher-centered instruction. It is important for students to acquire a base of knowledge before they try to apply it, and teacher-centered instructional methods will tend to be more appropriate for this. Although the lecture is the traditional form of teacher-centered instruction, teachers may also use textbooks, newspapers, the internet, or CD-ROMs to accomplish this goal. After this, it is desirable to move on to activities in which the students are required to do something with the knowledge they have acquired. Group discussions, individual problem-solving exercises, and case studies are all student-centered instruction methods that force students to analyze and evaluate situations based on what they have learned.

Role-plays
In a role-play, students are required to assume the roles of the various parties in a debate or discussion. This kind of instruction is especially useful for subjects in which it is

- 33 -

important that students understand and empathize with the parties concerned; in a discussion of industrial layoffs, for instance, it might be helpful for students to see the pressures acting on both the management and the laborers. It is very important that students are well prepared for their roles, and that the subject of the role-play is appropriate for the age group and the progress that has been made in the course. Lastly, teachers should take great care to emphasize that students are merely acting out roles, and that any disagreements should not be personal.

Class discussion
Class discussion is an effective teaching method when going over difficult concepts or covering material on which there are varying viewpoints. Sometimes, teachers might want to organize discussion by giving an agenda or a list of questions to be collectively answered, while other times teachers may want to allow the conversation to flow where it will. One of the main concerns in a large class is that some students will dominate discussion, while others will remain silent. Teachers may want to make participation mandatory to remedy this, or they may want to divide the class up into smaller discussion groups. Teachers may also find class discussion more profitable if they plan ahead and provide students with a list of the topics to be discussed before the day of the discussion.

Group work
Group work may be an effective way of encouraging students to master difficult material, because it forces them to describe the material to one another and agree on concepts. Group work also helps develop social skills and the ability to debate objectively and fairly. Teachers may want to select the groups themselves, to ensure that there is the desired distribution of males and females, of high and low ability students, and so that any disruptive students will not be grouped together. It is essential that groups be held responsible for presenting their work either to the teacher or to the rest of the class,

so that time is not wasted. In addition, teachers will want to set a series of small goals for groups rather than one large one, so that students are continually required to demonstrate progress in their work.

Games and simulations
Games and simulations are an excellent way for students to model complicated business processes and thereby better understand some difficult concepts. Moreover, they are a fun way to conclude a unit while still ensuring that students have mastered the material. There are plenty of games available that deal with running a simulated business. Differentiation is key when assigning games to a class; teachers want to avoid creating unfair teams or creating situations in which some students will be embarrassed. On the other hand, game situations are more likely to encourage cooperation among students of different ability, as they strive to win a contest. As with other activities, it is essential that directions are clear and exact, so that controversy and confusion can be avoided.

Case studies
Teachers can effectively use case studies to solidify conceptual knowledge that has been taught in a particular unit. In a case study, the teacher provides specific information, and students are required to analyze and evaluate the information. For example, students might be presented with a business plan and asked to describe its strengths and weaknesses. When developing case studies, a teacher should make sure that the information is comprehensible to all the members of the class and that no untaught concepts are required to perform an adequate analysis. It is also important to limit the amount of information given: too much data may confuse students and detract from the power of the exercise. Finally, teachers should ensure that there are some areas of the assignment that require creative thought, rather than simply recitation of the course material.

Assignments

Teachers will typically assign students a task or series of tasks to solidify and assess learning. Class assignments encourage students to manipulate and analyze course material. When making assignments, teachers should make sure to have a clear idea of what knowledge they are seeking to reinforce. Assignments should have varying degrees of difficulty, such that the least able students can attempt everything and the most able students will feel challenged. If research is required to complete the assignment, the teacher should have established the means for the students to perform this research. Finally, teachers should always grade every particular part of an assignment separately, so that students will have a better idea of what is expected of them, and in what areas they need to improve.

Investigative assignments
A teacher should keep a few things in mind when developing an investigative assignment for his or her class. First, it is better to assign several short tasks than one long task; students are more likely to become confused and flustered by long and unclear assignments. In addition, the teacher should leave some of the questions open-ended, so that students can distinguish themselves by their enthusiasm and understanding. Teachers might consider whether a particular investigation would be better carries out by a group or by an individual. Some investigations are more beneficial when students have a chance to talk amongst themselves, whereas in others it may be essential that a student handle every element him or herself. Teachers should make clear requirements about the way the investigation should be presented; it is wise to vary the format throughout the course, so that students gain experience giving speeches, writing reports, and creating visual presentations.

Differentiation
In classes that consist of students with varying abilities, it is crucial that a teacher practice differentiation: that is, distinguishing between students and adjusting the class material to engage all of them. This of course is a great responsibility for a teacher: more time must be spent planning, and teachers must guard against settling for lessons that appeal strictly to the middle level of the class. Besides differentiating between students, teachers must also differentiate between classes. Some classes may have a different "character" than others, depending on the time of day when they are held and their composition. Differentiation is especially important in classes because they are frequently available to all students, regardless of aptitude.

Teacher/parent relationships

Teachers too rarely make use of students' parents and run into problems later in they year as a result of not communicating properly with them. It is important to start every school year by sending a letter home with your students. This note should generally welcome the student to your class and give your contact information. This is also a great chance to make any requests for equipment or help that you might have. Some teachers ask parents to send them a list of their child's strengths and weaknesses. It is always a good idea to inform parents at the beginning of the year about your policies on homework, grading, and assessment. In addition, an early note is a good chance to mention whatever supplies the students will need for class.

Diversity and Multiculturalism

Cultural diversity

Particularly in a school setting, counselors will often work with students from varied cultural and ethnic backgrounds. Knowledge of the belief systems, perspectives, and sensitivities of an array of cultures and ethnicities is invaluable when working with students from varied backgrounds, particularly in a group setting. The foundation of this knowledge lies in recognition of the far-reaching influence of culture, as well as personal biases and perceptions that the counselor might have. Counselors should also be aware of misunderstandings and miscommunications within the group that might be culturally based, and work with the group to resolve these misunderstandings. In this context, students in the group can also gain an appreciation for different cultures, and an acceptance of the practices and belief systems within those cultures. A group counselor who possesses a knowledge and sensitivity of diverse cultures is a valuable resource in the school community.

As America becomes more culturally diverse, the schools will often be comprised of a mix of different races, religions and socioeconomic levels. Counselors need to be cognizant of not only the existence of this mix, but also the significance of these factors in the learning environments of students. One of the factors that counselors should be sensitized to is that certain ethnic groups may be victims of social and economic hierarchies, which can affect the availability of technology and other education-related amenities. Counselors can act as non-judgmental liaisons for students if they are aware and sensitive to some of the situational differences that are often defined by race. They can also work with groups of students on such issues as assertiveness and empowerment. Other factors include issues that arise for second-language learners as well as religious and cultural premises that may affect student interactions with others and with lesson materials.

An important foundation for counselors to broach the subject of culture is to first define what culture is, and what it affects. Below are some of the key components of culture:

- Beliefs or belief systems that define one's place in society, the world, and the cosmos
  o These beliefs can then translate into assumptions and practices regarding social status, personal empowerment, and relation to material wealth
- Perception of life experiences and how those experiences can affect life choices
- Value systems including family, career, and education
- Religious beliefs and practices
- Definitions and circumstances relating to belief in life's purpose
- Accepted behaviors for self-validation
- It is also important to remember that cultural distinctions are often rooted in historical tradition, supported by generations of practice and affirmation. Working with a culturally diverse population is best approached by recognizing and respecting the roots of culture.

Multicultural counseling

In the process of developing the counseling relationship with a student or students, it is important to recognize if it is that of multicultural counseling. Multicultural counseling occurs when the race or ethnicity of the student(s) is different from that of the counselor. The multicultural counseling relationship will necessarily involve two sets of expectations, perceptions, social environments, beliefs and backgrounds, often beyond the usual disparities between two people. Sensitivity to possible culturally based differences can be helpful with communication, expectations and goal setting. The five major cultural groups identified by the Association of Multicultural Counseling and Development (AMCD) are:

1. African/Black
2. Asian
3. Caucasian/European

4. Hispanic/Latino
5. Native American

Other cultural groups can pertain to gender, sexual orientation, religious beliefs, etc. Without falling into a biased taxonomy regarding multicultural counseling, it is nonetheless a consideration that can complement other factors in the counseling relationship.

Counselors who will be working with different cultural or ethnic groups are best served by not only receiving initial training in multicultural counseling, but also to attend workshops and other instruction in the field on an ongoing basis. Many schools and districts with a diverse student body require this of school counselors. Counselors who receive ongoing training in multicultural counseling will be less likely to impose their own belief systems and cultural insensitivity to the counseling relationship, and more likely to consider cultural differences when communicating and setting goals with students. School counselors and counselors can usually recognize when they are incorporating cultural sensitivity in their counseling methods by assessing the success of the sessions. If a counselor or counseling program is operating with multicultural competence, there should be no significant differentiation between success rates based on cultural factors.

Multicultural counseling incorporates three distinct levels of competence. The initial, foundational level is that of awareness. Counselors can begin to build multicultural competence by first becoming aware of the effects of culture on worldview, behaviors, etc. It is also a good first step for counselors to be aware of their own preconceived notions about culture(s), as well as aspects of their value system that are culturally based. Building on this, counselors can come to a knowledge, respect and understanding of other cultures, realizing that cultural assimilation is not always the recommended course of action for students. Cultural

sensitivity includes refraining from imposing dominant beliefs and attitudes, as appropriate. Learning to balance social protocol with cultural expression is a valuable skill that counselors can learn and teach to students. Lastly, counselors can increasingly develop skills that enable them to implement effective and appropriate strategies when working with students from diverse cultures.

Counselors who are cognizant of, and sensitive to, cultural differences will more likely develop strategies and hypotheses that are absent of cultural biases. Developing hypotheses that are not culturally slanted will allow counselors to more objectively plan and assess intervention strategies. Multicultural sensitivity enables counselors to design and deliver lesson plans that are free from stereotypical icons or remarks, as well as when and how to generalize instructions to diverse groups of students. With increased sensitivity, counselors can also design activities and strategies that are inclusive of diverse cultures, or individualize activities as appropriate. An example of an inclusive activity would be one that elicits student responses about a recent event on campus that they have all shared in. An individualized activity could be asking students to write about holiday traditions in their home, which would inherently allow students to respond from a cultural perspective.

Sensitivity to cultural differences can be especially pivotal when consulting with parents and teachers on a student matter, particularly when a student's family is from a different culture than that of the teacher and/or counselor. Often, the consulting/discussion group will be comprised of the student, his/her parent(s), the counselor, the teacher, and possibly a school counselor. Counselors need to be especially sensitive to key factors that may include:
  • A parent who lives in a culturally isolated household or neighborhood

- The student who is inherently bi-cultural
- The culture of the teacher/counselor
- The culture of the counselor

Counselors should create an environment that is conducive to comfortable communication and open to input from all parties. Counselors should be cognizant of and sensitive to the cultural significance and perception of the issue at hand, as well as to best ways to address the problem within the cultural contexts represented.

Addressing cultural biases or stereotypes
In the process of facilitating a discussion among parents, student, teachers, and other parties in a consulting discussion, counselors may find that one more individuals may be communicating or acting from a paradigm of bias or stereotyping. This may develop into a resistance to resolution, particularly if the problem is culturally based. Any discussion toward resolution may be hampered by one or more individuals acting out of cultural bias. Counselors may need to challenge the individual(s) by pointing out the specific words or behaviors that perpetuate stereotypes and the negative effect that these actions have on the intervention process. Counselors can remind the group of the shared desire for resolution, and how stereotyping can detract from the purpose of the gathering. They can remind participants that the well-being of the student will be best served by collaboration and refraining from expressions of cultural bias and stereotyping.

Multicultural competence
Cultural and ethnic diversity in the school environment often results in disparities in peripheral areas, particularly if issues of oppression and bias are not addressed. Some of the peripheral areas that can be impacted by culturally based hierarchies include academic achievement, literacy competence, AP course participation, career planning, and most significantly disparities in standardized test results, which can negatively affect college opportunities, and ultimately income level. Counselors who have been trained in, and operate within a paradigm of multicultural sensitivity can significantly mitigate these disparities by acting as a liaison between the student body and school officials. In this capacity, counselors can act on students' behalf when there is a culturally-based misunderstanding, as well help students develop strategies for bridging cultural gaps. Counselors can also consult with school staff and officials on pinpointing practices that may inherently pose a disadvantage for certain cultural groups.

For counselors to be competent in multicultural counseling, it is important for them to develop a sensitivity to the significance of the distinguishing characteristics the define culture(s). A good foundation for this sensitivity is for counselors to conduct self-investigation and self-reflection on their own cultural background. Counselors can develop an understanding of how their cultural and ethnic background has contributed to their value system, their traditions and rituals, their view of the individual's place in the larger society, and many other personal traits. Likewise, cultural history can reveal how particular cultures or cultural traits have played a part in social hierarchy. Counselors who are aware of their own ties to culture will be better able to understand the significance of culture in students who come from a different cultural background. A counselor with this valuable foundation can be an important liaison for students who need to balance culture tradition with assimilation.

The issues of diversity in the counseling and school environment are complex and multidimensional. As a society, our collective knowledge of diverse cultures and the issues of multiculturalism is continually evolving. Therefore, it is advisable for counselors to periodically attend workshops and seminars on the subject at least throughout their work as a school counselor. Each workshop or seminar will help to expand a counselor's knowledge of and sensitivity to diverse cultures. From these events, counselors will better learn how to work with students and their families in the school counseling environment. They will learn strategies and terminology that reflect sensitivity and understanding of the scope of culture in general, and the specifics of particular cultures. Fortunately, many professional organizations are aware of the need for ongoing training in multiculturalism and will usually offer numerous opportunities for the school counselor.

The benefits of meeting with other counselors on a regular basis, by joining organizations dedicated to increasing cultural sensitivity, can greatly add to the knowledge base formed from attending workshops and seminars. Also, the knowledge gained from periodic attendance at workshops can sometimes dissipate in an environment where it is not necessarily endorsed. Meeting with peers can repeat and validate this knowledge and provide the opportunity to implement and revise strategies, in an environment of learning, before applying these strategies in the classroom as the counselor/teacher. The combined expertise of the group can allow for shared ideas and strategies toward multicultural competency. Also, as a group, an organization of peers can collaborate on methods and strategies for combating oppression in the school and surrounding community through school counseling curricula and programs. These professional organizations include Counselors for Social Justice, The Association for Multicultural Counseling and Development, and others.

The ability to read, analyze and critically explore issues of culture diversity through a written medium offers benefits not necessarily present in a seminar, workshop or organizational meeting. Literature about cultural diversity can explore historical and current events through the eyes and perspectives of several cultural groups, because a written text like this is usually the culmination of research and interviews. Reading these texts, counselors can gain a comprehensive understanding of the historical factors and impact of events in relation to race, socioeconomic class, culture, gender and other groups who have been oppressed or victimized because of their particular culture. A good book dealing with these issues is Howard Zinn's A People's History of the United States, which contains personal testimonies and anecdotes about the subject. These personal stories allow for a first-person perspective on issues of social justice, giving the counselor a sense of empathy to bring to the multicultural counseling environment.

The benefits of reading literature that addresses issues of multiculturalism are generally two-fold: For one thing, literature on the subject of multiculturalism is always evolving, reflecting current research and other input. As with organizational meetings, literature dealing with cultural diversity is a compilation of the experiences and expertise of a number of people from a spectrum of perspectives. Counselors are well served to become cognizant of this evolving expertise, in multiculturalism as well as other aspects of counseling. Secondly, teaching or counseling in isolation from the continued input of others increases the risk of personal biases and perspectives coloring the curriculum. Any one individual inherently has a limited worldview, and no individual or group of individuals could possibly know all there is to know about other cultures. Consequently, continued exposure to viewpoints and perspectives beyond his/her horizon allows counselors to be aware, sensitive and able to respond appropriately to a diverse student body.

A checklist can provide a rubric for counselors to assess their own level of multicultural awareness, sensitivity and competence. For counselors commencing their own edification in multicultural sensitivity, or those who are relative new and beginning the process of multicultural training, checklists can provide a set of goals to attain in the process of becoming more aware of multicultural issues. Counselors can see which issues or concerns are in need of further work, and can take advantage of the available resources for developing in these areas. Once these goals are attained, counselors can periodically review the checklist to ascertain if they are continuing to incorporate the guidelines and strategies represented by the checklist, and again refer to outside resources if indicated. The Association for Multicultural Counseling and Development, as well as other agencies, publishes appropriate checklists that address such issues as behaviors, knowledge, sensitivity, and awareness.

The first step in becoming more culturally aware is to recognize the need to do so. Counselors who work with a diversity of races and socioeconomic levels can first recognize those differences in a lateral manner, and invest the time and attention to understand the roots and ramifications of the differences. There are cultural sensitivity training sessions available, possibly through the school district. Although this cultural sensitivity is becoming more commonplace and even required in some districts, counselors and their programs will be best served by a proactive approach. Some counselors reach beyond the school district to surrounding cultural enclaves, to better understand the nuances of a particular culture. Some counselors take further action by becoming involved in addressing policy and practices that serve to better the overall academic achievement of a particularly underserved group, although the effectiveness of this is not clearly validated.

Counselors working with diverse cultures can increase and enrich their sensitivity by understanding the fabric and terminology of a particular culture, as well as developmental theories pertaining to that culture. Understanding culture includes a working knowledge of the history, traditions, strengths, needs and resources of a specific culture. Counselors can act as consultant and liaison by assisting students who are facing misunderstanding and misrepresentation by school staff, students, public media, etc. Understanding the semantics and terminology of specific cultures can be particularly helpful in mediating between cultural groups, as well as encouraging communication and sensitivity between groups. Counselors who approach diversity with a fundamental knowledge of specific cultures and the impact of culture can provide a role model for dynamic multicultural understanding and communication in the school environment. Understanding the impact of culture in particular can lay a strong foundation for multicultural sensitivity, as counselors, students and school personnel begin to recognize the cultural bases for many misunderstandings.

Cultural sensitivity can provide counselors with not only the ability to recognize culturally based differences, but also the capacity to recognize culturally based disparities within the school environment. Counselors can first observe interactions relating to cultural differences, and then address those interactions, maintaining sensitivity to both the minority and the majority cultures. Counselors can involve school staff and counselors in discussions regarding the methods and policies for addressing cultural differences and conflicts among students as well as between teachers and students. Certain school practices can lead to an appreciation and celebration of these differences. These practices can include talking with students, talking with parents, and an ongoing respect of and sensitivity to cultural premises. Increasing cultural awareness within a school environment can lead to a rich, dynamic school environment, and further support the value of a well-designed counseling program.

Counselors striving to attain a healthy school environment of cultural sensitivity can begin the process by presenting a professional demeanor toward all students and other members of the school community. It is important to recognize that cultural and socioeconomic differences can affect behaviors and appearances, and to avoid responding negatively or differently to these manifestations. It is also important to remember that every person, including the counselor, lives with certain presuppositions, and to be cognizant of these presuppositions while developing an increased understanding of cultural differences and misunderstandings. Some of the bases for these misunderstandings include racism, stereotyping, socioeconomic oppression and discrimination. Additionally, cultural differences could be race-based, gender-based, belief-based or based on other distinguishing characteristics. Being aware of these cultural layers and learning to respond with dignity and respect can provide a healthy example for the school community.

Language limitations

Counselors who have been sensitized to cultural differences, and trained in strategies for addressing these differences in the school environment, nonetheless sometimes experience difficulty finding appropriate terminology to communicate with school staff, counselors, students and the rest of the school community in this regard. There are no clear-cut guidelines to facilitate this; however, counselors can first recognize that cultural differences can stem from historical traditions, racial or ethnic classifications, economic status, and cosmology, to name a few factors. These differences can affect how people view and respond to life experiences, and often divide populations into groups of similar experience and perception. Awareness of some of the roots of cultural diversity and cultural bias can help the counselor develop terminology for addressing issues of diversity, and for integrating cultural sensitivity into various aspects of the counseling program.

Teaching a multicultural class

One of the great aspects of teaching in most American classrooms is the diversity of the student population. This diversity can be a great advantage to a class, though it can also be an obstacle if it is not handled properly. Too many teachers take the easy way out and make their instructional methods the same for all students, when it would be to their benefit to modify their methods to best suit the student. Research has found that teachers are most successful when they focus on academic achievement, and allow their students to maintain their cultural differences. The best teachers are also those that attempt to cultivate in their students a fair-minded view of diversity; that is, a pride in their won culture and respect for the cultures of others.

Gender discrimination

Teachers need to be aware that not all discrimination in the classroom is based on race or ethnicity. Too often, teachers make assumptions about their students based on gender. Although research has shown that there are some difference between the learning styles of males and females, every child should receive the same chances to grow and develop in the classroom. Often, discrimination can be totally unconscious, the result of cultural assumptions about the interests, strengths, and weaknesses of boys and girls. This is harmful if it inhibits children from pursuing the fulfillment of their potential. The result of gender discrimination can be low self-esteem, low achievement, and even open conflict.

There are a number of ways, both intentional and unintentional, that teachers may discriminate against students because of their gender. Research has shown that teachers tend to give boys more attention and approval than they give girls. There seems to be a broad cultural assumption that boys are better suited to mathematics and science, while girls are better at reading and the arts. Teachers often expect boys to be more assertive and active, and girls to be docile and passive. Boys are more frequently asked to

- 41 -

assume leadership positions in the classroom. Boys are also more likely to be punished harshly for breaking the rules. In general, girls are criticized more for deficiencies in skill, while boys are more frequently reprimanded for bad behavior.

There are a few easy ways that every teacher can make his or her classroom a more equitable environment for students of both genders. The most important thing is to be conscious of discrimination, and make a point to avoid treating students differently. Specifically, teachers should make sure to assign leadership roles to both boys and girls, and to discourage students from breaking up into groups that are segregated by gender. Teachers should encourage their students to participate in those activities that are considered atypical for their gender; that is, boys can be encouraged to pursue the arts, while girls can be pushed to excel in science and math. It is always a good idea to reinforce instances of intergender cooperation as they occur in the class.

Sex and gender
Many people confuse sex and gender. Whereas a person's sex is strictly dependent on his or her sex chromosomes, hormone balance, and genital anatomy, gender refers to the psychological and social parts of being a male or female. Every individual has a sexual identity that is out of his or her control. To a certain degree, gender is also out of the individual's control, as it is a result of the way the individual is raised and how society treats that individual. Still, many people make conscious decisions to alter their gender identity. Some people simply feel more comfortable as a gender other than the one they have been raised as, and they may alter their dress, appearance, and behavior to suit their new gender identity.

Assessment

Student Health and Well-being

Abuse and neglect
Students who have been abused, neglected, or who have been witness to abuse within their family are inherently at risk of decline in any or all of the areas of physical, mental, social, spiritual or economic health. Often students with a history of neglect or abuse display chronic behavior problems including anxiety, depression, substance abuse and/or other emotional or mental disturbances. Further, victims of childhood abuse or neglect often feel a deep-rooted sense of shame or embarrassment, which translates to chronic social and emotional isolation. They often exhibit poor academic performance and retreat from normal activities with friends and fellow students, particularly if they have been helpless bystanders to abuse that has been perpetrated against a parent or siblings. Counselors find that there is often a clear correlation between at-risk behavior in school, and abuse or neglect in the home.

Social health
When counselors refer to social health, they mean the ability of an individual to interact with other people effectively, to develop positive relationships, and to adequately fulfill social roles. Individuals who are socially healthy contribute in the affairs of the community, live peacefully among other people, and are sexually healthy. Social health has major effects on all the other aspects of a person's life. Studies have shown that individuals without strong social ties are more likely to abuse substances, to have heart disease, and even to develop cold infections. Furthermore, individuals who become ill are more likely to recover if they have support from friends and family.

Psychosocial development
Self-actualization: In order to reach your highest potential, you have to satisfy a number of basic needs. To illustrate this,

counselors have set up a pyramid of psychological health, so that individuals can see what conditions must be met before they can excel. Before anything else is accomplished, your physiological needs for food, water, shelter, and sleep must be met. Then, if these needs are satisfied, you can work on achieving safety for yourself and your loved ones. When this is accomplished, you are free to develop loving relationships and fit into a society. These relationships are a necessary foundation for self-esteem and a healthy respect for other people. The person who has satisfied all of these needs is said to be ready for self-actualization, the fulfillment of his or her potential.

Individual values

All individuals have a set of values, criteria by which they understand and judge the world. Sometimes, though, individuals may claim to have a certain set of values even though they appear to act on another. In order to clarify your values, it is a good idea to consider carefully the consequences of your choices and ensure that they are moral and positive. Counselors define individual values as being either instrumental or terminal: instrumental values are ways of thinking that a person holds important, for instance being loyal or loving; terminal values are goals or ideals that a person works towards, for instance happiness. The values of an individual and even of a society are constantly changing, so you have to be sensitive to the values that you are promoting with your choices.

Self-esteem

Self-esteem is the way that you think about yourself. Every person wants to feel as if he or she is important and valued in society, and as if they are living up to their potential. Having healthy self-esteem is not only derived from these feelings, but it makes it possible for you to do the things necessary to make yourself happy and content. Most counselors agree that an individual's self-esteem is largely determined during childhood. Low self-esteem often haunts those who have been abused in the past, and can unfortunately lead

people to seek out relationships in which they are treated poorly. One technique that many counselors recommend for boosting self-esteem is positive thinking and talking. Even if it feels forced, studies have shown that encouraging the mind to take an optimistic viewpoint can eventually make good self-esteem a habit.

Emotional intelligence

In recent years, counselors have determined that what is known as emotional intelligence may be just as important as an individual's IQ. According to the psychologist Daniel Goleman, there are five areas of emotional intelligence: self-awareness, altruism, personal motivation, empathy, and the ability to love and be loved. Studies have shown that individuals with a high level of emotional intelligence will succeed at work and in developing positive personal relationships. An individual's emotional intelligence is not the same throughout his or her life, and many businesses have begun taking active steps to develop the emotional intelligence of their employees. Essentially, developing one's emotional intelligence requires listening to one's feelings and respecting them.

Moods

Moods are emotional states lasting for a few hours or days. Though every individual will have bad moods from time to time, some are better at managing their moods than others. Researchers have demonstrated that the most effective ways to solve a problem, and hence emerge from a bad mood, are to take immediate action, think about other successes, resolve to try harder, or reward oneself. Individuals who try to distract themselves, perhaps through socializing, will find that this only partly improves their mood. The worst things to do when you are in a bad mood are to vent at another person, isolate yourself, or give up. Using alcohol or drugs to escape a bad mood is also an ineffective way to feel better.

Empowering students

The idea of empowerment encompasses the distribution of resources, but is rooted in a larger context of social relationship and dynamics. Culturally based oppression often depends on acceptance from both the dominant culture and the oppressed culture to be perpetuated. Historically oppressed cultures sometimes adopt ways of thinking and behaving that originally were enforced by violence or other extreme means, but have continued because of cultural identity. Likewise, historically dominant cultures adopt ways of thinking and behaving that perpetuate a false sense of superiority. Counselors can assist students from oppressed cultures or in other situations where they feel disenfranchised, in developing personal empowerment by encouraging them to relate to others from a position of recognizing that individuals, and groups of individuals, often share many similarities and are connected at a fundamental level. This kind of thinking transcends the historical relationships, and forges new interpersonal connections, giving empowerment to previously disenfranchised groups.

There are several key areas of personal dynamics and self-image that are impacted through empowerment:

- Individuals begin to relate to others based on commonalities of experience and belonging, rather than on preconceived notions of difference.
- Individuals begin to recognize social dynamics objectively, rather than to internalize them.
- A sense of empowerment and recognition of social dynamics can significantly reverse students' thinking, from that of victim to that of change agent for social justice.

Once individuals understand that it is the dynamics, and not any inherent inferiority, that contributed to their social status, the implications for personal growth can be exponential.

Counselors who work with students toward empowerment are literally giving them back the power that was missing because of culturally based beliefs, attitudes and practices. Empowerment should be understood as not hierarchical, such that the oppressed group is now the dominant group, but rather as egalitarian, ensuring fair distribution of resources and opportunity.

Counselors can help students feel empowered by pointing out their membership in the larger community, and helping them to develop ownership and responsibility for their actions. Counselors can begin by discussing the parameters of group membership, noting that each of us belongs to several groups. Students can recognize that they belong to groups identified as students, community, culture, gender, etc. This enables students to transcend limits of identity. Counselors can then point out that social dynamics involve the whole community, affecting individuals in myriad ways. This allows students to broaden their understanding of social processes. Students should also be encouraged to take personal responsibility for their academic progress, as well as other actions and behaviors. Counselors can work with students in developing new behaviors that reflect a stronger self-confidence, a perception of membership in the larger community, and a realization that they can positively contribute to that community.

Counselors working with students toward empowerment can first provide them with the knowledge and perspective that will allow them to approach their goals and circumstances differently, allowing them to consider different/better results. Even though students can understand their community membership in theory, often, particular events or circumstances become discouraging symbols of validation for the status quo. Counselors can partner with students in confronting these circumstances, addressing them on a problem-specific basis, from an enlightened and empowered perspective. A good problem-solving strategy includes the following key steps:

1. Identify the problem.
2. Work together to set a goal that will mitigate or solve the problem.
3. Develop incremental actions toward the goal.
4. Identify available resources for achieving the goal(s).

Counselors can also provide support and encouragement, reminding students of their strengths, their desire to change their circumstances, and the support and resources available.

At-risk students

Recognizing that at-risk youth are generally overwhelmed and under-supported, counselors can be particularly effective by providing students with numerous opportunities to develop empowerment and self-confidence. When setting goals with and for students, it is important to set achievable, short-term goals to ensure success by the student(s). Each success should lead to further and larger successes and counselors can provide scaffolding goals and challenges. Counselors can also encourage listening and cooperation among family members by their own willingness to take a back seat and emphasize the importance of collaboration and teamwork, facilitating when appropriate. In terms of advocacy, counselors may be aware of policies or procedures within the school system that inherently poses an obstacle or inequity for at-risk students, and may need to intervene on behalf of the student(s). This is another way that counselors can model empowerment.

Building character in students

One of the many responsibilities of a counselor is building the character of the students. They should always set high expectations for good behavior in the lives of the students. However, if students are expected to behave and act in a certain way then they must see examples of good behavior happening in the environment around them. What happens at home cannot be controlled but what happens at school can. Students should be able to see staff members using caring words and having a positive attitude. Changing student's attitudes can have a major impact on their work habits and achievement. Character building is something that can be carried with a student for the rest of their life. Responsibility, kindness, caring, trustworthiness, and integrity are character traits students will need as they continue through school and adulthood it does not stop in elementary school.

Peer relationships

Adolescent students are simultaneously developing a sense of self-worth and self-identity, while at the same time developing close ties with peer groups. It is important for the counselor to assist the student in balancing the significance of peer relationships with the evolvement of his or her own self-definition. Students in this age group often develop a sense of ethnic identity before that of self-identity. While the role of a peer group can bolster and validate a student's ethnic or cultural identity, it is also important to develop personal and individual goals. Counselors can work with adolescent students to help them identify personal goals as well as changing ideas and perceptions. The effect of commonality of beliefs and behaviors can sometimes deter development of individuality. Nonetheless, because peer relationships are very important to this age group, counselors should also encourage and endorse healthy peer relationships.

Dysfunctional relationships

Dysfunctional relationships are those in which the behavior of the participants does not lead to positive communication or honesty. As one would expect, people who have substance abuse problems or addictive

- 45 -

behaviors are more likely to be in a dysfunctional relationship. Sometimes, one party may have an inaccurate idea of healthy relationships and will make unfair demands on the other. If there is not trust in a relationship, sometimes jealousy will cause a person to become paranoid and overly dependent on the other. These kinds of unhealthy relationships exist in every section of society, because they spring from personal psychological problems that are universal. Unfortunately, dysfunctional relationships can be very difficult to leave.

Codependence
A codependent individual is one who allows him or herself to be used to achieve satisfaction by someone with an addiction. Codependency causes a person to ignore his or her own needs in order to serve someone else's. They will change their identity, undergo unpleasant experiences, and even give up their friends and family in order to serve the other. People with low self-esteem and their own set of addictions are more likely to become codependent. In order to escape from a codependent relationship, an individual must realize the worth of his or her own life as well as his or her inability to change the other person. Codependent behavior has at its heart a simple desire for love, though this desire is poorly expressed.

Violence
Youth violence is a major problem in American society; homicide was the second leading cause of death among people between the age of 10 and 24. Youths may be at risk of committing violent acts if they have antisocial beliefs, a low IQ, poor behavioral control, a history of aggressive behavior, or an involvement with alcohol and drugs. Oftentimes, adolescents become violent if they were raised by an authoritarian parent, if they come from a low economic class, or if they have been witness to violence in the home. Adolescents can minimize their risk of being involved in violence if they maintain strong, positive ties with their family and school, if they stay involved in community

activities, and if they display an intolerant attitude toward violent behavior.

Oftentimes, individuals who have suffered some traumatic brain injury are more likely to display aggressive behavior. The abuse of alcohol or drugs will also increase an individual's tendency towards explosive rage. Scientific evidence has shown that many prescription medications, especially painkillers, anti-anxiety drugs, anti-depressants, steroids, and over-the-counter sedatives, may increase the risk of violent behavior. Males who commit violent crimes appear to have lower levels of serotonin in their brains, and males with a high level of testosterone are thought to be more prone to violence. As one would expect, individuals who suffer from psychological problems like schizophrenia are more likely to become violent.

In addition, children of abusive parents are much more likely to engage in violent behavior as they grow older. Although scientists believe that this is in part because such children fail to learn other coping mechanisms, there is also speculation that aggressive tendencies may be inherited. However, even if a child grows up in a nonabusive home, if they live in a violent community they are more likely to become overly aggressive. Children who perform poorly at school or who are ostracized by their peers are also more likely to become violent. Individuals who display violent behavior at a young age are often rejected by their community, which only exaggerates the problem.

There is a great deal of research to suggest that the portrayal of violence in television, films, and music can incite impressionable individuals to commit similar acts. According to some statistics, the average American child will be exposed to about 40,000 deaths and countless more acts of violence during his or her childhood and adolescence. It has also been clearly illustrated that poverty, unemployment, and gang involvement often lead to violent acts. The risk of violence seems to be inversely proportionate to the chances that an individual has for success in society. It should be noted that violence seems to be tied to economics rather than to race; no racial or ethnic group has been shown to have a greater predisposition to violence.

Often, students who feel disenfranchised will act out by bullying or otherwise victimizing other students. This sense of separation can result from a student feeling isolated from peer groups, cultural groups, family, or other groups from which the student feels excluded. This sense of exclusion may precipitate the student attacking other students, with bullying, ignoring, harassment, etc. This sense of isolation may also be a precipitator of suicide, or attacking the self. Students may intensify this attacking behavior by bringing weapons on campus, or inciting physical fighting. Recent years have seen more covert and violent victimization on school campuses. Counselors and other school personnel need to be attentive to any incidents of bullying, which can escalate into more intense forms. Bullying and other victimization may be more prevalent among certain groups of students, and should provide the counselor with the opportunity to address ubiquitous attitudes and behaviors.

Any act of bullying or other victimization implies a power hierarchy. The victim is perceived and treated as powerless against the perpetrator, and each act of victimization further endorses that hierarchy. Often, social injustices and inequalities in a community or school environment provide fertile ground for bullying and victimization, which perpetuates the inequalities. If a comprehensive program to balance inequalities is not implemented, the bullying and victimization will most likely continue. Counselors can begin to address chronic victimization problems by educating students and pertinent adults about how to effectively break the cycle of victimization. Victimization can also take the form of gossiping or excluding certain individuals from group activities. Although some schools have rules specifically prohibiting victimization, counselors can provide a valuable service by working with the parties involved to recognize and stop the cycle of victimization.

One of the factors that makes it difficult to predict violent incidents is that many students who display violent behavior do so on an impulse, resulting in most violent incidents being unplanned. Generally speaking, students who feel disenfranchised, helpless, or threatened will sometimes act out by perpetrating violent acts or behaviors. Often, violence will be perpetrated by feelings of desperation or an irrational fear that others may be threatening harm. Males are generally more likely to commit violence than females, and the highest incidents of violence fall between the ages of 15 and 24. Lower socioeconomic status is also a common factor in violent tendencies. In addition, if a student has a history of violence, s/he will be more likely to commit violence. Lastly, students who have disorders related to conduct, ADHD, hallucination, delusions, etc., will be more likely to commit violence.

Most of the research completed on the violent tendencies of students has been completed by governmental and FBI profilers and analysts, and made available to counselors and other educators to mitigate the possibility of future occurrences. There are four basic classifications of threats of violence identified by the FBI:

1. Vague threats that imply violence. The threat is implied in the terminology, but not specified. Time and place are not generally specified.
2. Veiled threats of violence. The terminology is more specific, but time and place are still not specified.
3. Conditional threats of violence. The terminology refers to violence if certain conditions are not met. A common example of this is extortion.
4. Direct threats of violence. These

threats are clearly stated and straightforward. The terminology is in the form of a warning, specifies a target, time and place.

According to government publications, the likelihood or seriousness of a threat can be generally divided into three sets of criteria:

Low-level threats are generally categorized by vagueness, a lack of specificity, etc. Students may make a general, indirect statement of threat with little or no detail, and little or no specific plan to carry it out. Minimal risk is associated with low-level threats.

Medium-level threats are more direct and plausible but do not appear to be realistic. They may contain details about time and place, but lack evidence of comprehensive planning. A medium-level threat may include phrasing that indicates seriousness, but lack the specificity to make it happen. The risk level of a medium-level threat is higher than a low-level threat, but generally does not pose imminent danger.

High-level threats are distinguishable by their high levels of specificity, and comprehensiveness and plausibility of a plan. High-level threats should be taken very seriously, and school officials should always contact the local authorities.

The FBI has developed a four-pronged model of threat assessment that focuses on the student making the threat(s) and his/her particular circumstances:

- Prong 1 assesses the behavior and emotional dynamics of the individual, including signs of alienation, poor anger management, poor coping skills in general, lack of trust, or marked changes in behavior.
- Prong 2 assesses the circumstances of the family and home of the student, including a lack of limits or lack of monitoring, access to weapons, lack of intimacy and/or volatile relationships within the family, particularly between the student and parent(s).
- Prong 3 assesses the student's perceived marginal place in the school community, evidenced by bullying, a lack of attachment to the school, inflexibility about culture, and a pecking order among the students.
- Prong 4 assesses the student's other connections, including peers at school, use of drugs or alcohol, and other outside activities or interests.

Counselors should be assured that incidents of campus-wide student violence have declined in recent years. Nonetheless, there is always some possibility of a student or students committing violent acts that harm or affect the campus as a whole. Unfortunately, there are not always clearly identified indicators of potential campus-wide violence. Most experts agree that this type of wide impact violence is usually the culmination of several factors in at-risk students. The best preparation strategies for counselors include both individual intervention for at-risk students and developing an intervention plan for the school. On the individual level, counselors should always work with students to mitigate their violent tendencies or fantasies, regardless of whether or not they appear to pose a threat to others. On the campus-wide level, counselors can work with school officials to develop a rubric for threat assessment, as well as an intervention plan to minimize the casualties should a campus-wide event occur.

Counselors can provide at-risk students with opportunities to develop healthy dynamics and self-validating experiences among their peers as well as with significant adults. Threat assessment teams can be formed and trained to focus on preventative strategies.

Peer mentor groups should be established that will allow both at-risk students and students not considered at risk to interact under the guise and facilitation of the counselor. These groups can provide an insulated environment for learning healthy strategies for coping with bullying, neglect and other forms of abuse. Counselors can teach healthy interpersonal skills within these groups. Counselors can also collaborate with local authorities and community groups to provide opportunities for at-risk youth to have positive experiences with adults and outside groups. At-risk students can be encouraged to join community support groups such as Big Brother/Sisters. Counselors can also encourage family members to develop connections with available support groups and resources.

Conflict resolution

It is inevitable in life that you will come into conflict with some difficult individuals. Many people persistently spar with others because they have a personality disorder based on low self-esteem or illness. For the most part, you will not be close enough to an individual to try and change them in any permanent way. Therefore, in most cases of conflict counselors recommend acknowledging the other person's viewpoint, and then finding a way to either avoid or circumvent that person. If confrontation is necessary, you should state your feelings honestly and politely. If possible, try to avoid making confrontations unnecessarily personal. Sometimes it helps to have a third party mediate an especially contentious dispute.

Types of abuse

Partner abuse
Sadly, about one in five women will be abused by a romantic partner during her life. Indeed, domestic violence is the largest cause of injury among women. Women are considered to be battered if they are the victims of repeated and persistent physical abuse. This is usually accompanied by a tremendous amount of psychological stress. Battered women are often unwilling to admit that they have been abused, and so the health care professionals who treat them are unaware of the abuse. Alcohol and stress are the reasons most often given by men to explain why they abuse their partners. Many of these men are not violent anywhere but in the home. Partner abuse seems to become more common the poorer a family becomes, and the more crowded their home becomes.

Child abuse
Although statistics have shown that impoverished parents seem to abuse their children more often, child abuse remains a problem among every socioeconomic group. Child abuse can be physical, psychological, or sexual. Sexual abuse includes virtually any sexual contact between an adult and child, whether it is kissing, fondling, oral sex, sexual intercourse, or just suggestive conversation. Pedophilia is the clinical term for any sexual abuse of a child that is perpetrated by an individual other than the child's parents. Incest, on the other hand, refers to sexual contact among members of the same family. Oftentimes, children that are psychologically or sexually abuse may develop physical symptoms, or begin to act out in society.

Substance abuse
Since the prevalence of substance abuse among youth is increasing, and the spectrum of illegal substances includes many possibilities, counselors should be at least generically educated on common legal and illegal substances and behaviors associated with substance abuse. Counselors should also be aware of local resources available for students involved in substance abuse. Although school guidance counselors cannot be expected to be experts on substance abuse, it is nonetheless a good idea to be cognizant of behaviors and other signs of possible substance abuse and be able to discuss the possibility with the student. However, students will not necessarily readily admit or discuss substance abuse, so the counselor should still be prepared for referral if

necessary. In addition, counselors should be aware of how substance abuse affects academic performance and mental ability, in order to best address these issues in a student for which substance abuse appears to be a contributing factor.

The Center for Disease Control not only considers alcohol destructive to adolescent health in itself, but also believes that it contributes to other behaviors that are damaging to adolescent health. Specifically, the CDC suggests that alcohol contributes to unintentional injuries, fights, academic problems, and other illegal behaviors. Over time, alcohol is blamed for liver disease, cancer, cardiovascular disease, neurological damage, depression, anxiety, and antisocial tendencies. The rate of alcohol abuse among adolescents has fluctuated a bit in the past years: whereas 50% of high school students admitted to regular drinking in 1999, only 45% said that they were regular drinkers in 2003. Of these, 28% stated that they engaged in regular heavy drinking.

The Center for Disease Control maintains that adolescent drug abuse is an ongoing problem that needs to be addressed. Besides the health risks associated with the drugs themselves, the CDC asserts that persistent drug use contributes to failure in school, fights, antisocial behavior, and unintentional injuries. Prolonged drug use can also be responsible for depression and anxiety. The CDC also maintains that drug use contributes to the HIV epidemic, insofar as those who share needles are liable to contract the virus, and drug users in general tend to engage in risky sexual behaviors. The statistics kept by the CDC state that marijuana use among teenagers decreased from 26% to 22% between 1997 and 2003.

According to the Center for Disease Control, every day about 4000 American teenagers try smoking for the first time. Assuming that conditions remain as they are today, about 6.4 million of today's children will eventually die from a smoking-related illness. The CDC reports that in 2003 22% of high school students smoked cigarettes regularly, and 15% smoked cigars on a regular basis. In addition, about 10% of high school students were users of smokeless tobacco. For the most part, students seem to be more likely to smoke cigarettes of they are from a poor background, and if they have parents or friends who are smokers. White males are far more likely to use smokeless tobacco than are any other demographic groups

Although students may be hesitant to self-report or even to recognize substance abuse, counselors can facilitate this recognition and self-reporting through a series of questions. The following questions target alcohol abuse and are identified by the acronym CAGE:

> C – Questions about cutting down. Ask the student if s/he has thought s/he should cut down on alcohol/substance use.
> A – The annoyance factor. Ask the student if s/he becomes annoyed when people criticize his/her drinking.
> G – The guilt factor. Ask the student if s/he ever feels guilty about the amount of alcohol/substance consumed.
> E – Alcohol as the eye opener. Ask the student if s/he ever needs alcohol to get going in the morning or to calm his/her nerves.

Counselors should also have regular access and referral to the Physician's Desk Reference to maintain current knowledge about drugs, alcohol, and possible side effects.

The following questions can be used as a guide for encouraging students to recognize and self-report substance abuse. Counselors can ask the following of students that may have a substance abuse problem:

- If they are taking over-the counter or prescription medications.
- The reason they take the medications.

- Any other medications/drugs they take.
- How long they have been taking these medications.
- Side effects, including severity and when they noticed the effects.
- If they drink alcohol.
- How they are affected by alcohol.
- About their drinking and substance habits – alone, with friends, etc.
- If their alcohol/substance use has affected their personal, financial, professional or legal circumstances.
- If anyone in their network of family/friends has asked them to stop using drugs/alcohol.
- If they attempted to quit alcohol/drug usage.
- If an attempt to quit caused withdrawal symptoms.

Psychological issues

Loss

One thing for counselors to remember is that a loss is still a loss, even though it may be as severe as the loss of a parent or as seemingly trivial as failing a class. Divorce of parents can be a particularly devastating but unfortunately a commonly experienced loss for young people. In addition, friendships are very important at this age and the loss of a friendship can be very upsetting and experienced as a major loss. What is significant about these different types of losses is that students/young people feel loss just as intensely as adults do, and that each loss needs to be grieved and processed. Students need to move through the grief, and on to acceptance. By understanding that a sense of loss can be experienced regardless of the precipitating event, and by knowing about the grief process, counselors can provide the support and the guidance to move students through the loss and on to acceptance.

Grief

The grief process encompasses the following five major stages:

1. Shock and denial usually define the first stage of the grief process. Counselors can guide students toward identifying their fears.
2. The second stage is usually anger that involves indignation and questioning of why this loss was perpetrated on them. It may include thinking they did not deserve the loss.
3. Guilt is generally the third stage, evolving to a sense that the student's actions or inaction may have caused the event leading to the loss, and therefore they did deserve the loss.
4. The fourth stage is that of hopelessness and depression. This tends to be the longest stage and may include feelings of sadness. As this stage becomes less intense, this is usually a signal that the student is nearing readiness to move on to acceptance.
5. Acceptance is the fifth stage in which the student adjusts to his/her new life circumstances.

Throughout the process, counselors can assure and remind students that these feelings are normal, and that life will resume to normalcy for them. This is not intended as a denial of their feelings, but rather as an assurance that the grief process is a process, and not a permanent state. Counselors can work with students in the grief process, remembering that there are four major tasks that are accomplished during grief:

1. Accept the reality of the loss, both emotionally and intellectually.
2. Experience the pain, both internally and externally.
3. Acclimate to life after the loss, accepting help from others as appropriate.
4. Assimilate the loss and reinvest energies elsewhere.

Counselors should be watchful for the stages and tasks involved with the grief process and be prepared to refer to the student to outside or specialized resources if the situation becomes overwhelming or too complicated for the counselor to be of assistance.

Stress

Stress can be a rather vague word. In a health education setting, stress refers to the response that the body makes to any demand placed upon it. These demands may be physical, mental, or emotional. The things that are creating these demands are called stressors. Stressors can be academic examinations, health problems, heavy physical loads, or even happy occasions. Eustress is the term used by counselors to describe positive stress; that is, stress that encourages the individual to adapt, grow, or develop. The opposite of eustress is distress, the negative forms of stress. Distress is stress that is harmful to the individual, and in some way prevents him or her from living to potential.

Many individuals become so used to the high amount of stress in their lives that they become used to it and do not try and remedy the situation. There are a few warning signs that stress may be a problem. For instance, individuals experiencing chronic fatigue, headaches, diarrhea, indigestion, or sleep problems may be over-stressed. Self-medication, including the use of non-prescription drugs, can be a sign that stress has reached a problematic level. Individuals under stress frequently have a hard time concentrating, and may feel irritable or apathetic. They also tend to exaggerate the importance of their work to others, and can become more prone to accidents. Stressed individuals often exhibit extreme behavior, for instance in eating, drinking, or working.

Every individual should periodically assess the level of stress in his or her life, regardless of whether he or she believes stress to be a problem. One way to do this is by asking and honestly answering a series of questions of oneself. First, how often in the past week or two have you felt out of control? To what degree do you feel confident that you will be able to solve the problems in your life? To

what degree do you feel that things are going well for you? How often have you felt hopelessly behind in your work? If you ask these questions and discover that the incidences of hopelessness or loss of control outnumber those of well-being and confidence, then stress may be a serious issue for you. Managing stress is not a matter of eliminating life's problems; rather, it is altering the way events are perceived and handled.

Biological theories: One of the most popular biological theories of stress is general adaptation syndrome. This theory postulates that everybody strives to maintain a stable physiological state, known as homeostasis. Stressors are those things that disturb this state. In order to restore this state, the body develops adaptive responses. These responses typically have three stages. First, the body registers alarm and temporarily lowers resistances; blood pressure may increase, and the levels of some hormones may rise. Next, if the stressor continues, the body creates a resistance by attempting to maintain normal processes. Finally, assuming the stress has carried on long enough, the body enters a state of exhaustion and may not be able to sustain activity.

Cognitive-transactional model: The cognitive-transactional model of stress considers the relationship between stress and health. These two factors are interdependent: stress can diminish a person's health, while poor health can increase a person's stress. According to the cognitive-transactional model, stress is a problem when its demands exceed the ability of physical health to deal with them. From this perspective, stress is seen to be relative: what may a debilitating event for one person will be easily overcome by a person in better health. This simply echoes what counselors have already thought about stress, that it is largely dependent on self-perception and self-esteem. Of course, even the healthiest individual will have stressful moments for which he or she is unprepared.

Causes: Inevitably, every individual will undergo a certain amount of stress owing to the rough passage through various stages of life. Indeed, leaving childhood, going through puberty, leaving home, or getting married may be the most stressful event one ever undergoes. Naturally, the level of stress involved with any particular change will depend on a number of internal and external factors. Some researchers measure specific events in life-change units, or the estimation of the stress caused by each change. The death of a parent or romantic partner is one of the highest-ranking events, but even changing one's residence is considered a notable source of stress. Any individual who registers over a certain number of life-change units in a single year is liable to develop significant health problems.

Research has consistently shown that students are among the most highly stressed individuals in any society. The stressors among students are very consistent, as well. They include test pressures, frustration with personal achievement, problems with friends and romantic partners, pressures of competition, and constant change. Students in their first year at a new school typically experience a decline in self-esteem. This stress may be responded to physiologically (sweating or trembling, for example), mentally (obsessively analyzing stressful situations), behaviorally (perhaps by crying, eating, smoking, or drinking), or emotionally (becoming anxious, fearful, or depressed).

Among students, the highest levels of stress are typically documented around the time of mid-term and final examinations. Incidences of cold and flu also skyrocket during this time, as elevated stress levels weaken the body's immunes system. As one might expect, the students who are most likely to develop destructive test anxiety are those who feel they are likely to perform poorly, whether this self-perception is accurate or not. Studies have shown that the most effective way to combat test-related stress is to teach students easy means of relaxation, like controlled breathing and meditation. Students trained in these techniques report lower levels of anxiety, as well as higher test scores.

Physical illness or disability can have a profound effect on an individual's ability to deal with stress. Of particular concern for teachers is the relation between learning disabilities and stress. Approximately ten percent of Americans are afflicted by learning disabilities, and the problems they create can be just as much emotional as cognitive. Individuals with learning disabilities frequently are disorganized, easily frustrated, hot-tempered, clumsy, emotionally immature, physically restless, and easily distracted. Students with learning disabilities often have above-average intelligence, so it may be especially frustrating for them to underachieve. Teachers should monitor their students for these symptoms, and try to defuse any stress that is the result of a blameless disability.

Not every stressor is related to the personal life of the individual; sometimes, a person may experience stress because of things that are done by or happen to other people. Discrimination is one common societal stressor. Since discrimination is difficult to combat by oneself, it is often a source of chronic frustration for individuals who experience it. Rising rates of violence in the United States may also be a source of stress for many people. Various studies have documented how the increase in violence in American inner-cities has resulted in health problems for many of the people who dwell there. These kinds of societal stressors may actually be more dangerous to the individual than personal stressors, because there is no obvious way to eliminate them.

Experts define stressors as acute, sequential, intermittent, or chronic. Acute stressors are those that happen one time and are extremely intense. The death of a parent is the classic example of an acute stressor. A sequential stressor occurs in regular progression, which may either increase or decrease in intensity.

The adaptation to life as a parent is a good example of a sequential stressor. Intermittent stressors are those that are moderately intense and occur at regular intervals, like paying monthly bills or undergoing periodic examinations. Finally, a chronic stressor is an intense source of stress that is constantly occurring. Individuals who live in low-income, high-crime neighborhoods are said to be subject to chronic stressors.

Coping mechanisms: The various ways that individuals try to adapt and respond positively to the stresses of life are called positive coping mechanisms. These are healthy, mature ways of dealing with problems, and come in four common forms. Sublimation is redirecting any socially unacceptable drives into more appropriate activities. Turning one's anger into art, for instance, is sublimation. Religiosity is the process in which the individual reconciles hardship as being a part of God's will or some divine plan. Humor, of course, is a very common way of dealing with stress. Altruism is the act of converting a negative experience into a positive one. People afflicted with lung cancer who speak publicly about the dangers of smoking can be said to be turning a bad experience for them into a positive experience for the community.

There are a few simple exercises that anyone can perform to avoid being overwhelmed by stress. First, you should be able to recognize the symptoms of your stress; for instance, you might develop backaches or nausea when you are stressed out. It can be very helpful to keep a journal, so that you can express your feelings and work on trying to understand why you get stressed and how you can avoid it. It never hurts to rehearse potentially stressful situations before they occur, so that you will be prepared for action. Sometimes it can be helpful to put stressful situations in perspective: ask yourself if the current problem is likely to seem such a big deal in a week, a month, or a year.

Stress-resistant individuals: Over years of research, counselors have developed a good picture of the kind of individual that is able to withstand stress most effectively. These stress-resistant individuals typically try to find an immediate solution to their problems rather than wallow in self-pity. They often have explicit personal goals, which they constantly remind themselves of as they make progress. In order to achieve these goals, they will typically rely on organization and conscientious problem solving. They will generally not be large consumers of caffeine, nicotine, alcohol, or drugs. They will regularly engage in some sort of focused relaxation, like meditation or controlled breathing. They will also tend to seek out and enlist the aid of others.

PTSD
Posttraumatic stress disorder is the clinical term for the prolonged response of an individual to some extremely stressful event or situation. Although for a long time PTSD was only considered as occurring in veterans of war or survivors of violent acts, it is now roundly acknowledged that any number of events, from sexual abuse to the death of a loved one, can result in PTSD. Oftentimes, PTSD can be triggered many years after the original event by some other event that reminds the individual. In order to escape the horrific psychological pain of the event, individuals will become numb or afraid, or may develop a strong chemical dependency. The best way to minimize the damage of PTSD is to seek psychological help immediately after any traumatic episode.

Consulting

National perspective concerning education

It is vital that counselors are aware of the national perspective concerning education. They need to know what is expected of them, the staff and their school. Counselors should know what the expectations are and make sure they are trying everything to meet those standards. The nation has certain goals that they expect schools to achieve and counselors need to know what is expected of them and ensure their school is moving in that direction. When a counselor knows what the national expectation is, they can look at their school and ask whether they have the means to achieve those expectations. If they do not then they will know what their educational needs are and find the means they need to achieve those goals.

Subcultures and countercultures

It is well known that effective counselors know how to shape and lead an effective school culture. Counselors can easily get the impression that the school is under one culture. This is highly unlikely because of each school will contain a wide variety of personalities and opinions. A school can have multiple organizations that make up a culture, subculture and even countercultures and each one is the one who wants to define who the school is. The most common example of this is in secondary schools where there are several departments and subjects. Many of the departments make up a culture and possibly within the department are subcultures. This can be an extremely difficult challenge for a counselor trying to understand and gather information about the school's culture and trying to set goals and expectations.

School community

When becoming a part of a school community, a school counselor can take proactive steps toward developing a collaborative relationship with other members of the community. These steps include:

- Recognize that the school staff is in a fiduciary role of implementing the academic goals of the school and the district.
- Be open to the evolution of your role within the school community, as opposed to imposing preconceived ideas about your role on the school staff.
- Become familiar with the rules and expectations of the school community.
- Recognize that any operational entity will have both explicit and implicit hierarchies, and become aware of those levels of authority and power.
- Cultivate alliances and friendships through shared agendas and recognition of individual strengths.
- Develop effective and collaborative vehicles of communication with members of the school and the larger community.
- Maintain objectivity when working with any educator or family member.
- Refrain from provocatively challenging the authority of an educator or community member.

Curriculum

Before a counselor can decide which curriculum to use or design, it is important to decide what the curriculum goals are going to be. These goals should not be determined by only the counselor but also the staff and parents. They should use data that has been collected through assessments and decide what the areas are that need improvement. It is crucial to ask teachers what they want out of a curriculum and in what direction do they want their students to go. Parents should also be asked what they expect their children to learn when they are at school. A curriculum should be based on a group effort. It should focus on what everyone wants the students to achieve and what is best for the school. Many times the district will already have goals and the school can just add to those.

State functions
The development of curriculum at the state level involves creating guidelines concerning the development and implementation of curricula and ways of assessing student achievement. The state also creates the tests and other performance measures that are required for each academic subject. They should take a limited approach and focus assessment on language arts, social studies, science and math. There has been a movement toward assessments to test the student's ability to complete projects and open-ended problem solving rather than the tradition pencil and paper methods. It is also the responsibility of the state to provide the needed material and resources to local school districts. Often times the most desired resources are monetary support and technical assistance. The state must also decide the graduation requirements in terms of credits and competencies. These functions are general and allow the district more ownership in deciding what their needs and strengths are.

District functions
Each district can implement any program of study they feel is necessary for their schools, however, it would be to the district's advantage if the program is consistent for each grade level and uniform for each academic subject. If the district ensures a consistent and uniform program of study, this would help guarantee equity that all students across the district are getting an equal education. Another advantage is it makes it easier for a student to transfer within the district. A parent will not have to worry that their child is not on the same level with other students simply because they changed schools. The school district should create a mastery core curriculum that will explain the subjects that all schools will offer. A mastery

core will also explain the goals and objectives of each subject. However, there is still the freedom and flexibility for each school to development their curriculum using the mastery core for guidance.

School functions
After the school has received the curriculum's goals and objectives from the state and district, it is time for the school to m ake choices. The school's decisions will be made under the leadership of the principal and teacher leaders. The school will also collect the appropriate input from parents and then build a curriculum that is guided by the mastery core. The school should identify their goals and needs and then supplement any classes they feel are necessary to add in order to meet the student's needs. As a team, there will be a decision about the schedule, curriculum integration, and how to align and implement the curriculum. If this process is to be successful, it is important that the principal has strong leadership skills and is well informed and active in the development process.

Curriculum delivery
School counselors are in the valuable position of liaison between students and school staff. They work with students on personal and academic issues, and collaborate with school personnel on appropriate strategies in the classroom to best facilitate student learning and development. Although counselors may directly design curriculum or deliver guidance in a classroom setting, often they will act as consultants to school staff in designing curriculum, program development, or other related issues. The strength of collaboration between counselors and other school staff in developing curriculum and programs lies particularly in the inherent comprehensiveness of combining input from teachers who follow a standardized curriculum, and counselors whose job it is to solicit and assess student feedback. The general relationship is that the counselors will provide consultation to the teachers, who will in turn implement the curricular changes.

Counselors can help infuse personal guidance and development into standardized curriculum toward a much richer program for students.

In some cases, the best model for curriculum delivery that incorporates counseling guidelines is one of partnership between the counselor and teacher or teachers. The particular value of this model lies in the fact that each partner is able to contribute his or her expertise in curriculum delivery. An example of this is teaching social skills through role-playing, which can be designed around a historical setting. In this particular model, the counselor would contribute a set of guidelines for social skills, based on the age of developmental level of the students. A history teacher would plan the lesson around the historical period indicated by the grade level, and a drama teacher could contribute expertise regarding performance and role playing. This collaboration would culminate in a lesson that would address students' different modes of learning, while delivering curriculum as well as counseling guidelines.

Student knowledge
Counselors can and should encourage the furtherance of student knowledge, either through synthesis between disciplines, or through sequential learning within a particular discipline. Counselors and teachers can communicate and collaborate, both within a grade level, and between grade levels, to develop lesson plans that encourage students to form correlations between counseling curriculum and academic curriculum. This can also extend to correlation between disciplines, such as between history and narrative or between math and music. Teaching in the classroom can include somewhat of a Socratic approach, encouraging student curiosity about the connections between disciplines. Counselors can also work with students to strive for the next level of sequential learning within a particular discipline, by making and facilitating those connections within the lesson plans. Sequential learning strategies

contribute to future student success as they move to higher grade and school levels.

Knowledge and intelligence

Benjamin Bloom
Benjamin Bloom and his team of researchers redefined education by declaring that it is not simply the acquisition of knowledge, but the development of three distinct spheres of knowledge-based skills. These spheres are the cognitive, affective, and psychomotor, and they are known collectively as Bloom's taxonomy. The cognitive sphere is the ability to make a sequential reasoning, and depends on the individual's knowledge and comprehension of a given topic. The affective sphere has to do with the way the individual reacts emotionally, and their ability to imagine other emotional states. The psychomotor sphere has to do with the ability to physically manipulate a tool or instrument.

According to Bloom, the development of every sphere of knowledge (that is, the cognitive, affective, or psychomotor) passes through six successive levels. At the first level, knowledge, one can recite facts or concepts from memory. The next level of knowledge is comprehension, in which one can demonstrate an understanding of facts through organization and comparison. After comprehension comes application, in which the individual can use the acquired knowledge to solve new problems. One then acquires the ability to analyze the new information, breaking it down into parts and identifying causes or motives. After analysis comes synthesis, in which one can compile information in a different way, and propose alternatives to some of its parts. Finally, one should be able to evaluate the new knowledge, developing opinions about it that can be supported with reasonable arguments.

Intelligence and abilities
Too often teachers recognize intelligence solely in terms of verbal and mathematical ability. Recent research has shown that there a number of different ways to be intelligent.

- 57 -

Instead of focusing on reading ability alone, teachers should try to identify creativity, innovation, group maintenance, visualization skill, strength and dexterity, reasoning skills, problem-solving skills, curiosity, and persistence. These are all forms of expressing intelligence. By becoming attuned to their students' various strengths and weaknesses, teachers can determine the best way to present their material.

Howard Gardner

The renowned Harvard psychologist Howard Gardner determined after long research that there are eight major forms of intelligence. They are logical-mathematical (ability to reason deductively and inductively, or to see rational patterns), linguistic (ability to read and write easily, and to appreciate subtle differences in language), musical (ability to discern pitch and rhythm), spatial (ability to create visual-spatial representations of the world), bodily-kinesthetic (ability to use the body to solve problems, make things, and convey ideas), interpersonal (ability to work effectively with others and empathize with them), intrapersonal (ability to work effectively by one's self), and naturalist (ability to distinguish among and use effectively the various features of the environment). Gardner is currently exploring a ninth intelligence: existential (the capacity to reflect on questions of life, death and ultimate realities).

Knowledge based skills

Affective skills

An individual's level of affective skill refers to how effectively an individual can recognize, understand, and handle emotions, relationships, and other social interaction. Affective skills allow an individual to feel a certain emotion as a result of a certain situation or stimuli and then respond based on that emotion. Some of the factors that can be used to measure how well-developed an individual's affective skills are include determining how well the individual receives emotional stimuli and how well the individual

responds to those stimuli. It is also important to determine how easy it is for the individual to acknowledge the worth of a particular situation, relationship, or individual and whether or not the individual has an organized and well-conceived value system. An individual's ability to receive and respond to emotional stimuli can be measured by how aware the individual is of a particular stimulus, how willing the individual is to acknowledge that particular stimulus, and how focused the individual is on that stimulus. An individual's ability to assign value to a situation and uphold a value system can be measured by how motivated the individual is, how the individual behaves, and how consistent is that individual's behavior. For example, a student that always comes to class and clearly always pays attention may have well-developed affective skills.

Cognitive skills

An individual's level of cognitive skill refers to an individual's ability to gather and understand information. Cognitive skills allow an individual to comprehend and apply knowledge that they have already gathered in other situations. Some of the factors that can be used to measure how well-developed an individual's cognitive skills are include determining the individual's ability to retain knowledge, comprehend knowledge, apply knowledge, and evaluate knowledge. An individual's ability to retain knowledge can be measured by testing the individual's ability to remember certain facts and information through exams or simply asking questions. An individual's ability to comprehend knowledge can be measured by an individual demonstrating a concept in a different form, explaining a concept in more detail or simplifying a concept, or predicting a result based on a particular concept. An individual breaking a concept down into individual parts and demonstrating how those parts make up the whole can also show comprehension of a particular concept. An individual's ability to apply knowledge can be measured by an individual demonstrating that they can use a particular concept for a real-life purpose. Finally, an individual's ability to evaluate a particular piece of knowledge can be indicated by the individual showing the value of that knowledge.

Psychomotor skills
An individual's level of psychomotor skill refers to an individual's ability to control his or her physical movements as well as his or her coordination. In other words, psychomotor skills are the ability that an individual has to control his or her simple and complex motor functions. Some of the factors that can be used to measure how well-developed an individual's psychomotor skills are include how well an individual performs physical skills and acts, how precisely can the individual perform those skills or activities, and how natural do those activities seem to be for the individual. An individual's ability to use physical skills can be measured simply by how much difficulty the individual has in accomplishing a particular complex physical activity such as climbing a rope or assembling a model. How precisely the individual can perform those skills or activities can be measured by determining the quality of the result of the individual's physical activity and how long it took the individual to reach that result. For example, if the individual has constructed a model plane, does the model look like a plane, are its wings and other parts attached correctly, how long it took to assemble, etc. Finally, an activity is natural for an individual if the individual can perform it without thinking.

It is extremely important for an individual to be able to use a combination of his or her affective, cognitive, and psychomotor skills together on a day-to-day basis as each type of skill is essential to the overall functioning of a healthy individual. An individual that has mastered his or her psychomotor skills may be in excellent physical health, but the individual's overall health as well as the health of the individual's family will suffer if the individual is unable to make effective relationships and understand basic and complex concepts. The situation is the same for an individual that can only make effective relationships or who can only understand complex concepts as it will be significantly more difficult for the individual to perform everyday functions if the individual has poor control over his or her psychomotor skills. For an individual to maintain the physical and mental health of the individual and his or her family, the individual has to be able to use a combination of different skills.

Academic development

Since school counselors are primarily concerned with personal issues that affect academic performance, they are often expected to devote a percentage of their time to developing programs that deliver guidance and instruction to all students. Incorporated in these programs are strategies that address such topics as academic performance, career planning and social skills. Counselors may also be asked to contribute to curriculum implementation. School counselors are expected to contribute significant resources to teaching. Although the guidelines for counselors contributing to curriculum implementation may differ between schools, there are generally understood percentages, based on age groups. In elementary school settings, 35 to 45 percent of the counseling program should be devoted to curriculum implementation. In the middle school milieu, the percentage is 25 to 35 percent. High schools generally expect 15 to 25 percent of the counseling program to be devoted to curriculum implementation.

Instruction methods

Socratic method
The Socratic method of instruction is patterned after the pedagogical style of Socrates, the ancient Greek philosopher. The Socratic method consists of a free-form conversation in which the teacher explores the ideas of the student by asking him or her a series of questions. In order to be effective, a Socratic dialogue must have the full

- 59 -

participation of students. Teachers should also be comfortable with some long silences in class, as one of the results of an effective conversation is that it forces students to stop and think. Likewise, there must be some flexibility on a teacher's behalf if a Socratic session is to be productive; the improvisatory nature of the conversation means that the subject matter may differ wildly from what the teacher had anticipated.

Direct teaching

The direct teaching model for counselors follows the format of instructors in the school whose job is primarily teaching, but differs in the type of information and curricular area addressed. While standard instruction focuses on information-based academic areas, direct teaching by school counselors most often focuses on life and social skills. Referring to appropriate topics for each age and grade level, counselors can plan and deliver lessons most useful for specific developmental levels. Elementary students might benefit from a lesson on friendships or on independence, while middle school students may need lessons on anger management, conflict resolution, or stress management. For high school students, these lessons could expand to incorporate planning for their future. Some topics under this umbrella could include college preparation skills, career planning, and goal setting. Other topics appropriate for high school students fall in the category of relationships and responsibility.

Competency-based instruction

Most vocational classrooms now feature what is known as competency-based instruction. Loosely defined, competency-based instruction is a style of teaching in which progress is determined by students' mastery of skills rather than some arbitrary time limit. For example, in a business class, the teacher will ensure that every student is reasonably adept at making a basic budget before moving on. In a teacher-based classroom, a certain number of days would be allotted to each subject, and the teacher would adhere to this

schedule whether students learned or not. Research has shown that a more learner-focused style of instruction, like competency-based instruction, ensures that students will retain the most of the curriculum. Teachers using competency-based instruction methods will be required to issue periodic assessments, so that they can gauge whether students have mastered a particular concept or skill.

Interdisciplinary approach

The interdisciplinary approach is used to encourage learning across the curriculum. Lessons are set up to make thematic units in all learning subjects. Each subject will be connected to this thematic unit. The teacher is making links between each subject. When this method is used, the student is able to learn without fragments during day and at the same time have a stimulating learning experience. The teacher chooses a topic or theme and then brainstorms activities to do in each subject area that revolve around this topic. Questions are then thought of in order to serve as the scope and sequence. The teacher can determine a grade by evaluating standards of performance levels or by using rubrics that evaluate the students' completed work assignments.

Parental involvement

Increased parental involvement and awareness strongly correlates with increased academic success in students. There is also a significant benefit to students who are able to dovetail their school experience with their home experience, by parents becoming more involved in and aware of students' academic requirements. When parents are able to supplement classroom instruction with additional teaching at home, their children generally perform better and are more engaged at school. Counselors and other members of the school staff can cultivate parental involvement through a number of vehicles. Open house events and parent-teacher conferences are common modes for increasing parental involvement. Other recommendations are parent resource centers, phone calls or even visits to the home as appropriate. If the school community as a whole recognizes the value of parental involvement and endeavors to forge a partnership with parents on a regular basis, the overall student achievement can be expected to improve.

There are numerous arenas in which counselors can encourage and recognize the importance of parental involvement in students' academic achievement. Augmenting those events in which parents are invited to visit the campus, counselors can build on this involvement by including parents in planning and decision making programs as appropriate. Another suggestion is to research the talents and skills of parents, and develop a volunteer pool. Educators and counselors will need to give specific directions for participation, and can diversify the selection of areas in which parents can contribute their time and expertise. Counselors can also acknowledge parental involvement through written newsletters, or at school events. Counselors should focus on the mutual goal of academic success, and recognize the parents' contributions. Counselors can distribute additional academic resources to parents. The school should be portrayed as welcoming to families. Counselors may want to coordinate transportation and baby-sitting for parent visits.

Parents are often hesitant about getting involved with the school functions because they often feel they are not important and their opinions do not count. In some cases parents may have had a negative experience involving a principal or other school functions, therefore, it is the responsibility of the counselor to make those parents feel valued and important not only to the school but to their child before discussing any type of involvement. An effective counselor knows the value of parental involvement and realizes they must invite, recruit and motivate all parents to get involved. Many

times when these efforts do not work, a counselor may have to offer incentives or rewards in order to get parents to take that first step toward involvement. Involving a parent does not mean they have to speak in public or put on a carnival, it could as simple as donating time to repair something in the school.

Counselors can set a welcoming tone each year, by proactively welcoming parents and encouraging participation in their students' academic lives. The following are some effective modes for setting this tone:

- Send a welcome letter at the beginning of the year that includes a calendar of events, and invites parents to participate.
- Provide a resource brochure or informational handout with general school policies and the counselor's role in the students' lives.
- Distribute informational resources explaining the counselor's role, the counseling program(s), community resources and pertinent contact information.
- Send event and meeting calendars on a regular basis, which could include contact information for support resources, including that of the counselor.
- Generate a school newsletter that will give parents and the surrounding community information with information about school resources and possibly include peripheral articles or notes of interest.
- Schedule new-family meetings right before school starts.

Special needs of students

The first step that an educator should take when determining the best way to meet the special needs of a student should be to determine exactly what the needs of the student are. If the student is performing poorly, the educator needs to determine whether it is because the student does not understand the material or because the student is unmotivated by the material. Each student is unique in his or her ability to learn and comprehend the material and therefore it is important for an educator to determine the cause of the student's poor performance. Once the cause has been identified, the teacher can determine how much assistance is needed. If the student's needs can be met through techniques such as one-on-one attention or assigning special projects, this is usually the best course of action. However, if the student has needs that require solutions beyond simple changes in curriculum, such as potential psychological or physiological disorders, the educator may have to discuss other options with the child's parents.

As defined by the ASCA, the school counselor should address the following functions in his/her role as facilitator and advocate for student needs:

- Lead and facilitate activities of the comprehensive school counseling program.
- Collaborate with other student support personnel to deliver appropriate services.
- Provide services to both students with disabilities and traditional students.
- Provide individual and group counseling.
- Work with staff and parents to develop an understanding of students' special needs.
- Refer students as appropriate to auxiliary resources in the school system or in the community, to address needs not met in the context of the counseling program.
- Advocate for the rights of students with disabilities in the school and the community.
- Assist school staff with issues related to students transitioning between grade levels.

- Serve on interdisciplinary groups that assess students who may have undiagnosed special needs.

Inclusion

A great deal of time is spent trying to equip teachers to handle students labeled "exceptional" for one reason or another. Furthermore, Public Law 94-142 mandates that schools must identify those students that require special treatment, whether from being extremely gifted or disabled. Many schools, however, feel that the best way to handle exceptional students is simply to include them in the regular classroom. Advocates of this program assert that specialists can come in to the class and help exceptional students as necessary, and that otherwise these students will benefit from being in contact with students of a wide range of ability. However, many classroom teachers feel overwhelmed when they are asked to instruct a very wide range of students.

IDEIA

The Individuals with Disabilities Education and Improvement Act (IDEIA) was enacted to ensure that eligible school-aged students receive the opportunity for a reasonable education. Eligible students are defined as those students who exhibit any single or combination of 13 identified disabilities. Reasonable education is distinguished as allowing students to make reasonable educational progress, and not necessarily to achieve highest possible performance. Eligible students can receive a free appropriate public education (FAPE) under IDEIA. The Act stipulates that these eligible students receive an education that is designed around their intellectual and physical levels. It is also mandated that the delivery of the curriculum be specially designed to meet the particular requirements of students. If the disability presented by the child has minimal or non-negative effect on learning, then the student may not be eligible for IDEIA resources, but may be eligible for reasonable accommodations under Section 504.

Autism, deaf-blindness, deafness, and hearing impairment

Autism is a disability that affects social interactions as well as verbal and non-verbal communications. It can present with repetitive activities, stereotyped movements, resistance to changes in routine or environment, and unusual responses to stimuli. Most autism is evident in children before the age of 3. Academic performance may be mildly or severely impacted by autism, depending on the range and intensity of the symptoms.

Deaf-blindness refers to significant impairment in both hearing and vision. The combined impairments can result in severe suppression of development, learning and communication, well beyond that which would result from deafness or blindness alone.

Deafness refers to a hearing impairment that is sufficiently significant to affect the processing of linguistic information through hearing, with or without amplification. Academic participation and performance are affected accordingly.

Hearing impairment refers to a permanent or fluctuating condition that adversely affects the educational performance but does not qualify as deafness.

Developmental delay, emotional disturbance, and mental retardation

Developmental delay refers to a significant cognitive lapse between ages 3 and 9 that cannot be accounted for by any other identified disability.

Emotional disturbance refers to a spectrum of symptoms that encompass a general inability to cope or learn which presents over a long period of time and to a marked degree. Symptoms include an unexplainable inability to learn, inappropriate behaviors or feelings under normal circumstances, a tendency to develop physical symptoms or fears that correlate with personal or academic

problems, the inability to foster satisfactory interpersonal relationships with peers or teachers, and a general mood of unhappiness or depression. This condition adversely affects educational performance accordingly. IDEIA includes schizophrenia in this category.

Mental retardation refers to a significantly sub-average intellectual functioning that may exist with deficits in adaptive behavior and manifest during the developmental period.

Multiple disabilities, specific learning disability, orthopedic impairment, and other health impairment

Multiple disabilities refers to a combination of impairments such as mental retardation with either blindness or orthopedic impairments whereby the student's educational needs cannot be accommodated in the traditional classroom. Excluded from this group is deaf-blindness.

Specific learning disability refers to a disorder whereby one or more of the basic psychological processes inherent in using or understanding spoken or written language causes a person to have difficulty in linguistically communicating or in performing mathematical calculations.

Orthopedic impairment refers to physical impairments that adversely affect a student's academic performance. Included in this category are loss of a limb, clubfoot, cerebral palsy, and disease-related conditions like poliomyelitis and bone tuberculosis.

Other health impairment describes the presence of such chronic or acute health problems as diabetes, epilepsy, ADD, heart conditions, or sickly cell anemia, that adversely affect the student's educational performance.

Special education appropriation

Generally, the steps involved in appropriating special education accommodations for a student include:

- 63 -

- Student will be recommended as needing special accommodations or additional instruction by parents/guardians, the school system, school personnel, or a state agency.
- History of student learning problems will be reviewed with parents/guardians, school counselors, school educators/special educators.
- Counselor should request written consent from parents/guardians to conduct further, formalized assessment.
- Students is formally assessed through tests administered by psychologists, special educators, specialists such as audiologists, etc. to determine the specific special needs and the extent of the special needs.
- Student eligibility for special accommodations is determined from results of assessment.

If student is eligible, counselor will develop an individualized education plan (IEP) that will address student needs.
Counselor will implement an FAPE in the least restrictive environment (LRE) as determined by the parents/guardians and educators.

Gifted students

Not all exceptional children are designated as such because they are disabled in some way. Many students are considered exceptional because they are more intellectually advanced than their peers. Gifted students may be able to think faster and to solve more complex problems than their peers. They may be able to think creatively and empathetically, and to have profound insights. According to the Education Consolidation and Improvement Act of 1981, gifted children are those that surpass their peers in reasoning, leadership, artistic, and academic fields. These students, according to the government, are entitled to special treatment from the school so that they can fully develop their abilities.

There are three basic types of programs designed to serve gifted children:

1. Enrichment programs are those that extend the regular classroom work, either by providing more topics of study or giving a deeper treatment of the material covered in the normal class. Enrichment seems to work best when it capitalizes on the interests of the student.
2. Acceleration programs are those in which the student moves ahead to content that normally he or she would receive later in life. This may involve grade skipping or early entrance to school.
3. Affective programs are those that are designed to address the social and emotional needs of gifted students. These students may have greater trouble assimilating into social groups because of their intellectual differences.

Teachers may find that helping gifted students work to their potential is just as difficult if not more than helping their disabled students achieve. One way to help gifted children succeed is to give them some independence, and allow them to determine enrichment materials. It is also a good idea to partner gifted children with one another, so they can work on social development while not sacrificing academic difficulty. Gifted children should be challenged; sometimes it may be good to let them struggle with advanced subject matter rather than continually gliding through less complex material. Gifted students should not be required to spend too much time going over material they have already learned. Finally, gifted students should be given the chance to develop their critical thinking skills through independent study.

Role as community liaison

Culture diversity
There are numerous cultural factors that can

affect the counseling relationship. One of the primary factors is the differentiation between group-oriented cultures and individual-oriented cultures. Students who come from a culture that values the group above the individual will necessarily approach communication, goal setting and decision-making from a completely different perspective than one who comes from a culture that values the individual above the group, such as traditional Western culture. Culture can affect how the student perceives the role of the counselor, in a spectrum that may span from helper to intruder. Students from various cultural backgrounds may communicate more with body language than verbally, and could perceive the counselor's communication similarly. Culture can affect students' time orientation, sense of self, and the ability to make decisions. This is particularly significant when counselors are working with students from a historically oppressed culture. Counselors can develop appropriate strategies for developing a student's sense of empowerment in harmony with his/her cultural values.

Diverse American families

Although many people may still consider the stereotypical American family as middle-class and white, variety is really the norm when it comes to family arrangement. All of the different cultures that combine in American society bring their own ideas of the family. In African-American households, for instance, women are often seen as the head of the household. In Chinese-American families, both husband and wife may be expected to work even of the wife does not get to make as many decisions. In Latino families, wives are seen as the keepers of wisdom, even if they defer to their husbands on practical matters. Furthermore, many American families now have a single parent, or two parents of the same sex. According to most studies, the most important factor in the development of children is the stability and love in the family, not its particular composition.

Race

In addition to biogenetic factors of race, race can also be defined by a spectrum of factors that may include socioeconomic grouping, distinctive traits and behaviors associated with a particular group, language, traditions and rituals. Individually or as an aggregate, these factors often play a part in racial discrimination and segregation. Members of a school community may segregate other members based on all or some of these factors. These segregation practices may extend to certain groups based on economic status, academic achievement, level of fluency in English, or certain disabilities. In this sense, race can be viewed as a political and psychological concept. Counselors working in the school community to dissipate cultural biases and misunderstandings will be well served to recognize that race is a concept, defined primarily by these behavioral and economic factors.

Ethnicity

In contrast to race, ethnicity is rooted in national origin and/or distinctive cultural patterns. Ethnicity is based on more easily identifiable factors. Groups of students with the same ethnicity share the same general ancestral background. A group that shares ethnicity will often share religious beliefs, attitudes toward family, school and career, and observations of customs, traditions and rituals. These beliefs and traditions are often reinforced by the fact that individuals who share an ethnicity often socialize together, providing a continuum of culture. However, counselors should be sensitive to the fact that individuals can present degrees of assimilation, developing practices and beliefs that differ from their ethnic origins. Ethnicity is generally associated with family, although it can also be defined by religion, race, and cultural history.

Oppression

Although oppression may be rooted in cultural or racist biases, it is usually manifested by inequities of power or benefits. The general psychological basis for oppression is a fallacious assumption by one group that another group is intrinsically inferior or unacceptable for a particular quality of life. Unfortunately, these misperceptions often are perpetuated by the vehicles that result from them. Individuals or groups who possess the power or benefits, e.g. better paying jobs, better access to technology, better access to transportation, etc., inherently define oppressed individuals as inferior by their lack of these quality of life indicators. Oppressed groups also often internalize this definition, further perpetuating the oppression and exploitation. Oppressed individuals or groups will often accept their subservient position in the school or work environment because they do not feel empowered to challenge the dominant group. Oppressive tactics include exploitation, intimidation, and occasionally violence.

Oppression can take many forms that fall under five general umbrella categories. The first category is that of individualized oppression, which encompasses oppression stemming from assumptions of inferiority in another person based on race or culture. This process extrapolated to the group level becomes cultural oppression, which is comprised of actions or attitudes toward a cultural group that result in the targeted group changing its behavior to be accepted. Systemic or institutional oppression denotes hierarchical practices that inherently discriminate against certain groups in the distribution of resources. Oppression that is internalized by the targeted group is insidious because it is the dynamic whereby the group believes and acts on its own perceived inferiority. Conversely, external oppression describes actions or beliefs targeting a particular group because they are perceived by others as inferior. Instances of oppression can fall under one or many categories combined.

The terms below identify oppressive belief systems targeting specific groups. Often public schools and other societal entities practice unfair distribution of resources based on these perceptions:

Ableism – targeting persons identified by different abilities/disabilities
Ageism – targeting persons younger than 18 or older than 50
Beautyism – targeting persons who are obese or otherwise fall outside of expected appearance norms
Classism – targeting persons based on income level or class of work
Familyism – targeting persons whose family falls outside of expected norms, such as single parents, same gender parents, foster families, etc.
Heterosexism and Transgenderism – targeting persons who are homosexual, lesbian, bisexual, two-spirit, intersex or transgendered
Linguisism – targeting persons because they do not speak the dominant language, or do so with a marked accent
Racism – targeting persons of another color or mixed race
Religionism – targeting persons who do not practice the dominant religion
Sexism – targeting persons of a different sex

Social justice
Social justice incorporates awareness of inequalities based on cultural, race or ethnicity, and the practices to rebalance the distribution of resources. Counselors who work with diverse student groups will be well served to recognize when and if those groups have been historically oppressed. This historical oppression usually reveals practices and attitudes that have been accepted and ingrained in the larger community as well as the school environment. Counselors can systematically and diplomatically address these practices and attitudes, toward creating social environments that support social justice. Examples of these practices and attitudes can include testing that does not allow for second language learners, lesson plans that use examples that are only familiar to certain cultural groups, etc. Counselors can work

- 66 -

with students, school staff, and the surrounding community toward establishing an environment of social justice.

A campus that endorses and supports social justice does not differentiate between members of diverse cultures, races, economic status, special needs, sexual orientation or gender, religious background, appearance, or second language speakers. Counselors can facilitate this kind of campus through their work with individual students, and by working with the particularities of the data system. All members of the community will expand their commitment to social justice and educational equity when the systemic data-driven approach is initiated at the school, which will increase the probability of all students having equal opportunities within the school counseling program. The counseling program in particular is a prime area in which to model equal access to resources by advocating and affirming all students with no attention to personal characteristics that define each student. By promoting social justice, campuses provide a model for the surrounding community.

Multicultural sensitivity

Counselors can offer their expertise and act as liaison to the surrounding community by including parents and neighbors in discussions and events promoting multicultural sensitivity. It is usually the responsibility of the counselor to coordinate this community outreach, and can take many forms. Counselors can develop peer mediation services, family counseling services, or hold workshops in the community to discuss cultural diversity. One of the key goals of a community outreach program is usually to increase multicultural sensitivity and communication, not only within the community but also within and surrounding the school campus. Since school campuses are often diverse, and the neighborhoods often culturally isolated, school counselors can provide the vehicle for transcending cultural differences and

encouraging multicultural understanding. Another method for involving the surrounding community is to hold programs, such as talent shows, on campus and invite the parents and neighbors.

Because members of a student body are in many ways required and expected to assimilate the dominant culture, counselors working with these students may be only vaguely aware of the expectations, belief systems and practices of a student's native culture. By developing and maintaining relationships with members of the surrounding community, counselors can be exposed to cultural practices and assumptions that are more pronounced because neighborhoods tend to be culturally isolated. One of the advantages of this exposure is the counselor's understanding of cultural elements that may underlie student attitudes and behaviors. Counselors may also gain insight about cultural identity from adults in the neighborhood that students would be less likely to reveal, partly because of inherent role dynamics between the adult counselor and the adolescent student. Counselors can also find out about cultural holidays, traditions and events in the neighborhood, and be able to talk about these with students.

Career planning and conflict resolution

One of the qualities that differentiate school counselors from teachers is their training and knowledge base both in areas pertinent to school-age children, and in appropriate expectations for each age and grade level. Although conflict resolution is a valuable skill to learn at any age, the delivery method and context will differ greatly between age levels. Counselors are particularly knowledgeable about this. Examples of this, touching on different ends of the age spectrum, is teaching young children how to get along with their friends with a puppet lesson; and for high school students, possibly role-playing to address relationships with parents. Also for high school students, it is important that they be given a wealth of information about career and college planning, which is an area about which school counselors are quite knowledgeable. They can talk to high school students about setting goals, researching options, and long-range planning.

One of the common tasks of a business teacher is to provide students with career advice and counseling. Because of a business teacher's area of expertise, students have a right to expect that teachers will be able to dispense valuable information about careers. In order to do so, a business teacher must stay apprised of changes in the job market, and must be knowledgeable on the responsibilities and functions of various professions. This is not to say that a business teacher must be an expert on every career—on the contrary! One of the most valuable functions a teacher may perform is directing students to on-line or text resources on a certain profession, or setting up a meeting between a student and a member of the community currently working in the student's area of interest.

Career clusters

One of the main uses of the system of career clusters as devised by the United States government is to provide vocational educators with a simplified way to look at the skills and standards for various types of jobs. The government has developed extensive paperwork regarding each of the sixteen skill sets, complete with specific training required and skills that must be acquired. Oftentimes, vocational teachers will administer a questionnaire to students that determines which career clusters best suit their interests and aptitudes. Then, with the help of the available literature, the teacher can work with the student to develop a plan for attaining the skills necessary for employment in their chosen field.

In this extremely specialized modern economy, it is useful to consider various "clusters" of careers that have similar

attributes. The United States government has established sixteen career clusters: agriculture and natural resources, arts/audio/video technology and communications, architecture and construction, business and administration, education and training, finance, government and public administration, health science, hospitality and tourism, human services, information technology services, law and public safety, manufacturing, retail/wholesale sales and services, scientific research and engineering, and transportation distribution and logistics. These clusters have been created in part to aid vocational educators, who may be overwhelmed by the variety of potential careers and can benefit from a system of summary.

Specialization
Specialization means dividing a particular job up into its various components, an allowing one worker to specialize in each. Although this idea has been around for centuries, it has been taken to another level by factory managers. Industrial engineers in the modern era may divide the manufacture of a product by process, workers, geographical location, or chronology. They may plan to develop certain parts of their operation in places where it is most cost-effective, or in the places where the workers are already skilled in the appropriate ways. They must also have plans in place for any errors or insufficiencies that may occur. The United States, because of its diverse geography, offers great opportunities for specialization.

Family and consumer science careers
An educator that is attempting to teach his or her students how to find the appropriate career and the skills that might be necessary for that career may want to begin by offering some examples of different careers. It is important for the class to examine a diverse sampling of different careers because family and consumer science skills can be applied to virtually any setting and it is essential for an educator to teach his or her students methods of determining how various techniques can

be applied. For example, a construction worker might not need to know about food, textiles, or housing design, but he or she still needs to know various problem-solving techniques. It can also be extremely useful if students can get some hands-on experience applying family and consumer science concepts to the tasks associated with various careers.

Some of the specific careers that individuals might be able to use their family and consumer science skills in include food management, financial management, human resources, public relations, tailoring, dressmaking, etc. Regardless of which career an individual chooses, there is usually some combination of skills that an individual can use both in his or her day-to-day living and in his or her career. An individual in food management can use knowledge about nutritional needs, the proper handling of food, and the temperatures and the amount of time necessary to prepare various foods. Financial advisors can use information regarding how to assess resources, determine the best way to cut costs, and determine how much an individual needs to save before retirement. Human resource and public relations managers can use their social skills and their knowledge of time management, resource management, and of human development and psychology to carry out their responsibilities more effectively. Finally, tailors and dressmakers can use their knowledge of various textiles and textile design to construct better garments.

CFO
The chief financial officer of a business is responsible for figuring out what the company's financial needs are, and then determining how to satisfy those needs. The CFO is also responsible for communicating the financial activity of the business to the shareholders, employees, and management of the business. In order to do his or her job effectively, the CFO will have to establish the best capital structure for the company. Capital structure is the particular blend of

cash, debt financing, and equity financing that the company uses to continue operations. The CFO will also have to maintain good working relationships with commercial and investment banks. The CFO assists in the creation of sales and expense forecasts and budgets.

Receptionists
A receptionist is charged with providing the company's face to the outside world, whether by greeting visitors or answering phone calls. Obviously, this job is quite important, as every business wants to make a good impression on the outside community. Therefore, a receptionist must always maintain a professional and courteous demeanor. Receptionists will also be required to sort and direct mail that arrives for the people they represent. More generally, a receptionist is a source of general information for visitors as well as for fellow employees. If a receptionist can provide basic information, it will save time and money for senior employees who have other, more important tasks to take care of.

Employment trends
The particular trends in the job market will always be unique to the part of the country in which a business teacher is working, so there is no substitute for staying aware of the employment situation by monitoring the local news and classified ads. That being said, a general trend in the United States over the past few decades has been the loss of manufacturing jobs, coupled with a rise in the demand for technology workers. The service industries in the United States have also seen a sharp raise in employment in recent years. Students can be assured that careers in computer technology will continue to be lucrative and easy to acquire. Students should also be prepared, however, to move to a different location in order to find the career they desire.

World of work

Work standards

It is very important that an employer enforce clear standards for employees. In order to do this successfully, the employer needs to make sure that standards are posted visibly and that employees are introduced to them during orientation. Employers should also lead by example by following all the rules themselves. Employers should strive to present the image to their employees that their business prizes accuracy and honesty. Finally, a good way to ensure that employee work standards will be attained is to set certain performance goals and reward employees for reaching them. Work standards may have to do with customer service, accuracy in bookkeeping, cleanliness, punctuality, productivity, or safety.

Employee rights

There are four main categories of employee rights: rights associated with collective bargaining and unions; rights having to do with working hours and pay; rights having to do with workplace safety and worker's compensation; and rights having to do with discrimination in the workplace. The rights that employees have today have been codified by federal legislation. Before that, however, employee rights were established first by state law, and later by negotiation between unions and employers. Some of the specific rights enjoyed by employees are the rights to distribute union literature, the right to negotiate wages and working conditions in good faith, and the right to work without being treated differently because of race or gender.

Ethical behavior

One of the most important missions of the modern counselor is to show students what constitutes ethical behavior in the workplace. Put simply, ethical behavior is just good business sense; customers that are lost to unethical behavior are a much bigger concern to a company than any short-term profits that may be gained from the behavior. Companies work hard to earn reputations for ethical behavior because they know it will help them in the market. To this end, they discourage lying to customers, employee theft, and misuse of company time. If a business teacher can instill a good sense for business ethics in his or her students, then he or she has given them perhaps the most valuable tool for success in the contemporary workplace.

Unfortunately, making ethical decisions in the business world is often quite difficult. Business teachers should recognize this fact, and equip their students with a good decision-making process. The first step in the process should be defining the problem; students may often jump to conclusions about a problem without ever articulating it to themselves. Next, students should be trained to consider the various alternative solutions to the problem. Making a list on paper is a good way of externalizing choices. After this, students should get in the habit of identifying the consequences of the various proposed solutions. Consequences may be both short-term and long-term; as every businessperson knows, losing a customer in the name of short-term profit is always a bad decision. Finally, students should determine whether they have enough information to make decision, and if not they should have the discipline to acquire the information they need.

Promotion

One of the most important tasks of a manager is the selection and training of new employees. Promotion from within is a straightforward concept, but besides indicating that a company tries to advance its own employees, it has come to mean more generally the philosophy of establishing loyalty among employees. Many businesses claim to have a promotion-from-within policy because it is attractive to employees, though the company may do a considerable amount of hiring externally. Sometimes the current employees of a company simply are not appropriate candidates for management. Furthermore, if a new area of business opens

- 70 -

up for a company, it will always make more sense to hire an external candidate who specializes in that area.

There are social and psychological advantages to promotion besides any increase in pay. Companies have various means of determining when employees will be promoted or given a raise. Some companies use a merit-rating system, in which every employee is evaluated at a certain interval. Employees are assessed for their dependency, initiative, handling of responsibility, appearance, production, use of resources, and the amount of supervision they require. If an employee seems to have demonstrated positive progress in these areas, he or she will receive a raise or promotion. Some critics of this system suggest that it often tends to degenerate into a system of automatic rewards, without the accompanying evaluation.

Open competition
In the matter of hiring, most companies these days have what is known as an open competition policy. That is, they fill vacancies or make promotions based on who is the best candidate, not on any predetermined criteria. Obviously, this policy results in the best employees being hired, and therefore seemingly in the best interests of the company. However, repeatedly hiring external candidates can have a demoralizing effect on a company, especially if current employees feel they are not being given a fair chance at promotion. If a company cuts staff development programs and then hires a series of external candidates, the workforce may have serious grievances. Most companies, though, find it to be in their best interests to encourage the development of their present staff.

Peer relationships
It is essential to maintain solid relationships among employees if productivity is to be maximized. Oftentimes, individuals who focus intensely on their work can actually undermine an organization by alienating their coworkers and inhibiting the flow of knowledge throughout the company. As a manager, it is crucial to monitor the relationships among staff and ensure that positive communication is taking place. Many businesses devote time to building the relationships among staff, as they feel that taking a bit of time away from work to develop trust and friendship in the company will ultimately lead to greater productivity in the long run.

Sexual harassment
Sexual harassment is any inappropriate verbal or physical conduct of a sexual nature, specifically when it is directed at an individual because of his or her gender. The Supreme Court has determined that sexual harassment violates the protections for employees that were set forth in the Civil Rights Act of 1964. There are also state laws against sexual harassment. In order to prove that sexual harassment has occurred, a plaintiff must be able to demonstrate that the alleged harassment was either severe or consistent enough to affect their work, and that the employer is liable because of their knowledge of the harassment. In many cases, the courts have leveled extremely harsh punishments against businesses that neglect to stop or punish sexual harassment.

Rate of pay
Large corporations may use a variety of measures to determine the rate of pay for their employees. Wages are the employee's pay based on hours of work or on the specific units of work that have been finished. A salary, on the other hand, is pay based on time at work, when that time is measured in weeks, months, or years. Salaries are generally paid on a weekly, semi-monthly, or monthly basis, and are typically reserved for managerial positions. A guaranteed annual wage (GAW) is the amount of guaranteed hours of work in a year that a company promises its employees. A GAW may be important in businesses that tend to have varying production demands throughout the year. A bonus is simply anything awarded to

- 71 -

an employee for special performance, especially when the money is derived from profits.

Overtime pay is usually one and one-half times the normal wage, and is paid for hours worked in excess of the normal amount. Usually salaried employees are exempt from overtime pay. Incentive pay is given to employees as a reward for meeting certain production goals; it is usually offered as a means of stimulating increased productivity. Profit sharing is any system whereby employees are entitled to a certain amount of the company's profits, whether in cash or as contributions to their pension plans. Insurance, in this context, is any group, life, health, or disability insurance paid for by the company. Paid vacations, of course, are time off from work in which the employee continues to receive full pay.

Seniority system

When union members are allowed to vote on their company's system for promotions and raises, they almost uniformly select the seniority system, in which decisions regarding advancement and elimination of employees are made based on the employee's length of service. Of course, this system does not always work in the best interests of the company; those employees who have been around the longest may not be the most qualified for advancement. However, a seniority system may seem like a good objective alternative to a merit-based system of promotion that they feel is unfair or prejudiced. The seniority system also tends to induce a certain amount of complacency among employees, who may feel that they do not need to do anything but wait for their inevitable promotion.

Termination

Termination of employees may take a number of different forms. Many workers are considered terminated because they retire. For the purposes of the company, the money that an individual receives after retiring is money that was earned during the period of

service, and has simply been deferred until the employee became inactive. Retirement plans are influenced by the state of the economy, the rate of unemployment, the life expectancy, and the rate of inflation. Another kind of termination occurs when workers voluntarily leave a company to work somewhere else. In the American business community, mobility is much greater than in countries (like Japan) where loyalty to an employer is more carefully cultivated. Termination of employees may also take the form of layoffs, motivated by poor performance or declines in the industry.

Recruiting

Screening is always the first part of the recruiting process. Some companies have recruiting officers that travel to universities to interview potential employees. In any case, it is important that the firm have a good set of minimum requirements, and that they do not bother to interview just anyone who is interested in a job. An able recruiter should establish close relationships with people at the place of recruiting, so that he or she will have an available reference for candidates. Usually, resumes are used to screen candidates at first. Business analysts all agree that it is best for a company to have an immediate idea of a candidates weaknesses; being placed in a job for which one is unqualified is as bad for the individual as it is for the company.

Job-hunting

As part of preparing students for entry into the job market, teachers need to show them the various places to look for jobs. One of the best places to find a job is still the classified ad section of the local newspaper. However, there are now many on-line listings for jobs as well. These are constantly changing, so business teachers will want to keep abreast of the most popular sites. Many part-time and odd jobs will be advertised on bulletin boards and message boards at local supermarkets and libraries. Magazines and trade journals often have job listings, too. One of the most obvious yet often overlooked ways to get a job is simply to ask for one. If students are interested in working for a particular company, they should have the skills and wherewithal to call and inquire about openings.

Application forms

Large businesses can be overwhelmed by the volume of resumes that they receive, whether they are advertising vacancies or not. For this reason, it often makes sense to compose a standard application form that every prospective employee will have to fill out. This allows the business to inquire directly about the things that are important to them, rather than allowing candidates to mention anything they believe to be significant. By law, application forms cannot inquire about age, marital status, arrest records, gender, religion, citizenship, or nationality. All of these things are considered possible sources of discrimination in hiring. Application forms should be concise and clear, so that managers can look through a large number of them quickly.

Resumes

Basic concepts

A resume may be the most important document that students will ever compose in their lives, so it is essential that business teachers give them the skills to construct thoughtful and effective ones. It is essential first of all that students have an idea of who the target audience is for their resume. If they are applying for a babysitting job, for instance, they would want to highlight different aspects of their background than if they were applying for an internship with their local congressional representative. A student should think of the resume as a marketing tool, in which the product being sold is him or herself. To this end, a resume should make clear the unique and positive attributes of the student, without going into too much detail. After all, a resume aims to earn an interview, not necessarily a job. Too many resumes are overloaded with accomplishments, to the point where they are either unbelievable or unreadable.

Language and grammar: There are a few stylistic points that students should keep in mind when they are composing a resume. First, they should always use short, bulleted statements rather than lengthy descriptions. After all, they can expect that their potential employer is going to be looking over a large number of resumes, and so they need to make the information immediately accessible. A resume should try to use as many "action" words as possible, rather than using forms of "to be" or passive verbs. If the student is applying for a job in a particular field, then it may help to demonstrate some knowledge of the terminology associated with that field, as well as to display any experience doing the kind of work that will be required. Finally, and most obviously, a resume must contain no grammatical or spelling errors!

Opening paragraph: Since managers will read many letters of application, students need to be equipped with some tools to help their letters stand out from the pack. The most important place to distinguish oneself is in the opening paragraph. Rather than use some formulaic introduction, students should be encouraged to pique the reader's interest with an anecdote, or a clever way of mentioning how the job came to his or her attention. Certainly, a letter of application should stay on the subject, but too many students damage their chances for employment by merely filling in the blanks of some cover letter model. Instead of doing this, the savvy applicant will indirectly demonstrate his or her intelligence and familiarity with the company without boring the reader with empty praise or false modesty.

Job objective: Every resume should begin with a job objective. The job objective sets the tone for the rest of the resume by answering three key questions: what position you are seeking to find, who should be reading your application materials, and how to interpret your resume. In order for this to work, of course, a job objective must be clear and precise. One should not say something like, "I want to improve myself and work as part of a cohesive team." Of course this may be true, but a potential employer needs to hear exactly what you want to do for his or her company, so that he or she can be start visualizing you in that position as he or she reads the rest of the resume. A strong objective, with action verbs and precise terminology, immediately separates a quality resume from the pack.

Job descriptions: Too often, resumes include long, detailed descriptions of the duties and responsibilities the applicant held at a previous job. For the most part, these summaries should be avoided in favor of lists of achievements at that job. The main reason for this is that a simple job description does not convey to the resume reader that the applicant is particularly good at his or her job; in many cases, it may simply tell the reader things about a certain job that he or she already knew or could have guessed. It is much better to alert the reader to whatever success you may have had in a previous position, or to indicate any special privileges or duties that would not normally be considered part of the job.

Summary of qualifications: After a job objective is given, an effective resume will provide a brief Summary of Qualifications; that is, a list of the three or four best reasons for you to be considered for the job. This is the place to mention the most impressive and relevant attribute that you have. This might include your experience, your credentials, your particular expertise, your work ethic, or your personality. Note that a summary of qualifications does not have to reference specific achievements. This is not to say, however, that it should be general. On the contrary, you should take this opportunity to highlight any skills that make you different from every other applicant, and worthy of special consideration.

Work history: The work history section of a

resume is your opportunity to showcase whatever experience and training you have already acquired, so long as it is pertinent to the job for which you are applying. Even if a job you have had is not directly relevant to your desired job, it is a good idea to briefly list it to avoid giving the impression that you have been unemployed for long periods. If there are gaps in your employment record, it is a good idea to indicate that you were not just lying about during this period by entering something like "student" or "personal travel," and then giving a brief summary. Job candidates should avoid mentioning rehabilitation, unemployment, or personal illness unless it is necessary.

If you have been promoted at a past job, the work history section of your resume is the right place to indicate it. Future employers will naturally be impressed by candidates who have apparently thrived in their past jobs. In order to effectively show these promotions, you can create separate entries for each position you have held—just make sure to list the name of the company for each, so that people reading your resume won't think you simply changed businesses often. If in fact you have worked for a number of companies over a brief period of time, you should try to minimize the impression of flightiness this might give by simply listing the employment agency you were working with, or indicating that you were performing strictly contractual work by including a title like "consultant" or "contractor."

Achievements: Every resume should include a list of whatever achievements either indicate particular skills relevant to the job or general personal qualities that will be appreciated in an employee. In fact, a successful resume will simply frame every job description in terms of achievements; that is, instead of describing responsibilities held and tasks performed, a good resume will list skills acquired and advances made. The idea that you are trying to convey by listing achievements is that you have the skills to do the job, you enjoy and are proud of these skills, and you hope to do more of the same in the future. For this reason, it is a good idea to downplay any achievements that may seem irrelevant to the job for which you are applying, and especially those that may make it seem as if you are overqualified.

One of the quirky things about writing a resume is that, even though it lists your past achievements, it is actually supposed to be a document about your future. That is, an effective resume should be designed to suggest your ability to do whatever work you are aiming to do, rather than show your past successes in their best light. Therefore, the accomplishments that you list should be those that will be the most impressive to your desired employer, not those that you happen to think are noteworthy. A good resume should always lead off with a statement of purpose, so that whoever reads it knows immediately what you would like to be doing. Then, you should design the rest of the resume as if it were an advertisement for yourself, showing how you can fill the role you desire.

Things to avoid: One of the most important things a student can learn about composing a resume is how foolish it is to lie on one. Resume lies can take a number of forms, from misrepresenting your duties and position at a former job to claiming to have degrees that you have not obtained. No form of misrepresentation is acceptable on a resume; besides being immoral, it is bound to catch up with you. The advent of high-powered search engines has made it quite easy for companies to check up on the claims that their applicants make, and any candidate who lies on their resume can be assured that if it is discovered during the selection process they will be disqualified, and if it is discovered after they have been hired they will most likely be terminated.

In order for a resume to net the desired job, it should be oriented to promote the idea that you are capable of performing that job. In other words, you should avoid bragging about

skills you no longer wish to use, or describing jobs you no longer wish to perform. Say, for instance, that you had a managerial job in a restaurant in which you were frequently called upon to wash dishes; it would be foolish to apply for another managerial position by mentioning how great your dishwashing skills are. This is not to say that one should lie about one's job history, but simply that one should only advertise what one has an interest in providing to a future employer. Nondisclosure (that is, not mentioning something) is not the same things as lying.

Some students will have been a part of many organizations, received many awards, and just generally have acquired a number of tings to list on a resume. They should be discouraged from including everything. A proper resume will take its cues from its statement of purpose; in other words, if a certain achievement does not support your desire to do the work you are aiming for, it has no place on your resume. Including too much information will only confuse whoever reads the resume and may result in that person not reading it any further. This may be of particular concern if you are applying for a job for which you feel overqualified. Many times, individuals in desperate need of a job apply for positions that are below their level of training. They may feel concerned that their full resume will put off potential employers; it is perfectly all right in such a case to omit certain data, as long as the resume remains truthful and does not contain any large gaps in the employment history.

Cover letters
In order for a letter of application (or cover letter) to have the desired effect, it must be tailored to its audience. This means finding out the name and title of the person who will read the letter, even if it requires a bit of research to discover this information. A proper cover letter should also give the reader a bit of insight into the author; including some personal experience or anecdotes is a good way to distinguish one's

letter from the rest. In this line, it is important to try and disguise whatever letter form the author may be using. Many applicants are helped by using available models of application letters, but it should never be apparent to the reader that a cover letter "formula" is being used. A cover letter should always strive to represent the individuality of the person it represents.

There are a few essential tips that concern the composition of all cover letters. First, a cover letter should always refer the reader to the applicant's application, or to any other documents that may be contained in the same envelope. A cover letter should always end with a clear and courteous offer for an interview, and should of course include the same contact information as the resume. It goes without saying that any letters of application should be scrutinized closely for spelling and grammatical errors. An accomplished cover letter will be professional without being boring, and interesting without being too casual. Students should be encouraged to have a friend or mentor read their cover letters before submission.

Job interview

Preparation
In order to be fully prepared for a job interview, a candidate must have considered three areas. First, the candidate must have a general understanding of his or her own skill, strengths, and weaknesses. This is essential so that he or she can decide whether the job is truly an appropriate one for him or her. Next, the candidate must have prepared for the questions he or she is likely to be asked, both those that are standard to a job interview (for instance, why he or she would like the job, or what he or she already knows about the company) and those that are unique to the company. So that these last questions may be answered effectively, the candidate should also have spent some time researching the business as well as the job that is available. If possible, it is good to know a bit about the person who will be conducting the interview.

Once an individual has scheduled an interview with a particular company, he or she should seek to find out as much about that company as possible. There are a number of ways to go about this. First, he or she can simply ask the company to send along any brochures or promotional literature that might be helpful. He or she might also try to contact other businesses that work with the company, to ask them their opinions. A very simple way to procure some information is to do an internet search of the company, or to search at the local library for articles about the business. Finally, one can make use of one's own business network, to try and discern what the reputation of the business is in the local community.

Objectives
Too often, students assume that a job interview is always given with an eye towards getting a particular job. While this may be the usual case, it is also perfectly appropriate to interview for a job so that one can discover more about it, as well as about one's place in the job market. Many times, individuals will interview for a number of jobs they have no intention of taking, for the sole reason of polishing their interview skills. It is important to decide before an interview exactly what your objectives are. One danger that candidates run when they interview only to seek information, however, is that they will discover mid-interview that they would like the job and they have not done adequate preparatory work for the interview. For this reason, it is best to always be as well prepared as possible, and settle the question of objective before the interview begins.

Listening skills
One common misunderstanding of job interviews is that they are simply opportunities to go through a rehearsed monologue of one's skills and achievements. In actuality, one's ability to listen well may be more impressive to a potential employer. The candidate should make sure not to interrupt

- 76 -

the interviewer, or fill in blanks in their sentences. If one is not sure about something the interviewer has said, it is always better to ask for clarification than to pretend comprehension. Too often, candidates are so focused on what they intend to say that they do not pay adequate attention to the tone and nuance of the interviewer; a well-prepared candidate should never have to worry about forgetting his or her lines.

Areas of questioning

Any candidate who has not got any questions about the employer during the interview is, whether intentionally or not, conveying the idea that he or she does not really care about the company. A candidate should always inquire about a few key areas. First, who are the business' chief competitors, and how does the business distinguish itself? What is the leadership structure of the business, and how long has the present leadership been in place? What particular issues or problems is the business dealing with at present? Does the company have a particular set of values? What is the "culture" of the company? Have there been any major changes in the business or in the industry as a whole that will affect the business in the near future? Questions like these convey to a potential employer that the candidate has a real interest in the business.

The questions that are appropriate to a job interview will depend on what job is being offered; a manager will need to ensure that the candidate has whatever skills or training is requisite to the job. Still, there are some general questions that are appropriate for just about any interview. For instance, most managers like to ask a candidate why they are interested in a job, or where they first learned about the vacancy; these questions give the candidate a chance to speak at length about his or her interests and goals. It is important for a manager to ask questions that require more than a simple "yes or "no," so that he or she can gat an idea of how the candidate's mind works. Asking for opinions, or for a description of some past experience, is a good

way to draw the applicant's personality out.

In a job interview, closed questions should be the easiest to answer, although they may not necessarily be the most pleasant. Closed questions are those that require just a one or two word answer. Such questions might include whether the candidate has a college degree, what their grade point average was, or whether they have ever done similar work before. Usually, these questions are asked simply to verify information that is listed in an individual's resume, or to introduce lines of conversation that will then be developed more fully. As a candidate, one should avoid elaborating too fully on these kinds of questions, particularly if such elaboration might be seen as making excuses or qualifying negative aspects of a resume. One should simply answer these questions and move on.

Open questions are those that require more than just a simple one-word answer. An open question might invite a candidate to describe a past work experience, or to detail what it is about the company that interests him or her. These are good questions for well-prepared candidates, because they give him or her a chance to accentuate positive aspects of his or her resume, as well as to avoid mentioning qualities that might be viewed less favorably. One of the common dangers of these questions, however, is that they may lead to vague responses. If the candidate feels unsure exactly how to answer an open question, there is nothing wrong with politely asking the interviewer to narrow it down, or breaking it down him or herself into some simpler parts.

Leading questions are those that the interviewer poses with an eye towards introducing some further line of conversation. Leading questions can be very dangerous for a candidate if he or she is not well prepared. As an example, an interviewer might insinuate that one of your previous bosses was unfair or incompetent. While this may or may not be true, sometimes interviewers will use such a line of questioning to determine whether a job candidate is likely to be overly critical of authority, or to pass the buck. The best thing to do in an introductory interview is to try and remain diplomatic when presented with opportunities to be critical. A good candidate will not suggest that he or she is incapable of criticizing others, but will always emphasize his or her own responsibility as the most important concern.

Clothing

Perhaps the most important thing a job candidate can do is present a positive image with his or her dress. Although what is appropriate clothing will vary from job to job, it is generally agreed that a successful candidate will ensure that no aspect of his or her appearance will be uncommon for people in that profession. This may seem a rather soulless idea, but one should remember that the point of a job interview is to convey the impression that one can easily assume the role and responsibilities of the job. Even if one is supremely qualified otherwise, it will be difficult to convince a potential employer of this if one's first impression is wildly outside the norm. In a similar line, it is crucial that a candidate have performed the appropriate hygiene regimen before the interview; bad breath and body odor can kill job chances before the interview even starts.

Interview process

The first in the series of job interviews is the screening interview. During their screening interviews, a company is just trying to narrow down a large field of potential candidates. These interviews may not be performed by the same individuals that will conduct later interviews, and they may even be performed over the phone. For this reason, candidates should always be prepared for a screening interview. This means having a copy of one's resume and cover letter close to the phone, and being able to provide succinct answers to basic questions. The main point of a screening interview is to ensure that candidates have the basic qualifications and skills to be further considered for vacancies.

After the initial screening interview, a candidate should assume that his or her basic skills and achievements are known by the company. So, in the next interview (known as a selection interview), the goals should be to make clear what other skills the candidate will be able to bring to the business. If the selection interview goes well, there will be a final interview, the confirmation interview. In some cases, the confirmation interview may be simply a formality, in which the top executives get a chance to meet candidates who have already been approved for hire by the human resources department. Candidates who make it to a confirmation interview should just try and be polite, and not try too hard to sell themselves.

Reference checks and tests

Although checking references is not always a fun experience, it is an invaluable tool for learning more about job applicants. Most managers are astonished by the honest information they can find out about potential employees just by calling up their previous employers. Even if the company finds its applicants through a headhunter or employment agency, it is a good idea to check with the applicant's references. Companies may also find it helpful to administer psychological, medical, IQ, or dexterity tests to their applicants. It is a good idea to limit testing to those areas that are directly relevant to the position offered; IQ testing for a receptionist position, for example, might be unnecessary. Drug testing is also frequently employed by businesses, although it is illegal in some cases.

Orientation

Orientation is the process through which new employees are introduced into the culture of the company. Most businesses will include a partial orientation in the hiring process, so that employees can determine whether the job is a good fit for them. Once hired, though, employees will receive a full orientation, which usually includes the following:

- Company history and major operations
- General company policies and rules
- Outline of the organizational structure
- Rules concerning wages and payment, overtime, vacations, and holidays
- The economic and recreational services made available by the company, such as insurance or pensions
- The system for promotion and transfer
- The procedure to follow when the employee has a problem or a suggestion regarding the company.

Of course, no employee will remember everything he or she is told during a formal orientation. There are several other ways for them to become experienced on the job. In vestibule training, new employees are led through a brief course of training in an environment identical to the one they will be working in. This is a method of orientation often used by factories. On-the-job training is simply when the new employee learns his or her job by performing it. Apprenticeship is a common form of orientation in skilled jobs; here, the new employee is mentored by a veteran employee with long experience in the field. In management positions, orientation may take the form of job rotation, in which employees receive training in several different fields. "Assistant-to" positions give new employees a chance to tag along with some senior executive and thereby get a feel for the job.

Junior Achievement program

Junior Achievement is a combination of teachers, parents, and volunteers that seek to educate children about free enterprise, economics, and business. Junior Achievement runs programs for children all they away from elementary school through high school, in the hopes of preparing students for their future participation in the business world. At the high school level, Junior Achievement focuses on four areas: economics, personal finance, business and entrepreneurship, and work preparation. JA also offers a number of scholarships for students who have completed JA programs and plan on studying business or economics in college. JA is a non-profit organization funded by the contributions of corporations and individuals.

Vocational education

Vocational education is the training of individuals to perform certain jobs. Often, large communities will have separate schools whose sole purpose is to cultivate workplace skills. These schools may work in conjunction with local industries to tailor the students' education to the anticipated job market. Vocational classes and schools may also offer cooperative training opportunities, in which students gain first-hand experience in their field of interest. As industrial work becomes more and more specialized, companies are requiring extensive vocational training and on-the-job experience for their employees. Public vocational education is designed to enhance the entire life of the worker; to this end, non-vocational classes are required so that students can earn a secondary degree as they gain work skills and experience.
Acts and amendments

The Vocational Education Act of 1963, also called the Carl D. Perkins Act of 1963, broadened the government's conception of vocational education. It established some procedures to provide part-time employment to students, and established a federal advisory council on vocational education. It also set aside some federal money for the construction of local vocational schools. This act also established some work-study programs enabling students to get real-life experience while earning some school credit. Some amendments were made to this act in 1968, including some direct support for cooperative education and a renewed emphasis on postsecondary education. The amendments also included new provisions for funding an expanded vocational curriculum.

The Carl D. Perkins Act of 1984 was issued in the hopes of improving the basic skills of the labor force and preparing students for the job market by enhancing vocational education. Specifically, the Perkins Act sought to establish equal opportunities for adults in vocational education, and to aid in the introduction of new technologies in vocational instruction. In order to meet its objectives, the Perkins Act set aside money for research into vocational education, as well as money to ensure access to vocational studies for people with disabilities, adults in need of retraining, single parents, and ex-convicts. This act was enhanced in 1990 with the issuing of the Perkins Vocational and Applied Technology Act. This act sought to integrate academic and vocational studies, as well as to fund better technology in vocational classrooms and better cooperation between the business and education communities.

Business education

Business education has a host of applications for students. Although it is typically assumed to be only relevant for people who are planning to make or sell goods or services for a living, the skills that are essential to business are also used by charities, governments, and farmers, just to name a few. Students may reconsider their future plans after learning a bit about business, especially if they live in an area with seemingly narrow career choices. Business studies will acclimate students to the set of standards they will be held to in their future life as a contributing member of the economy. Moreover, the skills in manipulating numbers and creating and analyzing various graphs and charts will serve students well in many different endeavors.

In the past, business classes have relied mainly on case studies to give students some experience looking at real-world applications of business concepts. Unfortunately, business case studies have some drawbacks: they do not allow students to experience events as

they happen, they do not allow students to make business decisions themselves, and they do not allow students to test out what might have happened if different decisions had been made. It is a great aid to study, then, that computer simulations have been created. Business simulation software enables students to act out any number of scenarios, immediately see the results of their decisions, and adjust all kinds of variables to see their effects on business. Many teachers have discovered that this is an excellent way to show students how business concepts apply to real economic exchange.

Experiential education is simply the process of engaging students in real-life scenarios as a means of educating them. In business education, this might mean encouraging students to take on internships or part-time jobs so that they can gain first-hand experience of the business world. This notion of education as "learning by doing" has been around forever, but it has been seized upon by vocational educators as a means of making their subject matter vivid to students. In an effective instance of experiential education, students will be forced to describe and analyze their experiences when they return to the classroom. Many educators have noted the positive changes that occur when students are required to take full responsibility for their education; concepts that may be seen as boring when they appear in a textbook can become fascinating to students engaged in experiential education.

Cooperative education work-experience program

Cooperative education is a method of providing students with academic instruction and practical, hands-on experience at the same time. As the job market has become more competitive, employers have increasingly valued on-the-job experience, so cooperative education gives students the chance to earn valuable training while not sacrificing their education in other areas. Research has shown that cooperative education increases motivation and clarifies career choices for students. For employers, cooperative education helps create a trained workforce and gives business some control over school curricula. However, observers have noted that cooperative education programs are still stigmatized as "non-academic" by some, and may isolate students from the academic community at large.

Job-shadowing

Job-shadowing is one of the many ways that students can gain some experience in the workplace. In job-shadowing, a student simply follows along with a worker in the field in which they are interested as that worker goes through a normal day. Through shadowing a real worker, students can learn first-hand what skills they will need to hold a certain job and what exactly a job entails. Sometimes, students may discover that they are not as interested in a particular job as they originally thought. For instance, a research study showed that students that originally were interested in fire fighting often changed their minds once they realized the real, day-to-day life it would involve. One of the limitations of job-shadowing is that students only observe; they do not actually practice any job skills.

Local businesses

Teachers should be familiar with some ways of promoting their classes to the local community, so that they can develop helpful relationships with local businesses. One good way to do this is by interacting with the community advisory councils from local businesses and municipal groups. These are committees whose only purpose is to discover ways in which the business can create positive connections with their community. Obviously, a great way for them to do this is by setting up relationships with local schools, and so they can become a wonderful resource for business teachers. Through partnerships with community advisory councils, business teachers can set up mentoring, job-shadowing, or internship programs, organize class trips, or simply acquire useful information about contemporary business practices.

Skills

Keyboarding

In order to survive in the computer-driven business world, students will have to acquire basic keyboarding skills. While many business classes do not explicitly focus on keyboarding, every class should force students to complete a number of assignments that require word-processing throughout the school year, so that they can develop their keyboarding skills. There are a multitude of texts and computer programs to assist students in this endeavor. Unless a student is interested in becoming a secretary or in pursuing some line of work in which rapid typing is essential, the emphasis should always be on accuracy rather than speed. Students should be encouraged to review and revise their own work rather than rely on the spell-check function.

In order to keyboard properly, there a few basic pointers to keep in mind. First, it is a good idea to clear your workspace of everything that is not essential to the task at hand. You should sit all the way back in your chair, with your back straight and your feet flat in the floor. It is a good idea to place your elbows close to your body, and to have your forearms parallel to the keyboard. You should keep your wrists low, so that they just clear the keyboard. Your body should be positioned so that it is in line with the J-key. You should hold your head straight up, facing the book. With your left hand, you should place your fingertips on the A, S, D, and F keys, and the fingers of your right hand should be on the J, K, and L keys. Your right thumb should be poised above the space bar.

Macros

A macro is used by a computer to allow one to perform with one keystroke a commonly performed command that would normally take several keystrokes. Word processing programs often allow the use of macros for editing and formatting. Many users also create macros to insert often-used elements into their documents, for instance tables with a certain number of columns or of a certain size. Typically, word processing programs will have a recorder so that users can enter the commands that they want for their macro to accomplish, and then decide which keystroke will set into motion this action. Users of some programs can create a space for macros on the toolbar, so that they can be enacted with the click of a button.

Public speaking

There are a few basic strategies for public speaking that can allow even the shyest individual to represent themselves well in front of a crowd. First, it is essential to know both the room and the audience. This makes it possible to tailor one's speech and manner so that they will be appropriate. Next, a speaker should know his or her material well. It is always a good idea to try and relax before speaking. Many speakers find that it helps them to visualize their speech beforehand. During a speech, one should never apologize for being nervous or for any other problems; simply try to remedy these problems as quickly as possible. Finally, a good public speaker will concentrate on his or her message rather than on him or herself.

There is a variety of technological aids currently available to aid in public speaking. Probably the most popular of these is the PowerPoint computer software, which allows the user to create elaborate slide systems that can be projected onto a large screen to provide an outline for a speech. The same equipment that is used to project PowerPoint presentations can be used to project web page or word processing documents, as well. Many speakers enhance their speeches with audio or video footage, which can be manipulated and presented using basic computer software. Besides these more advanced forms of equipment, many speakers still use such old-fashioned props as overhead and slide projectors.

Telephone etiquette

Since an individual's first contact with a business may be over the phone, it is essential that employees be schooled in proper telephone etiquette. When an employee (a receptionist, for example) answers the phone for someone else, he or she should always identify him or herself and the company he or she represents. Then, he or she should always ask how the other person could be helped. It is important not to make commitments on behalf of other people; in other words, one should say that one will pass on the message rather than saying that one's superior will call back at a particular time. Finally, it is very important to always take accurate and legible messages that include a time, date, the reason for the call, the degree of urgency, the company the caller represents, and any other relevant information.

It is essential that students learn the proper way to defuse customer complaints and place calls. First, one must listen carefully as the customer outlines his or her complaint. One should remain calm and respectful, agreeing with the customer when appropriate, but never explicitly disagreeing. One should never interrupt or blame the customer for any problems. One should always apologize personally (this is more meaningful than apologizing on behalf of the company) and act quickly to remedy the situation. When placing a call, one should always plan the call and place it oneself. At the beginning of any phone call, one should briefly identify oneself and one's business, and describe the reason for the call in summary.

There are some general tips that students can learn to immediately improve their manner on the telephone. As far as one's voice, one should always strive for distinctness, so that every word can be understood. One should also try to cultivate warmth, naturalness, expressiveness, and pleasantness. Many writers on the subject recommend adopting a lower, mellower pitch to one's voice; they claim that this style of speech is more soothing to customers. In order to create a good image on the phone, employees should avoid using slang or chewing gum. They should never slam the phone down or fail to introduce themselves and offer a few courteous words. Last, and perhaps most important, employees should always keep the promises they make on the telephone.

Fax and email

Although the fax machine has been somewhat replaced by Internet technology in the past few years, most businesses still maintain fax service and use it often. Faxes are valued for being speedy and for immediately confirming their delivery, so that there is no anxiety over whether the document has arrived intact. Faxes require a cover sheet listing the date, recipient, sender, and total number of pages. E-mail is probably the most popular form of office mail these days. Although it is still seen as somewhat informal, the speed and ease of electronic mail makes it very popular in the business world. One can also attach a more formal document (for instance a word-processing document, a database, or a spreadsheet) to an email message and maintain a more formal appearance.

Civil Rights Act of 1964

The United States government has set up some laws to ensure that all citizens are given a fair chance at available jobs. The Civil Rights Act of 1964 decreed that it is illegal to discriminate against candidates based on their race, ethnicity, religion, or gender. Title VII of this act established the Equal Employment Opportunity Commission (EEOC), which has its goal an increase in job opportunities for women and minorities. Since its inception, the EEOC has been enhanced by the Equal Pay Act of 1963, the Age Discrimination in Employment Act of 1967, and the Equal Employment Opportunity Act of 1972. These are laws that apply to business, state and local governments, labor unions, and educational institutions.

Sexual stereotypes

Eliminating sexual stereotypes is a major concern of school counselors as it is important that an individual is able to disregard sexual stereotypes and recognize that an individual's gender does not necessarily affect the role a particular individual plays. In the early to mid 1900's, women were commonly seen as caretakers of the home and men as providers for the family. However, these roles have changed drastically over the past fifty to sixty years and it is important that individuals realize that it may not be realistically possible for women and men to play these roles any longer. For an individual or family to function appropriately, there are certain necessities that must be acquired and as the cost of living increases, it becomes more and more difficult for a single individual to provide for the entire family. As a result, both men and women need to share the caretaker and provider roles to satisfy the physiological, financial, and psychological needs of the family.

Balancing dual roles

It is important that an individual is able to balance his or her work and home roles because it is becoming more and more common for individuals to have to act as both caregiver and provider for the family. The ever more common presence of dual roles in society can be extremely difficult for an individual to balance, as there may be instances where work-related responsibilities and family-related responsibilities conflict with one another. Family and consumer sciences education attempts to teach individuals how to avoid and how to handle these conflicts through the use of successful life management tactics such as time and resources management, problem-solving and decision-making techniques, effective communication techniques, etc. Family and consumer sciences education also attempts to give individuals a basic understanding of what responsibilities and qualities are necessary for the successful completion of

each role so that individuals can set better
priorities and find better ways to plan their
lives.

Coordinating

Management and Organization

School mission statement

Counselors will be well served to refer to a school's mission statement when developing or revising programs or data systems. A mission statement represents the basic tenets, philosophies and goals of the school as a whole, which should be represented appropriately in its programs and practices. The mission statement can assist counselors when proposing programs or outreach efforts, so that the overall direction and mission of the school can be incorporated in the rationale for the proposal(s). Counselors may also be in a position to collaborate with school officials in developing or revising a mission statement, possibly to better serve a diverse population and/or the surrounding community. The statement should embody a collective result for all students, and provide a clear and concise focus that will frame future program development and evaluation as well as data collection systems.

Data-driven programs

Data-driven accountability of a school counseling program can provide counselors with ordered data and methodical strategies for strengthening appreciation for the program by the school community. Counselors can provide the following accountability information:

- Program evaluations or audits when asked about the comprehensive, standard-based program in place.
- Needs assessment results when asked about the specific needs of the student population based on the results of evaluations.
- Service assessment results when asked to provide examples of implementations that address student needs.
- Results or outcomes of studies when asked about the results of interventions.
- Performance evaluations when asked about counselor performance.
- The school counselor must perform the tasks of needs assessment, program evaluation, test program management and interpretation of assessment results, in order to effectively address the accountability of the counseling program to school boards, parents or other members of the community who may be concerned about the value of the program.

Counselors and other interested parties can view firsthand the effectiveness that data-driven accountability can add to the contributions of counselors toward student achievement. Data-based assessment that is designed around standardized categories can also assist state and national data management in evaluating their goals for equity in academic achievement. Information gleaned can assist counselors in identifying which programs were successful, and which programs could be improved. Data revealed in well-designed systemic programs can isolate particular academic areas, student issues or student populations that are not being well served. Counselors can implement strategies for program improvement, incorporating its assessment in the data system. As counselors are regularly able to evaluate and revise the process of setting goals and assessing their achievement, they can tailor the school counseling program to effectively and comprehensively serve the needs of the students, the school, and the community.

Counselors developing a systemic approach to counseling and assessment can first refer to those identified goals at the school, district, state and federal levels, in order to tailor the quantitative data in accordance with recognized goals for which the school is accountable. Some of the identified goals are as follows:

- National goals: reduction of attainment and achievement gaps, attendance improvement, likelihood of a drug-free school environment.
- State goals: national goals, some of which are identified above, as well as state-specific goals such as improving the rate of literacy, post-secondary matriculation, etc.
- District goals: at the district level, there may be additional goals to state and national that address key areas identified at the district level.
- Local goals: further focus on the needs of students and how those goals can be realized in students' lives.

Implementation of a data-driven program is uniquely delivered at each of the following levels within the school community:

- Individual levels focus on particular students, including crisis situations and student-specific situations, and can provide insight into issues experienced by the entire student body.
- Grade levels focus on age-specific experiences and may be best implemented by long-term planning.
- Classroom levels align the counseling program with the academic curriculum.
- School-wide levels call for coordination of interventions, toward benefiting the entire school.
- Family levels involve parents and/or guardians as equal partners in the promotion of student achievement.
- Community levels involve members of the surrounding area to form partnerships toward the promotion of student achievement.

The effective data-driven approach to improving student achievement is a collaborative endeavor shared by educators, counselors and other school personnel. Recognizing that each program strives for equal access, attainment, and achievement for the students, counselors can work with educators and other school staff toward a comprehensive data assessment system, and ongoing oversight and revision as needed. A holistic systemic approach utilizes inherent connections between programs. Education and counseling programs are connected by a related structure that allows for the alignment of content, delivery, and the reporting of results. The systemic data-driven counseling program is further connected to the school mission, inherently aligning it with the program goals, development, and evaluation of educational goals. All school-based programs are aligned with federal and state goals, and any counseling goals are aligned with ASCA standards that address goals and strategies to best target student needs. Through these combined efforts, students are supported toward their academic and career goals.

It is understood that the benefits of a data-driven counseling program include quantifiable accountability and assessment of professional review organizations. The ASCA views it as being clearly defined and sequential. This can also offer a holistic, comprehensive assessment of individual students. Counselors can provide the bridge between the systemic overview and the needs of individual students by working with the design of the data collection system toward one that promotes holistic development in students. This includes nurturing individual qualities in students, and cultivating the particular goals and skills identified in the data. Using the data-driven system for the planning of implementation of the program, counselors can partner with school members to develop a comprehensive program that identifies the needs of individual students as well as the student body as a whole. This type of program will benefit the students by giving them the confidence and leadership to pursue their dreams.

Counselors may find that an existing counseling program or other student services model may be data driven, meaning that statistics are routinely collected and presented, from which curricular and student services decisions are often made. Counselors may discover that either the data being generated is incomplete, or it is being organized and presented in a manner that does not reveal pertinent information about particular student issues. Data may reveal information about the entire student body without focusing on groups of students in need. Counselors can apply system analysis to the data system toward the goal of redirecting either the data collection or data presentation in a manner that will isolate student needs that can be addressed in the counseling program. By placing the student at the center of the system, data regarding school, family and community becomes more relevant. School counselors can also view the entire system, including subsystems, and the interconnectedness of those systems.

Schools that are regulated and data driven nonetheless recognize that targeting the whole student can include not only classroom delivery, but also extracurricular activities. Since the school is also a social system, it includes a hierarchy of activities and relationships that incorporate the entire school community. Standards-based educational programs can generate standards and competencies for classroom delivery, tutoring programs, extracurricular clubs, peer programs, mentoring programs, school sports, service learning projects, honor societies, and arts-music groups. The comprehensive education program can also include the contributions and considerations of parents, business collaborators, and pertinent outreach programs. The presence of absence of this kind of holistic inclusion can define a school culture in a way that either supports or hinders students' achievement. When developing a counseling program,

counselors should endeavor to support and enhance existing educational program approaches, to the maximum benefit for students.

Counselors who do not adopt the data-driven model of program development inherently place themselves out of the accountability sphere that includes the school and district. They may place the program at risk by not aligning it with the accountability paradigm. Counselors who are ethically responsible should garner the benefits of a data-driven system of planning and accountability. Counselors can embrace the systemic approach by utilizing the expertise of school counselors and district counseling resources. They can then serve as mentors for emerging school counselors. Counselors should take the time to research available information about data-driven programs and how they can best benefit the students and the counseling program. This includes learning how to analyze the data, apply it to existing strategies and programs, and revise intervention strategies accordingly. Although data-driven counseling does not replace individual counseling, it can provide valuable empirical oversight to assist the counselor in maintaining an effective and relevant program.

Counselors can apply the following steps to realize a program that embodies social justice with a mission of access and equity:

- Analyze data to identify need. Example: graduation rates may identify inequity between demographic groups.
- Develop goals. Example: graduation for all students.
- Align goals with school mission: sequential year plans for graduation involve all stakeholders.
- Integrate interventions. Example: utilize existing educational programs toward the goal of graduation for all students.

- Implement interventions at different levels: Incorporate interrelated and interdependent interventions at various levels.
- Collect data results: all levels of program intervention should be collected.
- Analyze data and present for evaluation: include goals met, goals not met, and discuss strategies.
- Revise programs if needed: make changes to program strategies in accordance with new data.

When developing assessment methods for a systemic approach, counselors may first want to refer to existing data from school and district databases as well as adequate yearly progress (AYP) reports for a baseline representation of academic achievement or other pertinent information. Qualitative assessment from focus groups, interviews and observations can provide a profile of key areas to be addressed. Counselors can then glean a basic understanding of what influences the access, attainment and achievement of students. Counselors may then want to choose the best format for assessment, incorporating best methods for garnering information, most comprehensive participation, and best feedback. They will want to look at those specific areas that will provide the clearest and most comprehensive picture of assessment of the program. Once the data is synthesized into a rubric, or other assessment vehicle, counselors can identify the students' needs more clearly and the areas that need to be addressed within the school community.

Data collection and sharing

One of the most crucial steps a counselor needs to implement in order to have an effective school is to have clear goals and objectives for curriculum, instruction and learning outcomes. It is imperative to the school's effectiveness that these goals are explained and well known to everyone that is involved with the student's learning. However, the goals can be well known but, how does a counselor know they are being achieved? One indicator of achievement is student assessment. Once the data has been collected on these a counselor can carefully examine the data and see if there are still weaknesses in the same areas or if there has been an improvement. Another indicator of achievement is the staff's opinions and attitudes. An open line of communication is crucial to any counselor wanting to achieve something more in their school. The staff can be able to tell whether a curriculum is working or if there is still room for improvement.

Counselors can make a significant contribution to both the efficacy and the equity of a school's curriculum by collecting and sharing data related to academic performance of the student body. This data can be invaluable in identifying chronic achievement inequities between racial, ethnic and/or socioeconomic groups. Counselors should work with school staff and counselors to identify these inequities and to implement strategies to rectify the disparities. This may result in changes to course offerings, and/or changes to the counseling program itself. Data collection may also identify strategies or courses of study that are successful. Since decision related to curriculum are often made by committee, including school boards, clear and accurate presentation of the information is vital to data being appropriately translated into curriculum or program change. Therefore, interpretation of the data is particularly important and should be conducted in collaboration with school counselors and staff.

The first area to focus on when collecting data is that of academic achievement. This kind of data can be gathered from standardized test scores, grade point averages, other academic-based scores or results, as well as retention and graduation rates. Secondly, academic participation can be quantitatively assessed by looking at data related to course enrollment, discipline referrals, suspension rates, incidents involving illegal substances, also positive data relating to parent participation, homework completion and extracurricular participation. It should be noted that retention/drop-out rates can form part of both the achievement and the participation databases. The third major area of focus for student data collection addresses those data related to graduation-readiness competencies. These competencies include such areas as number of students with four-year plans on file, students who have participated in such workshops as career planning, job shadowing, and conflict resolution. Students who have completed their academic goals also form part of the graduation-readiness competency data.

Utilizing data collected to determine inequities based on race, culture, ethnicity of socioeconomic status should first begin by including appropriate variables. While there may be significant conclusions to be drawn by simply comparing results divided by gender, race, socioeconomic status, second language learners and other major categories, more useful information may be gained by comparing results in different areas within cultural groups. For instance, results of second language learners that perform well on aptitude tests that are number based, but poorly on those that are language based, should be assessed to determine if the testing and/or the curriculum inherently results in a cultural inequity. This kind of data gathering can identify which programs, courses, and strategies are most and least effective for diverse students, and adjustments can be made accordingly. In addition, if students do well on standardized tests, and poorly in the classroom assignments and tests, this may be an indication of poor participation in the classroom.

Counselors can collect data through the following methods:

- Interviewing counselors, educators or members of stakeholder groups in a structured, semi-structured, or unstructured manner.
- Observing students informally and formally.
- Distributing written questions, rating scales and surveys containing open- and closed-ended questions requesting factual responses or anecdotal perceptions. This method may prove problematic for participants to complete in its entirety.
- Reviewing program records or schedules usually kept in a database format for easy retrieval and archival use.
- Quantitatively comparing the results of standardized tests with educator-generated tests to measure student performance.
- Analyzing performance indicators such as grade point average, classroom grade, attendance, and daily behavior.
- Studying products and portfolios of student performance in the classroom.

Research-based decisions

It is important for counselors not to rush and implement programs that do not have solid research and results. Many times new programs can just add more activities to the curriculum and not fit the needs of the students or they can conflict with what the school's mission is. Many research articles and journals can say that a certain program can bridge the learning gap however; it may not work in every school. Counselors need to stay focus and remember what works best for their school and stay on that course. An effective counselor should only use programs that can produce solid research-based results. It is always important for a counselor to know what the needs are for their students and school before making any huge program change.

Needs assessment

There will be times when a counselor is forced to face the pressure of making changes within the school. The first and most important stage in the pro
cess of change is using a needs assessment plan that provides important information about the strengths and weaknesses about the various educational programs and activities the school is currently using. If the counselor does not occasionally assess the current educational program then most likely he or she will be unaware of any needed change and assume all programs are working well and meeting the needs of everyone. This assessment will also help others understand the need for change. Once there has been a decision to change the program, alternatives need to be selected. One alternative is to replace the current program or just modify it. The counselor should choose the alternative that will best help to improve the school.

Needs assessment serves to analyze and identify needs of the school, the student body, and the community. An effective needs assessment will identify the particular needs of specific subgroups, and whether or not the needs of all groups and subgroups are being met. Comprehensive needs assessment will reveal areas to be addressed in the student body and its respective demographic subgroups, also in school community including parents, staff, counselors, local business, community organizations and community members. Counselors can analyze the results of needs assessment toward recognizing those students who are not reaping the benefits of various academic and personal programs in place on the school campus. Counselors can create effective, comprehensive counseling programs that will enable students to realize improvements in their personal and academic performance. Needs assessment can also assist counselors in better understanding the distinguishing needs of different subgroups and addressing the significant issues of the school community.

Assessing students allows counselors and teachers to understand the level their students are on, whether it is reading, math, science or social studies. Assessments can give an indication of what area students are achieving and in what areas they are struggling. If there is an area of great achievement then counselors can take that information and decide what exactly it is that this school is doing right in order to get these results. They can also ask themselves if there is anything else this school needs in order to help students keep achieving in a particular area. The same is true if after an assessment there is an area where students are struggling. Counselors can look at this data and ask why are students struggling and what are the needs that need to be met in order to achieve improvement. After all this data has been collected and needs have been identified then counselors can start setting priorities to ensure improvement will be made.

Counselors need to look at what the population is regarding their school. If there is a diverse population then there could be diverse educational needs as well. In a diverse population, there are people of all races and ethnicity groups and each race and ethnicity group has different expectations. It is so important that a counselor recognizes this and ensures that the groups know they are important and their voices will be heard. Another population group that should be recognized is the mobile population. If a school services a mobile population group, for example, a homeless shelter, it is important to recognize their needs may not have anything to do with education. Their needs may be just to keep their children fed. Another important factor in determining educational needs is gender. Boys and girls are different emotionally, mentally and physically and their educational needs are different too.

When a counselor is trying to determine which educational needs are the most important to meet, it is important that he or she looks at the community needs. Some communities need to know that when they send their children to school they are going to be safe; others may need to know that their children are getting the best education possible. Different communities have different needs. Counselors need to get involved with the parents and find out what they expect from their child's school. Ignoring the parent's expectations can have a negative effect on the counselor. The parents could start to complain and the leadership status of the counselor could suffer from it. It is also important to look at the population projections. These types of population projections can help give an indication of how fast the school is going to grow and which ethnicity groups are coming in. This is important because different ethnicity groups also have different needs.

School counseling accountability

A proactive approach to school counseling accountability includes clearly articulated parameters for responsibilities and duties, well-defined evaluation and assessment vehicles, and reporting the results of the evaluation to stakeholders. The following components contribute to a dynamic accountability model:

- Identify and collaborate with stakeholder groups. Take a proactive, collaborative stance.
- Collect data and assess the needs of students, educators and community.
- Set goals and establish outcomes as revealed by data.
- Implement effective interventions that address the goals and objectives.
- Design and implement effective outcome assessment for the interventions.
- Utilize the results to improve the counseling program.

- Share the results with students, parents, educators, school counselors, school boards, school counselors and supervisors, and community leaders.

Accountability studies
Accountability studies can enhance counselors' overall knowledge and awareness about the effectiveness of strategies or programs, so that they can provide valuable input to the decision-making process involved in new programs or practices. Based on the results of these studies, counselors may become aware of professional development or staffing needs. The quantitative data from the studies can provide the tangible rationale for these requests. Counselors who are well versed on the assessment results of their program are better able to network with other counseling professionals to share program results and increase their awareness of new intervention strategies. Accountability studies can be a valuable public relations vehicle for informing educators and the larger community about the accomplishments of the school counseling program and the focus of the school system for its students. Counselors who engage in accountability studies demonstrate a personal and professional commitment to ongoing standards of quality and success.

Although accountability studies can provide valuable information for the school counselor as well as the school community as a whole, there are inherent disadvantages and cautions associated with the studies. An obvious disadvantage is that the studies take time away from individual or group counseling, in order for the counselor to implement and assess the accountability model of evaluation. Although this time could be well justified by the overall benefits to the program and to the student body, these benefits can only be realized if the counselor is trained in utilizing the data, and spends the time on research and evaluation to garner any useful results. Counselors may have misgivings about utilizing accountability studies because they may produce results that are counterintuitive to implementation strategies that have proved successful in individual and/or group counseling. Some counselors may also be hesitant to perform accountability studies because of a perception of being micro-managed by the stakeholders requesting the data from the studies.

Program evaluation
The purpose of process evaluation, or program audit, is to determine if the program is appropriately implemented in all areas, and if that implementation is properly documented. The evaluation reviews whether there is implementation and sufficient documentation of all relevant facets of a comprehensive school counseling program. By providing an analysis of each component of the program, the audit identifies areas of strength and weakness within the program, and indicates how these areas compare with district or state mission statements. The following terms are used to evaluate areas of the program:

None: not in place
In progress: started but not completed
Completed: possibly not implemented
Implemented: fully in place
Not applicable: areas where the criteria do not apply

Service assessment
Counselors may be required to provide service assessment reports to guidance supervisors as well as superintendents and/or school boards. Although guidance supervisors may request general service assessments, school boards and superintendents may ask for more specific event-topic counts. These counts refer to specifically how a counselor spends his/her school time and in what capacity. Counselors are asked to document each time a student is contacted, receives any type of counseling service, and/or interacts with the counselor in any capacity. Reporting these counts may be in the form of a log or a simple count, and requires the counselor to maintain a weekly

or monthly recording of how many students receive general counseling as well as those individual sessions to treat depression, behaviors, anxiety, social skills, anger management, family changes, or conflict resolution. Counselors and school boards can appreciate the contributions of the counselor evidenced by quantified event-time counts.

The purpose of time logs is generally determined by the school, the district or other oversight entities. Time logs can provide valuable compliance documentation to counselors and school boards for funding purposes. Certain states and school counseling programs require the use of time logs in order to quantify the type of work being done in the school community and surrounding areas. Some school programs may require the counselor to spend a certain percentage of their time in meetings with students individually, in groups, or for guidance purposes. Counselors should set up the time log format in a manner that will best document the time spent in which capacity, and be categorized in a manner that will be most useful to the entity requesting the time log. The amount of time spent on any counseling-related activity should be documented and categorized as accurately as possible. Counselors may want to maintain daily time logs to effectively capture data regarding time spent.

Outcome assessment
In contrast to service assessment that quantifies time spent, a well-defined outcome assessment can provide a profile of the effectiveness of particular aspects of the program. Counselors should recognize that it is not intended as an evaluation of his or her performance, but rather a useful assessment of the program itself. Counselors can focus on the two key features of outcome assessment. It is not a professional evaluation of the counselor, a limit to his/her ability to perform the job, a requirement for standardized tests or curricula, or a prescribed process with no capacity for expansion. The assessment is:

- A vehicle for garnering information on program-related questions.
- The responsibility of an accountable counselor.
- An ongoing and evolving process.
- A cooperative outreach to other SCPAC members and stakeholders.
- A path toward better education for all students.

As a member of the school community, counselors can report outcome assessment in a way that will be best understood and accessible by the other members of that community. One of the ways that this can be achieved is by categorizing outcome results in alignment with the groupings established by the school. By presenting data that aligns with educational outcomes, the connection between the counseling and educational programs will be more clearly understood. Counselors may also want to provide access to outcome assessment to the larger school community. Results can be disaggregated to profile outcomes for grade levels, individuals or subgroups on the school campus. Some counselors may also provide online access to outcome results for students, families, or community, in a report card or other user-friendly format. By providing reasonable access to easily understood data, counselors can further cultivate the integration of both educational and counseling goals achievement.

When designing research or implementing new intervention strategies, counselors should consider outcome assessment in the initial stages of planning, and definitely before beginning an intervention. Otherwise, they are reliant upon pre-prescribed case studies, non-experimental design paradigms, or static-group comparison studies to analyze the effectiveness of the intervention. By planning for outcome assessment, counselors can tailor the assessment to the intervention. The optimal format for research design is random assignment of participants to treatment conditions. This will allow the

counselor to implement true experimental designs. Otherwise, with little or no control over assignments, counselors must rely on the results of a quasi-experimental or non-experimental design. The completion of pretests and posttests is also optimal, although not all counselors are able or need the dependent variable.

There may be occasion when a counselor may choose to develop an original outcome measure that directly addresses the application, or is most appropriate for the group. When posing questions to the group for responses to be used in the assessment, the following considerations should be incorporated:

- Use simple language and question the group members only on events or circumstances with which they are familiar.
- Each question should be specific, and any unclear terms should be specifically defined in the appropriate context.
- Counselors should always avoid yes-no questions since this limits the responses.
- Counselors should always avoid double negatives since this can confuse the response group.
- Questions should be posed individually, and not in combination with another question.
- Topic-specific wording should be consistent with the wording used in the discipline.
- Counselors should be sensitive to cultural differences.
- Learn to handle difficult response groups effectively.
- Second-hand opinions should only be acceptable if firsthand information is unavailable.
- Background information can be provided to remind the group members of a specific event or reaction.

Assessment terms

The following are assessment-related terms and their definitions:

Evaluation implies a measurement of worth, indicating that the effectiveness will be judged.

Evidence refers to all data that can be used to judge or determine effectiveness. It is either quantitatively or qualitatively derived.

Formative evaluation describes specific feedback received during a program implementation.

Summative evaluation refers to anecdotal feedback received during the evaluation process.

Stakeholder refers to any person or persons who are involved in or benefit from the school counseling program.

Baseline refers to data gathered at the onset of evaluation, to define a starting point.

Pretest describes an administered measure given before an intervention.

Posttest describes an administered measure given after the intervention has been completed.

Value-added assessment refers to the timing and final result of the intervention.

Role of the school counselor

The role of the school counselor has broadened and integrated, so that the goals and delivery of the counseling program dovetail with those of the school as a whole. School counselors as educators recognize that school curriculum delivery and achievement standards are quantifiable media to address the access, attainment, and achievement goals of each individual student as well as the student body as a whole. Counselors also frame their approach with a basic premise that students who are given rigorous curriculum and good support are capable of realizing their potential. Augmenting individual sessions and group workshops, counselors can participate in academic program planning. By integrating educational

and counseling goals, counselors can provide the bridge between personal success and academic achievement. The counseling program can provide finger-on-the-pulse assessment that profiles holistic achievement of the students, by operating within the accountability paradigm of the school.

Counselor's health and well-being

Disability law

For the most part, American disability law is regulated by the Americans with Disabilities Act of 1990. This law prevents discrimination against disabled individuals with respect to housing, employment, education, and access to public services. Interestingly, the ADA includes alcoholism as a disability. The ADA asks that reasonable accommodations be made to provide equal opportunities to disabled individuals. States are not forbidden from passing their own disability laws, so long as they do not contradict the ADA. A number of other acts have been created as spin-offs to the ADA: the Fair Housing Act, the Air Carrier Access Act, and the Individuals with Disabilities Education Act, to name a few.

Self-care

Most individuals, even if they have no medical training, are constantly diagnosing themselves and changing their behavior and diet accordingly. This can include taking aspirin for a headache, taking a nap to combat fatigue, or eating a piece of fruit to stimulate the digestive system. Doctors recommend that individuals perform basic tests (like breast exam, testicular exam, and skin exam) on themselves to determine whether they need formal attention. Other tests, like those for pregnancy or blood pressure, require some diagnostic equipment but can still easily be performed by untrained individuals. The most important skill to have when performing self-care, of course, is to know when to seek a more professional opinion.

Self-nurturing

Counselors have an extremely difficult job; they must motivate, coach, lead, attend meetings and maintain the mission and goals of the school. These job duties can feel rewarding, however, they can also be emotionally draining. Many times this can cause burn out among many counselors and in return have a negative impact on the rest of the school. In order for a counselor to perform their responsibilities effectively, they must remember they are individuals too, and need to take care of themselves. It is important for counselors to find a healthy balance between a work and personal life. Sleep, relaxation, fitness and a healthy diet will enable a counselor to be a well-adjusted person. When a counselor has found a way to balance their responsibilities, they become a healthier individual and in return a wonderful role model for staff members, students and parents.

School-based community

A school-based community involves everyone in the decision-making process including teachers, parents and students. Each team is responsible for a certain part that will improve the school, and with all three teams working together, it will promote a school-based community that focuses on trying to continue to improve the school. This type of community will help student behavior, performance and will encourage parents to take an active part in their child's education. When the teams are able to work together and make decisions it creates a feeling of ownership and responsibility. Everyone is aware of the school's goals and will know what direction they want the school to take. It may be difficult at times for everyone to agree on certain issues, however, the conflict may be reduced if individuals can agree on issues by using a "no fault" problem solving, collaboration and making decisions by consensus. These methods work better than voting because with voting there is an increased chance of individuals taking sides.

Enhancing school culture

Before a counselor can enhance a school culture, he or she must first achieve a good understanding and full knowledge of what the organizational culture is. After this has been achieved then the counselor can move on to the next step of enhancing it. If the school culture is not an effective one, it will be a challenge for the counselor to change it. The counselor must envision the future of the school, what is the goal that will make the school improve. A counselor must also make it a priority to meet the needs of the teachers and students. Enhancing the school culture will more likely be achieved if the counselor views a problem as an opportunity to find solutions not another burden. It will also be enhanced if teachers are encouraged to use creative practices and they are given opportunities to share their ideas and made to fill they are a vital part of the improvement of the school. The most important factor that will enhance school culture is staying focused on student achievement.

When a counselor is striving to build a school culture, it is important to have certain characteristics. School culture consists of everyone: teachers, students, parents and other staff members. One of these important traits is paying attention to the values of its members. These are the ideas and opinions of the member and what they feel is needed for the improvement of the school. One sign of an effective culture is the behavior of the members, whether or not they are positive and upbeat. Another sign is whether teachers are interacting with students and parents in a positive and effective way and vice versa. A strong culture also respects the written and unwritten policies and procedures. In order for the counselor to truly understand the school's culture they should take the time and perform group interviews, this way they can accurately understand the issues of the school.

Influence

Referent influence

If a counselor possesses a referent influence, this means others are able to identify with the counselor as a person. Certain characteristics that others can identify with are a strong character, outspoken personality and compelling leadership style. Characteristics like these may enable a counselor to gain cooperation from others even if teachers, parents and students may question the decisions made by the counselor. The qualities are positive and tend to make people want to react positively to another. However, there are no certain character traits that have a positive impact on everyone. While some groups respond positively to certain traits, others may view them as a sign of weak leadership. Another issue with referent influence is that if a counselor is in a position of leadership, their authenticity has already been established, and if certain traits are not there, then the probability of them developing is unlikely.

Reward influence

This type of influence means a counselor has certain rewards that can be given out to certain individuals who act and obey certain decisions a counselor makes. One issue with this type of influence it that a counselor may not have enough rewards to be able to distribute equally. There may occasionally be a time when rewards may be offered to an individual or group without having to distribute the same reward to others. However, this may seem like preferential treatment and in the education field this is not viewed favorably. Another problem that may arouse is the counselor may receive very little rewards to give from the school board and other bureaucratic agencies. Although these problems may occur, a counselor can develop their own variety of awards. These rewards can include a free period, an additional lunch break or support a new activity a teacher wants to implement.

Center for Disease Control reporting

Mental health and social services guidelines

The Center for Disease Control has provided some basic guidelines for schools seeking to provide adequate mental health care and social services to students. It is recommended that each school have an employee to oversee mental health and social services; some schools may benefit from having a guidance counselor, psychologist, or social worker. Many states require schools to provide a Student Assistance Program (SAP) for all students. Schools that lack either the population or money for such services should partner with local health agencies. Schools that can provide counseling services to students may benefit from offering assessments as well as family, individual, and group counseling.

Disease reporting

In order to stay abreast of any outbreaks of disease, the government has made it mandatory for health agencies to report certain diseases to their state department of health. Diseases that must be reported immediately by phone include anthrax, botulism, rabies, plague, and smallpox. Other disease, including AIDS, E.Coli, and gonorrhea, are to be reported within one business day. These laws apply to physicians, health care facilities, medical laboratories, and, in some circumstances, veterinarians. These individuals or groups also need to report it to the government any time they treat a pregnant woman for some chronic infection, like AIDS. For diseases that are less contagious or severe, the government provides forms for reporting.

Youth Risk Behavior Survey System

The Center for Disease Control has created the Youth Risk Behavior Surveillance System to monitor the negative health behaviors of youth and young adults. Specifically, the YRBSS monitors six categories of risk behaviors: those that contribute to unintentional injuries and violence; tobacco use; alcohol and other drug use; sexual behaviors that cause unintended pregnancy and sexually transmitted disease (including HIV); unhealthy dietary behaviors; and physical inactivity. The YRBSS gathers information by conducting a national survey in schools, as well as by having state and local health agencies conduct their own surveys. All of this data is collected, organized, and published in a national report

The 2003 YRBSS indicated that about 70% of deaths among individuals between the ages of 10 and 24 are caused by four things: motor-vehicle crashes, other unintentional injuries, homicide, and suicide. Many students admitted engaging in behaviors that increase the chances of such a death, namely riding with an intoxicated driver (30.2%), drinking themselves (44.9%), carrying a weapon (17.1%), and smoking marijuana (22.4%). In addition, in the year before the survey was conducted 8.5% of students had attempted suicide and 33% had been in a physical fight. Adults older than 25 are likely to die of cardiovascular disease or cancer, and many young adults are engaging in behaviors that increase the likelihood of such a death: 22% had smoked a cigarette recently, 78% had not eaten enough fruits and vegetables, and 33% had not gotten enough exercise.

Behavioral Risk Factor Surveillance System (BRFSS)
The Center for Disease Control has established the Behavioral Risk Factor Surveillance System to collect information on common health behaviors that may be contributing to illness and injury. The BRFSS originally was only used in a few states but has now been expanded to include the entire nation. Information for the BRFSS is collected by telephone survey. The primary focus of the surveys is to explore the prevalence of behaviors that lead to heart disease, cancer, stroke, diabetes, an injury. The information collected in these surveys is useful to health agencies as they develop policy and health-promotion programs. The BRFSS also helps health agencies to determine which groups are most likely to practice negative health behaviors.

The 2003 BRFSS was designed to pinpoint areas in the United States where particular negative behaviors were practiced more frequently. One of the most disturbing trends indicated by the BRFSS is that obesity is on the rise virtually everywhere; some states, including Alabama, Mississippi, Indiana, and West Virginia, report that over a quarter of their population is overweight. Not surprisingly, the area with the highest instance of diabetes, 11.1%, is in West Virginia. Also unsurprising is that more than twenty percent of the population in these obese states report they have fair or poor health; Texas and Kentucky have similar rates of dissatisfaction.

School Health Policies and Programs Study
The Center for Disease Control administrates the School Health Policies and Programs Study every six years. This survey is designed to measure health policies and programs as they are conducted at the state, district, school, and classroom level in elementary, middle or junior high, and senior high schools. The SHPPS specifically tries to determine the characteristics in each school of the eight school health program components: that is, health education, physical education, health services, mental health and social services, food service, school policy and environment, faculty/staff health promotion, and family/community involvement. The survey also seeks to determine who coordinates and delivers these components, and how the health programs have evolved over time. Information is typically collected via personal interview.

The last School Health Policies and Programs Survey was conducted in 2000. This survey provided a great deal of information about how various school health departments are working to improve health among students and reduce the risks of negative health behaviors. For instance, although 78% of states require health departments to give

- 97 -

lessons on avoiding tobacco, alcohol, and other drugs, only 48% give similar instruction suicide prevention. Injury and illness prevention seems to be most common at the high school level, though only 79% of high schools give direct instruction in physical activity and fitness, and a similar percentage give training in preventing unwanted pregnancy.

CDC adolescent risk behaviors
Unfortunately, two of every five deaths among American teenagers are caused by an automobile accident. Studies have shown that having teen passengers increases the risks for teen drivers, and the risk increases along with the number of passengers. Teens are more likely to underestimate the dangers of driving, and are more likely to speed, run traffic lights, drive while intoxicated, or ride with an intoxicated driver. Teens also have the lowest rate of seatbelt use. Most of these accidents occur on the weekend. The CDC recommends that parents restrict adolescent driving and work hard to ensure that drivers are sober and obedient to traffic regulations.

The Center for Disease Control maintains that the instance of obesity among adolescents between 12 and 19 has more than tripled in the past twenty years. This problem is blamed on simple caloric imbalance: individuals are consuming more calories than they are burning off. These problems can be exaggerated by a genetic predisposition to obesity as well as by bad health. Many overweight children also have high blood pressure or a high cholesterol level. Obese children are more likely to develop bone and joint problems, sleep apnea, low self-esteem, and social dysfunction. As they age, obese children are also more likely to develop heart disease, diabetes, cancer, and stroke
The Center for Disease Control asserts that a tendency to have unprotected sex and multiple sex partners places adolescents at a greater risk of contracting HIV and the AIDS virus. The risk seems to be especially bad for minority adolescents. Individuals are considered to be at special risk of contracting

HIV if they are regular substance abusers, do not have much awareness of the risks of HIV, come from a poor and/or uneducated background, or have dropped out of school. In order to combat this problem, the CDC has developed a number of programs to continue providing education to students in both classrooms and community centers. Many of these programs specifically target minorities.

According to the CDC, teens who become pregnant immediately decrease their chances for success in life. Teen mother have a reduced chance of finishing high school, and are more likely to spend their lives in poverty. The good news on this subject is that better contraceptive practices and more responsible behavior by adolescents have led to a reduction in the number of teen pregnancies, abortions, and birth rates over the past decade. However, these rates are still higher in the United States than in other developed countries, and they are especially high among African-Americans and Hispanics. The CDC has approved a number of programs that they say do a good job of educating and encouraging teens to make the right decisions.

Because they are more likely to engage in risky sexual activity with multiple partners, adolescents are more likely to contract a sexually-transmitted disease. The CDC believes that adolescents are particularly at risk if they are frequent drug users and if they do not have access to contraceptives or to sex education. In order to meet the ongoing needs, the CDC has developed programs to present important information to adolescents so that they can protect themselves, as well as so that they can seek treatment if they do contract an STD. Part of the CDC's mission is to increase the level of parental involvement in the lives of adolescents. The CDC has published a number of statistics indicating that when parents actively supervise their children's lives, the children are less likely to engage in dangerous sexual behavior.

The CDC has indicated a few ways in which schools can develop an effective physical education program. First, the CDC believes that all high school students should have to take a physical education and activity course in order to graduate. If possible, a school should have students participate in group/team activities, individual activities, dance, and aquatic activities. Surveys have found that the most popular team activities in high schools are basketball, baseball/softball, volleyball, and soccer. As far as individual activities, the most popular are walking, jogging, and jumping rope. The CDC recommends that students be given some kind of skills assessment test to determine their level of progress.

Health and nutrition services

In order to provide adequate health services, the CDC recommends that every school have a coordinator of health services, a full-time physician, a nurse, and health aides. Schools should have policies in place to deal with students who have HIV/AIDS. Staff should be allowed to administer medication to students, so long as the students have provided the appropriate documentation. Moreover, students should be allowed to self-medicate with prescription inhalers and insulin injections as long as they are supervised by staff and have filled out the necessary paperwork. To fully serve students, many schools will need to form partnerships with local health agencies, organizations, or counselors.

The Center for Disease Control offers some suggestions for how schools can effectively manage the nutrition services provided to students and staff. First off, health education at the high school should include some instruction on basic nutrition. Most high schools benefit from participating in the USDA National School Lunch Program, and many of these participate in the breakfast program as well. Schools should make sure to order the following healthy foods: skim or low-fat milk, fruit juice, vegetables, baked goods that are low in fat, and fresh fruits. In order to best serve students, schools should employ a full-time nutritionist and food service manager. All food service employees should receive some training in nutrition.

The Center for Disease Control has outlines a few ways that schools can be sure to promote the health of the faculty and staff. Many schools actually have an employee charged with overseeing health promotion for faculty and staff. Most schools allow the faculty and staff to use the exercise facilities maintained for students. Unfortunately, too many schools fail to provide physical examinations to employees. If possible, employees should also receive a tuberculosis test and a screening for illegal drugs. Many school districts provide funding for alcohol treatment, HIV testing, nutrition counseling, stress management therapy, and weight management therapy for their employees.

The Center for Disease Control has issues some basic guidelines for schools to incorporate families and the community into a school health program. First, schools need to communicate their health programs and services to families. It is important for parents to know what materials and services are being made available to their children. Many schools have a specific employee charged with acting as a liaison between the school and the community. Many schools benefit from a close working relationship with external health organizations and professionals. Many schools also open up school exercise facilities to members of the community. Schools should have a protocol in place in the event that a health educator needs to contact a student's family immediately.

Information Acquisition and Dissemination

Integration of developmental and academic goals

Counselors can best serve their students and the school system as a whole by continually integrating developmental goals with academic goals. Since students mature and move through the graded school system simultaneously, counselors should maintain a conscientious awareness of achievement standards in the areas of academic development, personal-social development, and career-focused development. These areas are inherently interdependent, and an effective counselor will consciously integrate them toward the holistic development of his/her students. The ASCA identifies three key strategies for this integration:

1. Counselors should be cognizant of the academic content in classes, and when those classes are being taught, tailoring his/her counseling sessions around the academic needs of the students.
2. Counselors should refer to the school documents and personnel for explicit and implicit goals and competency standards for the students.
3. Counselors can be proactive in enriching certain academic areas for students.

Information retrieval

Although a counselor may discover information over a period of time and through different methods, in the context of the counseling relationship, s/he should strive to obtain the following information:

- The precipitating situation or event: Specifically, the duration, intensity, manifestation and triggers.
- Developmental and environmental factors: For instance, socioeconomic and cultural settings, medical and emotional background, physical and emotional development, etc. This information can often be obtained from parents, teachers and other people connected to the student.
- Relationship specifics: Particularly, classmates and teachers, and how the student interacts within these relationships.
- Academic performance: What are the student's successes and failures in school? Does the student have difficulty in particular subjects, or an identified learning disability?
- Personal attributes and affinities: Ask about favorite activities, favorite subjects, talents, and strengths, and how these are incorporated in the student's daily life.

Treatment and methodology

Assessment of both the student and the situation in any counseling session(s) is very important in that it serves to provide the counselor with choosing both treatment and methodology for that treatment. A counselor will consider each student's developmental stage and environment to determine the best method for approaching a particular circumstance or problem. In addition, school or district policy can affect the counselor's methods, for instance whether to use formalize methods or to be more informal and flexible in developing a treatment for a particular student. Likewise, conducting the assessment can range from formal to informal, and can be rather individualized among counselors. A comprehensive assessment of student needs, the precipitating event or situation, and careful choice of approaches and actions based on this assessment is a very important factor in the success of a counseling relationship.

Assessment documentation

Well-documented assessment provides accountability for the success of the program in addressing student needs. Assessment reporting and documentation can also isolate and identify student groups that are not being served by current programs and policies. By disaggregating data, school counselors can reveal portions of the student demographic – such as those identified by race, ethnicity, socioeconomic status, and other defining categories – that are not being met. Counselors may also want to conduct longitudinal studies that will reveal success or failures of strategies within these subgroups. This kind of focused, delineated data can clearly point to underserved students, and the need for revisions in policy or program development to incorporate the identified students. The contemporary school counselor can serve as a leader in the creation and refinement of school programs that equally address the needs of all students. Documented assessment can provide the kind of tangible evidence that may be needed to garner school support for policy changes.

Academic vs. mental health institution setting

In contrast to assessment methods used in a mental health institution, assessment in an academic setting is less formalized and more geared toward establishing a trust and collaborative relationship with the student. In a mental health setting, the counseling session might be well served if the counselor asks direct questions to the client, in order to assess the problem(s). However, in an academic setting, an effective counseling relationship depends on not only the student's cooperation, facilitated by a less direct approach to assessment, but also incorporation of student needs not readily divulged. A counselor in an academic setting needs to be aware of, for instance, a student's body language when assessing the student and know how to approach treatment. It is important for the counselor in the academic setting to listen and observe carefully, and to engage in non-intrusive inquiry.

Intervention outcomes

In the absence of available success/failure rates for many intervention strategies, the onus is often on the counselor to document the outcomes of strategies used. In order to authentically and effectively produce this outcome assessment, it is at first important to document student responses during and/or after an intervention. In keeping with the assessment model, counselors should produce documentation that either quantifies or clearly identifies specific outcomes. Counselors should also be mindful of their role as an advocate for the students by realistically reporting successes and failures, so that program improvements can be made if necessary. By doing so, they can also provide a model for reflection and willingness to change. Counselors who provide authentic documentation and are willing to revise strategies are excellent candidates for added funding or other resources, and can provide comprehensive parameters for the role of school guidance counselor.

Assessment methods

Informal assessment: Informal assessment can occur in the classroom setting, in conversation with the student, or by observation. Although informal assessment does not lend itself to a standardized rubric, it nonetheless can provide a holistic profile of a student through such activities as games or storytelling. Some of the commonly used strategies for conducting informal assessment include not only games and storytelling, but also role-playing, opportunities for decision-making, writing exercises and prioritized lists. These activities can reveal a student's thought patterns and coping strategies, including those areas which a counselor identifies with specific treatment. Informal assessment can be particularly beneficial when working with an early or middle childhood student who may not be able to isolate and articulate difficulties. Counselors conducting informal assessment need to report their findings in a more comprehensive and less quantitative format that that of formal assessment.

Formal assessment: Formalized assessment is conducted through the use of standardized instruments and can be beneficial in identifying specific areas and treatments for intervention. Formal assessment operates within a rubric, or set of rubrics, that incorporate behavioral checklists, measurements of self-perception, value scales and inventories of interests, skills and interests. This type of assessment also provides the counselor with identification factors that is more targeted and specific than that of informal assessment. Formal assessment, because of its rubric-driven reporting, can sometimes provide counselors with a more objective evaluation of a student than would be gained from informal assessment. Counselors should be aware of, and trained in, an array of formal assessment methods. Results from a formal assessment may include data relating to significant behaviors or attributes that could be overlooked and therefore not addressed in an informal assessment.

Formative assessment: Formative assessment is the testing carried out by the teacher during the course of the school term. Its aim is to ensure that students understand the material, as well as to diagnose any gaps in their understanding. It should provide a clear view of the varying ability levels of the members of the class, and it should indicate some ways in which the teacher needs to improve his or her instruction. Formative assessment should often result in a different means of presenting information, or more time spent with troublesome material. It is a good idea to include self-assessment and peer-assessment, so that students can indicate how they feel about their progress in the course and alert the teacher to any problems in morale.

Oral questioning: One easy way for teachers to conduct a formative assessment in class is to briefly quiz students on the material covered. Indeed, whether it is to be done for a grade or not, it is generally useful to recapitulate the previous day's lesson at the beginning of class. Oftentimes, this can be best accomplished by allowing students to articulate the material and to critique one another's understanding. Some probing questions from the teacher can ensure that the recent material is understood in the context of the material that has already been learned. It is not always necessary to formally grade students on their participation or performance in an informal question-and-answer session; the main thing is to develop an idea of the students' progress.

Written comments: Perhaps the most important kind of formative assessment a teacher can provide is helpful written comments on student papers. This is the place for teachers to clarify the strengths and weaknesses of the student's work, as well as assess the student's progress in the class. Moreover, this is the perfect venue in which to differentiate between students; in order to keep all of the students motivated, teachers must set different standards for them, and indicate these standards in their comments. Comments should always be positive and supportive, but not at the expense of being constructive: simply assigning a letter grade is inadequate. The important thing when commenting on student work is to indicate areas for improvement without alienating or embarrassing the student.

*Summative assessment:*Summative assessment is carried out less frequently by the teacher; it is appropriate for checking knowledge at the end of a unit of study or at the end of the course. Whereas formative assessment is an assessment for learning, in that it helps the teacher to make positive adjustments to the course, summative assessment is an assessment of learning. It is likely that the means of summative assessment will be affected by the performance of students on formative assessments. It is important that summative assessments provide a comprehensive evaluation of students' mastery of the material, such that every area of knowledge is questioned and every skill is tested. Also, summative assessments should include questions of varying difficulty, so that students can distinguish themselves.

Self-assessment and peer assessment: It is always a good idea to incorporate some self-assessment and peer assessment into a class, so that students will be encouraged to think about their own progress relative to the progress of the class, as well as to stay focused on the goals of the course. Interestingly, students are usually much harder on themselves in their evaluations that they are on their fellow students. In order for self-assessment to be successful, the teacher must have clearly outlined the learning objectives of each activity. Furthermore, the teacher must have provided adequate constructive criticism, so that students will have a clear idea of where they stand. Sometimes, it may be useful to design a specific assessment checklist so that students will not resort to vague praise or criticism.

Choosing assessment methods
The following considerations should be incorporated in choosing an assessment method:

- How the test developer defines that construct that will be used, e.g. aptitude, achievement, etc. The counselor should not utilize the assessment in another context than the original one, since the results could be misrepresentative. The technical manual should also be studied in order to value the utility of the test as well as the reliability and validity of the scores.
- How other organizations reviewed the test. Professional literature is available to counselors that will provide reviews from other counselors and similar organizations.

The key factors that should be considered: Counselors considering a quantitative or qualitative assessment should analyze if the baseline and original population are appropriate for the student and whether the instrument can indicate a direction for intervention.

Cultural bias
In most school environments, there are a number of standardized tests that are administered to assess academic achievement and aptitude. Counselors can provide a valuable service to the school and its students by determining if tests are inherently culturally biased, and suggesting alternate assessment methods as appropriate. Some of the aspects of testing that should be reviewed include references to events or individuals that are specific to particular cultures, language-based assessment that does not allow for second language learners, etc. It may be indicated for the counselor to work with school counselors to develop alternative testing methods, or to work one on one with students from cultures that would be disadvantaged by a test. Counselors will be well served to obtain training and refer to outside resources for identifying culturally biased testing, and for choosing alternative methods. It is also important to understand how to communicate testing results to families of students from diverse cultures.

Counselors should be particularly vigilant about any personal biases that they may have that could obscure the assessment process. In other words, if a test is designed to assess student readiness for academic promotion, and half of the students perform at the readiness level, and the other half at below readiness, the initial reaction might be that the test was successful, and that half of the class is ready for promotion. However, if a counselor finds that lines of success or failure fall in a quasi-line progression toward eliminating or isolating a particular cultural group, s/he should guard against a personal assumption that the test validates cultural differences, and instead review the test and the testing process for cultural biases. Not only can these cultural biases negatively affect individual students, but the continued use of a culturally skewed test can also be

- 103 -

used to fallaciously document poor achievement by particular cultures, and further perpetuate academic oppression.

Additionally, assessment vehicles that are language-based, such as math word problems or reading comprehension tests, may intrinsically put second-language learners at a disadvantage. Counselors should be sensitive to this disadvantage, and offer students alternate testing methods. These methods may include written tests in the student's native language, or an interpreter present for testing. Translators may also be on hand to present the questions in both the dominant language and the student's native language, in order to assist the student in making associations between the native language and the dominant language. It is important that the testing environment be presented in a way that is comfortable, allows ample time for translation, and does not contain any implications of inferiority about second-language learners. Assessment of second-language learners should fairly and accurately test students' aptitudes, skills and abilities.

At-risk youth assessment
When a student is identified as being at-risk, the identification is usually made based upon overt behaviors or shortcomings. These may include poor academic performance, or inappropriate behavior. An initial assessment may point to the need for more native language materials or conflict resolution workshops. However, for some first- or second-generation immigrants, these outward circumstances may be noticeable, but not the underlying or most problematic issue. Often, the underlying issue can be masked by overt behaviors, until the need for treatment is long past due. Students from diverse cultures may be contending with issues related to isolation, sadness for loved ones left behind, bridging the gap between cultures, and other issues directly related to poor cultural assimilation. Although there are no clear guidelines per se for identifying such cultural factors, counselors should be aware of the possibility of precipitating circumstances when dealing with at-risk students from other cultures and/or countries.

Instructional assessments

Assessing learning objectives
Counselors can informally assess the effectiveness of a lesson, and the general level of student receptivity, by listening to student responses during the lesson and/or at the conclusion. However, a more formalized assessment can be more advantageous for a few reasons. If a counselor develops a written rubric before presenting a lesson, this rubric can provide a real-time backdrop for counselors to both assess and guide the lessons toward its conclusion. Having a kind of inventory for lesson objectives can provide an outline for the discussion that can be at least informally shared with students, allowing them to realize their strides. In addition, a written rubric can provide the kind of quantitative, formalized assessment vehicle that is very valuable in terms of building credibility with the school community. With clear assessment

information, counselors can experience increased collaboration and support from school staff, counselors and parents.

Designing an assessment rubric for school counseling classroom strategies first begins with defining the learning objectives. Also included should be the demographics of the group, expected learning outcomes, and clear criteria for measurement. Once this rubric is clearly delineated, counselors can target learning objectives with specific planned activities. They can assess the success of the activity by comparing student responses with the rubric criteria. It is important that the components of the rubric be clearly defined before the commencement of the lesson, in order for the counselor to design and deliver activities that will elicit appropriate responses. All of this can be conducted during the normal course of a classroom lesson, with its introduction, activity, and conclusion. A clearly written rubric designed well before the lesson will ensure a successful, non-disruptive assessment.

Lesson plan assessment results can provide a meter for the success of the lesson as well as the relevance of the learning objectives. If student responses have met the criteria set forth in the rubric, counselors can be fairly assured that the lesson or activity was relevant and targeted the expected objective. However, if student behaviors or responses do not meet the rubric criteria, there are several possible explanations that should be considered, individually or in concert. An initial consideration is that of the lesson or activity, to review its applicability to the group and to the objectives. Another consideration is the objectives themselves. Counselors should consider if the objectives were reasonable for the student group. The value of rubric with clearly defined components is realized if some of the criteria are met, but others are not. Counselors can then tailor the lesson or activity according to the results of the assessment.

Assessments for students with special needs

Even students with special needs must be regularly assessed so that teacher's can determine their progress and determine how best to serve them. According to the present system, students with special needs will be subject to all the normal state assessments, although some allowances may be made for them. These allowances may include un-timed exams or isolation during examinations for students with attention-deficit disorder. Students with severe cognitive disabilities may be assessed against their level of previous achievement, rather than at their grade level. Teachers may also discover that some students are better able to perform during oral examinations, or that students may respond positively to indirect questioning.

Program Development and Evaluation

Policy interpretation

Although most school policies and procedures are clearly delineated in written form, their interpretation can be less clear-cut, and can even vary between teachers and classrooms. One policy area that can easily vary between educators is that of allowing students to participate in counseling during time normally set aside for classroom instruction. Some teachers may be in support of students receiving counseling, and may be willing to let that student leave his/her classroom to do so. Others may also be in support of students receiving counseling, but may feel that it should not be done at the expense of classroom time, but rather after or before school. Teachers may also have differing opinions about collaborating with school counselors by implementing behavior modification strategies in the classroom. Counselors should be sensitive to these differences in opinion, and the spectrum of teachers' responses to the need for and implementation of a counseling program.

- 105 -

Copyright © Mometrix Media. You have been licensed one copy of this document for personal use only. Any other reproduction or redistribution is strictly prohibited. All rights reserved.

Collaboration for effectiveness

Because the average student to counselor ratio can range from 100:1 to 300:1, the accessibility of counselors is sometimes well below optimum. The moderate needs of many students can be eclipsed by attention paid to the more severe needs of a few. Therefore, it is advisable for counselors to consult with parents and school personnel in the design of effective prevention and intervention programs. Parents and school personnel experience day-to-day contact with students, and are able to observe them in the classroom and home environments. The combined student contact that parents, teachers and school counselors have can provide valuable feedback to counselors for designing programs and intervention strategies that will benefit the most students most effectively, augmented by individual sessions as indicated. Counselors who meet with the larger school community are able to maximize their efforts and therefore the efficacy of the school counseling program.

Dovetailing counseling and developmental theories

Since school counselors are working with students of different ages and developmental levels, they need to be sensitive to any developmental issues present as well as the overt topic. In the context of implementing strategies targeting the whole of the group, counselors may need to refine or revise their methodology in relation to the age group, or to the developmental level of its members. Within each age group are often inherent developmental crises such as separation anxiety, individuation, or self-worth, and counselors need to incorporate sensitivity to these crises in their topic-based strategies. A six-year-old will have different coping strategies than a fifteen-year-old, even though the topic for both may be divorce. However, these age-based sensitivities should not mitigate counseling strategies, but rather serve to make them more effective and more readily received. Some therapeutic strategies that have been successful in the school setting include cognitive therapy, reality therapy, Adlerian therapy and SFBC.

Counselors need to be cognizant of developmental stages as they implement strategies for different age groups and developmental levels. A recommended approach is to dovetail a particular developmental theory with sequential task order as standardized in the K-12 curriculum. Certain learned life skills and levels or awareness may be negated if a student encounters significant life changes after the strategy is implemented, or if the strategy is implemented too early. By incorporating the K-12 model with the particular developmental theory, counselors can build a comprehensive model of guidance that introduces sequential skills in a meaningful order. It is important for counselors to be aware of students' developmental level, before introducing a task or awareness that is beyond the student's capability or understanding. A good reference is the Adlerian-based framework of five key stages:

1. Understanding self and others
2. Development of empathy
3. Ability to communicate
4. Ability to cooperate
5. Responsibility

Dovetailing counseling and academic curriculum

While the school counseling curriculum is developed within the same parameters as standard academic curriculum, there are distinguishing characteristics and processes. One of this differences is that standard academic curriculum is generally developed to address grade- or age-based curricular goals, whereas counseling curriculum also incorporates behavioral strategies and expectations. Counselors can further augment curriculum with professional expertise and knowledge gleaned by reviewing professional journals or other resources. In terms of process, standard academic curriculum is often a collaborative product of committees that include parents, school staff and administration. School counseling curriculum is generally developed by counselors and teachers. However, many schools have liaison committees available to assist school counselors in developing curriculum. Nonetheless, all school staff should be aware of the goals and strategies employed in school counseling curriculum, as should counselors employ academic curricular goals within their development of school counseling curriculum.

Evidence-based curriculum
Counselors can facilitate students in meeting short-term and long-term goals by using either curriculum they have developed, commercially available curriculum, or a combination of both. There are several advantages of using commercially available curriculum, the first of which is that they are usually evidence-based, having been developed and revised in response to professional research and to tracked success rates. Counselors using this evidenced-based curriculum experience the added benefit of more widespread institutional support for an established, evidence-based curricular model. Counselors can collaborate with school staff and administration to select an appropriate commercial curriculum, and from there identify pedagogy that best addresses student outcomes. When commercial curriculum is selected and adopted, outcomes can be matched with appropriate pedagogical methods. Often these evidenced-based curricula provide both students and school faculty with the confidence and efficacy that result from utilizing established pedagogy.

School counseling curriculum standards
There are both state standards and national models from associations such as the ASCA for the development of school counseling curriculum. These models address expectations for grade and education levels, as well as school guidance models targeting regions as well as grade levels. A number of states have developed counseling programs that are derivations from national

recommendations, incorporating current literature as well as success rates for particular models or strategies. When developing school counseling curriculum, counselors will be best served by not only following these national and state models, but also by continuing to consider and incorporate recommendations from the school community. The local school community is often the best source for determining best strategies to improve the academic, personal, and career development of the students. Collaboration with a school advisory group can also facilitate development of a counseling curriculum that best meets students' needs and goals/expectations from the school community at large.

Overall theory for counseling
To ensure continuity within a counseling program, it is best to design strategies and activities within the tenets of an overarching theory for counseling. Within each counseling group or series of sessions, counselors should develop strategies that are within the context of a specific theoretical model. School counselors should be knowledgeable of a number of theorists and models, in order to opt for one that is applicable to the school setting. Human development theories can serve as a viable foundation for many program designs, as can peripheral models of developmental phases within age groups. However, not all counseling sessions or students will necessarily be well served within the same theorist or paradigm, so counselors should be watchful that a particular paradigm or theorist will address the situation or student group appropriately. Counselors should consider age levels and other defining factors in each counseling situation.

Role in school system

It is important for school counselors to remember that they are one member of the school personnel community. Their role is to provide individual or group therapy to student members of the community who are at risk for self-destructive behaviors, which usually include academic failure. It is the intervention focusing on the dangers of academic failure that serves as the linchpin of the collaborative goals of the entire school community, including the school counselor. For school counselors to be most effective and of value to their student clients, it is important to remember that the school counselor in serving his/her students is also serving the greater good of the school community. This greater good includes the safety of the student body, and the academic goals of the school and the district. Those academic goals can be reflected in test scores, retention, and other quantifiable data.

Particularly in a school counseling environment, any kind of intervention or therapy must be considered and delivered within the context of the larger school system and community. The primary purpose behind this is efficacy of treatment. Counselors who are working with at-risk students or students who are facing personal problems will gain benefit for the student and for the counseling program by collaborating with school personnel. This may include a collaborative consultation, or may just be a matter of available resources. Counselors may also want to serve as a liaison in suggesting student-orientated changes to the school system. Counselors can also adopt a holistic approach to therapy, within the context of the school community. It is important to remember that students are classmates and have classmates, take course work within a prescribed curriculum, and operate within the mandates of the school system. Therefore, when working with students, counselors should be cognizant of a student's daily routines and environment.

Responsibility to individual students
It is important to remember that the primary responsibility of the counselor is to the student body and the school community as a whole. This community includes parents, teachers, the student body and even other counselors. Within this context, counselors can and should strive to address the needs of individual students who will most benefit from individual counseling, particularly as it relates to their academic development and success. The counselor's role is to assess individual students to determine if one-to-one counseling would be beneficial, and then to implement that counseling if it appears it would be helpful to the student, particularly as it relates to his or her academic success. If a counselor feels a student is in need of additional therapy or therapy beyond an academic context, it is recommended that the student be referred to outside agencies or other appropriate resources.

Expectations concerning students
A counselor should set high expectations regarding students. However, it is important for the counselor to remember every student is different and the expectations should be set accordingly. One of the first considerations to take is the student's developmental level. A counselor needs to be aware if the student has any learning disabilities or is developmentally slow. Expectations should not be set too high especially if the expectations are not developmentally appropriate for the students. Another factor to consider is the instructional level for the students. Expectations should not be set so high that they go beyond the instructional level. A kindergartener cannot be expected to perform on the same level as a sixth grader. The opposite is also true; expectations should not be set too low that the students will be performing below grade level and not want to achieve anything higher than that.

Teachers' perceptions of counselors
School counselors and the work that they do may run the risk of being perceived as disruptive and counter-productive to the class. One of the ways to mitigate the chances for this negative perception, in addition to conversation and collaboration with teachers, is to understand and respect certain aspects of the classroom dynamics. Particularly for younger aged children, maintaining routine is

important to the continuity of the class, and therefore places the counselor in a role that is complementary and not disruptive. It is also important for counselors to understand and respect established rules of discipline and behavior standards in classrooms in which they work with students. By recognizing that classroom dynamics have been established and provide a continuum, counselors can fulfill a role of facilitator and gain the respect and trust of teachers and other school staff.

Individualized session strategies

An initial consideration for the school counselor is that of scheduling the session at a time that is least intrusive to the academic day, tempered by factors that are most beneficial to the student. Although the primary consideration is that of respect to the academic setting, the counselor also should be sensitive to student nuances, such as students who may be more receptive after school hours as opposed to during a time in the middle of the day. Beyond that, within the session format, the counselor needs to strategically incorporate the particular needs of the student within the context of developing and implementing therapeutic goals. It is important to couch counseling techniques in a way that will be most effective, such as considering a student's developmental or situational hindrances. Further, the counselor should develop rubric for assessing the success of the therapy.

Collaboration

An effective counseling group is reliant on the support, endorsement and collaboration of parents, teachers and school counselors. It is important that these individuals and administrative groups understand and support the importance and goals of the counseling groups. Counselors can work with parents and school personnel to sensitize them to the importance of counseling groups. One of the common concerns is that counseling groups ask students to spend time that could otherwise be spent in the classrooms. It is important to stress to

parents and school personnel that the time students spend in the classroom is generally more effective if students are allowed to address personal, time management and other issues in counseling sessions, that can hinder their performance and success in the classroom. Once counselors have established this understanding with parents and school personnel, they can unite in a partnership for the students' benefit.

SFBC

Parameters and purpose

The brief-counseling method, sometimes referred to as solution-focused brief counseling (SFBC), is often indicated in schools that are operating under regimented time constraints for counseling. In these schools, the SFBC counseling model can be one that is commonly applied. The parameters of these brief-counseling sessions are designed to mimic the parameters of longer individual sessions, but modeled for the indicated time period. The SFBC model also incorporates the unique particularities of the school counseling session. The model includes an opportunity for the student to concretely describe his/her particular situation, present any previous attempted resolutions, and then develop and implement an intervention. The SFBC model is most effective when the counselors utilize the time to endorse student strengths, successes and resources. This model is often found to be effective for students of diverse backgrounds or cultures.

Premises and strategies

Some of the key premises that underlie the SFBC model are as follows:

- Focus should be directed toward solutions, and not toward the problem(s).
- Within each problem is an identifiable exception that should be isolated and addressed when formulating a solution.

- Large changes often begin with small changes.
- Within each student are the resources needed to solve his or her problem.

The following are the basic strategies of SFBC:

- If the counselor determines that no problematic issue exists, s/he should be cautious not to create one.
- Counselors should develop tasks similar to those with which the student has found success.
- Counselors should be open to the necessity of changing strategies, if it is found that a particular strategy is unsuccessful with a particular student or situation.

These premises and strategies have been carefully researched and formulated by a consortium of counselors well versed in the SFBC model.

The strategies indicated for SFBC are based on the following set of core concepts:

- If the counselor develops and presents the goals in a positive context, rather than a negative one, the student's cooperation, collaboration and response are more likely to be forthcoming.
- In the SFBC model, a pragmatic approach is much more indicated than a theoretical one, i.e. focus on what works and not what the problem is.
- Counselors should be careful to formulate intervention strategies that can be reasonably attained within the allotted time frame.

Because of the nature and parameters of the SFBC model, counselors should encourage students to focus on present and future circumstances, and avoid past experiences as much as possible.

Counselors should focus intervention strategies on students' behaviors and actions, rather than reflective insights.

All of these strategies contribute to the efficacy and success of the SFBC model of counseling session.

First session
One of the goals of the first session of the SFBC model is for the counselor to present the student with a series of questions designed to elicit a response. These responses will form the foundation for developing an intervention. A recommended format for introducing these questions is for the counselor to first present the basic goals and premises of SFBC. Secondly, s/he will inform the student that questions will be asked, and that the questions could prove to be difficult or challenging. This precursor strategy often sets the stage for the student to be poised with a response to a challenge. The student's response will often provide the counselor with a starting place for intervention. This posturing will contribute to the efficacy of presenting the questions in the first session of the SFBC.

Establishing rapport
Foremost in the school counseling model is the establishment and the perception of a trust relationship between counselor and student. This includes, but is not limited to, developing a relationship of trust and cooperation. This trust and cooperation sometimes needs to be established over a period of several visits, and is augmented by a strict policy of confidentiality by the counselor, further contributing to the safe environment. The dynamics of identifying and addressing key or underlying issues can be very positive and productive in a counseling setting when the relationship between the counselor and student is established, during as many sessions as is reasonable. An added benefit of numerous sessions can be the student's receptiveness to the counselor's recommendations, ideally working with the counselor on possible resolutions.

Counselors are not only responsible for explaining their role in the session, but this explanation can and should serve to establish a relationship of trust and collaboration with the student. It is important for counselors to be sensitive to a student's age when explaining his/her role. In other words, for a younger student, the counselor might couch the discussion with the explanation that s/he wants to help the student feel better, whereas for an adolescent this type of explanation could easily be deemed condescending. For adolescent students, it might be advisable to first begin by asking the student of his perception of the goals and purposes of counseling, and then elucidate or clarify from there. Counselors will often be also responsible for explaining the role and purpose of counseling to parents, and need to be sensitive to this approach, particularly in relation to explaining to the student.

Because of the importance of peer relationships for students, they are often less likely to be receptive to recommendations or inquiries from adults. It is important for the counselor to develop a relationship of trust with the student. One of the strategies is for the counselor to listen carefully to the student's perception of a situation in order to develop and convey an attitude of empathy. Likewise, once a counselor has researched a student's background and situation or precipitating event, it is important to refrain from developing biases or expectations based on this research alone. Listening to the student's experiences and perceptions will allow the counselor to form a more realistic and comprehensive approach to resolution. As the counselor and student develop a relationship of tackling a situation in tandem, the counselor will not only encounter less resistance from the student, but also will benefit from the student's suggestion and collaboration.

For all age groups, it is important for the counselor to listen attentively, and to refrain from judgmental or negating behaviors or comments. For specific age groups, there are particular activities than can facilitate the establishment of a trust relationship between counselor and student. For younger children, playing and creative activities can provide a rich medium for developing rapport. Students in middle childhood and adolescence can benefit from playing sports or other games, toward developing a trust relationship with a counselor. Counselors should be versed in an array of rapport-building strategies in order to apply the best strategies for each student. Other strategies include drawing, collage-making and writing on a board. Counselors can facilitate the therapeutic benefit of these activities by isolating and discussing particular pictures or words, always remembering to be attentive and respectful to the student.

Student resistance
It is important to remember that the student has been referred to the counselor in most cases. Not only is the student not motivated to work with the counselor, but often confused and mistrustful of the purpose of the session. Counselors need to be sensitive to this apprehension by not immediately tackling the situation for which the student has been referred. One approach is to allow the student to begin talking to the counselor about an innocuous subject such as objects in the room. This will sometimes help the student to feel more comfortable in the counseling office, as well as alleviate the feeling that s/he is the subject of a therapeutic spotlight.

Self-referred students
In some cases, students will refer themselves for counseling. In this case, although the counselor should experience less resistance from the student, there are nonetheless legal and ethical issues to be considered. It is first important to refer to government and school regulations regarding self-referral. One of the issues to be addressed include when and how to obtain parental consent. Another issue is that of professional and ethical codes when counseling a self-referred student. Further, limits of confidentiality in counseling a minor

student need to be thoroughly researched and clarified before the counseling session(s), whether an individual or a group session. A counselor should be cognizant of all of the considerations and ramifications of working with a student who self-refers, before meeting with the student, and in fact may decline the session based on findings.

Confidentiality

The general rule of confidentiality, as denoted by the American School Counseling Association, specifies that counselors are mandated to protect the confidentiality of the student unless there is indication of intent to harm oneself or others. It is important to both the student and the integrity of the counseling relationship that this confidentiality principal be explained in a manner that is aligned with the student's age group and ability to perceive the explanation. This confidentiality ethic needs to be explained to parents also. The benefits of clearly explaining issues of confidentiality include the student's trust to divulge sensitive information, as well as the parents' understanding of the ethical obligation of the counselor to protect the student's confidentiality. It is also important that the student understands the counselor's obligation to breach confidentiality if s/he fears the student will harm him/herself or others.

It is important that the student not only understands the tenets of confidentiality, but also feels comfortable with the counselor's obligations and respect of confidentiality issues. Younger students may participate in a counseling situation with their parents present, but it should be clearly explained to both parents and students that information divulged in a session without the parents should be protected. Although young students need to understand that this confidentiality can be breached in the presence of threat to self or others, it is most likely more an assurance to parents that this aspect of confidentiality is in place. On the other hand, adolescent students are particularly sensitive

to protection of their confidentiality, and it is important that they be aware of the criteria for breaching that confidentiality. To best respect the rapport established with an adolescent, counselors could approach these criteria using humor or exaggerated examples, to best maintain the student's trust.

Promoting multicultural sensitivity

Often counselors are required to speak to large groups of students, and in this capacity can deliver lesson plans to diverse groups of students regarding multicultural awareness and sensitivity. Counselors can effectively improve the cultural climate in a school setting by promoting multicultural sensitivity and educating students about best practices for positive diversity. They can begin by defining and identifying cultural differences, as well as appropriate language and behaviors for addressing these differences. A lesson plan about multicultural sensitivity can first identify that culture may include or refer to race, ethnicity, gender, sexual orientation, different levels of ability, etc. Counselors can illustrate how culturally biased behaviors and attitudes can lead to oppression and conflict, whereas avoidance of these behaviors can contribute to the richness of a diverse student body. Counselors should also remind students of the negativity engendered by practicing and promoting oppressive behaviors among their families and other members of their own culture.

Counselors wishing to educate students on positive diversity and multicultural sensitivity can include both informational and reflective elements in their lesson plans. Informational elements can encompass the correct usage of multicultural terminology, identification of oppression and oppressive practices, identification of cultural differences and how they can affect interaction, etc. Counselors can explain differences of world view and value systems that are culturally based. Reflective exercises can be group discussions, testimony of personal experiences, or journal exercises exploring personal biases and assumptions. Counselors can also include examples of racism, ageism, ableism, etc. to identify cultural bias and illustrate its negative impact. Included might be identifying cultural bias in historical texts. The class can also discuss ideas for addressing oppressive beliefs and practices throughout the world. Lesson plans can alternate between informational lecture and reflective discussion to best engage the students in the topic.

Program evaluation

Formal and informal
Communicating with the student about the success of interventions, and progress toward therapeutic goals, should incorporate consideration of the counseling relationship. Student response to evaluation practices forms a part of the success of the intervention. Without student response, counselors run the risk of losing the student's trust. A counselor can determine if a particular student, in a particular environment, would be best served by an informal or a formal evaluation of progress. In a collaborative informal evaluation, both student and counselor are present and the counselor can observe and monitor student response. Formal evaluations take into account reports from parents and teachers, as well as the student's documentation of his/her success in a particular area. With either formal or informal evaluation of progress, the counselor should make it a practice to take into consideration the relationship that has been established with the student.

Cautions and safeguards
While counselor-generated evaluations are to some extent inherently subjective, there are several recommended safeguards to ensure a reasonable level of objectivity. In terms of the relationship to the student, the counselor should maintain a professional emotional distance, while still demonstrating sensitivity to student needs and his/her relationship with the counselor. The counselor should guard against becoming too emotionally attached to a student, to the point that it could obscure the counselor's ability to empirically evaluate the level of success of the therapy or intervention. It is also important that the counselor and/or counseling team develop evaluation techniques and rubric that will appropriately assess achievement of therapeutic goals. A single-case study experimental design may be recommendable. Another common suggestion is for the counselor to implement both formal and informal evaluation techniques to allow for better objective assessment.

Crisis management

A crisis is defined in part by the event, and in part by the response to the event. Generally speaking, a crisis is a situation that is perceived as overwhelming and intolerable by the individual(s) facing the crisis. Crises can affect people cognitively, psychologically, behaviorally and even physically. For an individual, a crisis may fall somewhere in the spectrum between failing an exam to full-scale disasters affecting the entire community. Although full-scale disasters necessarily affect entire populations and inherently pose overwhelming circumstances, counselors also need to be aware of the levels of crisis facing students vis-à-vis their coping skills. For most crises, which fall significantly short of full-scale disaster, counselors can employ intervention strategies to help students through the present crisis as well as to help them develop coping skills for future challenges. Early intervention will mitigate the possibility of traumatic response to a crisis.

Personal crises
Some students may be having personal problems during the school year that prevent them from working to their potential. When this is the case, teachers have an obligation to intervene and do whatever thy can to help the student. One of the most important things a teacher can do is to provide an example of a

stable and protective adult. If the student is struggling with a parent's divorce or with an abusive parent, it is essential for there to be a steady nurturing presence in their lives. In other situations, it may be important for a teacher to work with parents to help the student through a personal crisis. School counselors and counselors should always be available to help teachers who feel overwhelmed by a situation.

Suicidal behavior

Suicide is very prevalent among young people, and has been deemed the moist common cause of death for adolescents. School counselors working with youth need to be well versed on the factors and behaviors contributing to suicides. There is no guaranteed strategy to prevent suicide, and in fact, suicide may occur despite the best efforts in the student's network of support. However, counselors can take the stance of being informed and prepared in the event of suicidal behavior. It should be noted that suicidal ideation may be expressed differently among different cultures, and therefore counselors should respond to every potential ideation seriously. Some of the common circumstances precipitating suicide are alcoholism, depression, and a sense of hopelessness or helplessness. Counselors who observe suicidal tendencies should meet with the student regularly to discuss and work on the student's problems and state of mind.

School counselors need to be educated on potentially suicidal behaviors, and be prepared to intervene if necessary. These behaviors can include ideation, or any other behaviors that may indicate a student is contemplating suicide. All threats of suicide should be taken seriously. Counselors should consult institutional directives and state laws regarding responsibility for notification. In some cases, parents should be notified immediately, and may even need to pick up their child from school as soon as possible. In any case, students who are at risk for suicide should be in the presence of an adult at all times during the school day. Since the possibility of suicide can be extreme and immediate, intervention may include referral to an outside agency or institution. Counselors can work with parents and consultants in order to transition to treatment facilities and should be familiar with community services available.

Although there are infinite manifestations of suicidal thoughts, there are seven key identifiers that counselors should take note of:

- Communication, either spoken or implied, which incorporates suicidal thoughts and possibly includes themes of escape, punishment, or self-harm.
- Well-thought-out plans for dying. If the plans are feasible, concrete, detailed and specific, this may be a good indicator that the student is seriously contemplating suicide.
- Well-thought-out plans for self-harm or for murder. Remember, suicide is self-murder.
- An association of completed business, closure, or a note with the idea of dying.
- Extreme stress such as a traumatic loss, illness, failure, etc. Counselors should also be wary of significant anniversaries in a student's life representing past losses.
- Mental state indicators pointing to alcoholism, depression, or any recent changes in attitude.
- A sense of overwhelming hopelessness or helplessness.

The Center for Disease Control acknowledges that the rate of suicide among youth has declined during the past decade. However, the CDC still believes that the rates are still too high. Many adolescents become overwhelmed by stress, confusion, and depression, and consider taking their own lives. In fact, suicide is the third leading cause of death among people between the ages of

15 and 24. The majority of suicides among adolescents are males. Firearms were used in the majority of these suicides. An individual may be at risk of suicide if he or she is impulsive, aggressive, has a history of mental disorders or substance abuse, has a physical illness, has access to some means of committing suicide, or has recently suffered some personal loss.

Working with students who are presenting suicidal ideation includes reconnecting that student to his/her network of support. In the process of working with a student, a counselor can glean which activities and people in his/her life provide meaning, and contribute to an attitude of hope and resiliency. If a counselor deems that suicide is an imminent threat, the first consideration is the student's safety. This may include involvement of the parents, within the parameters of privacy mandates in this situation. Counselors can also encourage the student to reach out to his/her network of support for encouragement. This network could include parents, friends, church, coworkers, etc. As the student's ideation begins to subside, this network can also provide a grid upon which the student can reestablish positive connections. Counselors can remind students of their responsibility, purpose, and place in this network and in the larger community.

Crisis intervention

Since crisis by definition is a situation that is overwhelming and intolerable, crisis intervention serves to provide immediate support, and assist the individual(s) in developing the coping skills to meet the present crisis and similar crises in the future. It is good to remember that one of the factors that can contribute to a crisis is that the situation or event poses a new challenge to the individual(s). Some of the components of crisis intervention include:

- Defusing emotions to allow for exploring solution options.
- Interpreting the event or situation causing the crisis.
- Organizing the situation in terms of information, resources, etc. Proper preparation calms the student to be able to handle the situation.
- Integrating the event into personal experience. Assist the students in recognizing the life lessons to be realized.
- Recognizing the positive impact gained from a crisis, e.g. the coping skills gained, new awareness, etc.

Counselors can work with school staff and counselors, both at the school level and at the district level, to develop a crisis response plan, to be prepared for any crisis that may occur. Counselors should facilitate regular meetings with school personnel, parents and other professionals as appropriate, to educate them on crisis intervention both at the school and at the community levels. Crisis response teams should coordinate campus-wide and community-wide services as part a critical response team. Counselors can educate and prepare the team on strategies and methods for handling the crisis. The team should be versed on methods for crisis prevention, strategies to employ during a crisis, and post-crisis needs. The team should work together, with the counselor usually as facilitator, to develop a well-organized, systemic response plan. The coordination of the team and the crisis response plan should be implemented as a matter of preparation, and preferably not in response to an immediate crisis.

Crisis response plans need to address the possibility that normal logistical operations may be suspended, particularly in the case of a school-wide or community-wide crisis. Therefore, a good crisis intervention plan will allow for the following needs:

- Location needs: It may be necessary to establish a location for temporary counseling offices. This should be addressed by the team in anticipation of a possible crisis. Locations should also be established for a communication facility, first aid/treatment, emergency personnel, storage of supplies/food, and a break room or safe room.
- Communication needs: Crisis response teams will need to communication with other members of the team. They may also need to communicate with parents, as well as with the press. Part of the communication requirement will be the oversight and monitoring of team activities.
- Other considerations: An overall plan and assigned personnel for assessing the situation and assigning intervention tasks.

Counselor's role after trauma

Numerous kinds of traumas can affect a student population, from individual crises to those affecting the entire student body. Counselors need to be cognizant of the types and levels of trauma and how they impact students. It is prudent for them to be aware of the possible ramifications of trauma, how to identify these effects, and strategies for intervention. Counselors need to be aware of the scope of trauma, and the scope of the needed intervention. School-wide traumas can include natural disasters, school shootings, widespread gang activity, etc. Individual traumas may encompass family illness, depression, domestic abuse, and even suicide. Sometimes an individual crisis can escalate into a school-wide trauma, by culminating in a school shooting or a suicide. Counselors should be well versed in types of trauma and how to assess and treat its victims. This information should be ready knowledge, in the case of a trauma or crisis.

Legal guidelines

State and federal regulations

Federal statutes generally address the right of a parent to access records of a minor student. Both state and federal mandates dictate that parents have the right of access to privileged information, although some state laws mitigate that right in the case of abuse or neglect. It is important for counselors to be cognizant of both federal and state statutes regarding the protection of information relating to minor students. Since federal law generally protects the right of parents to view their minor child's school records, counselors should probably keep counseling records separate from school records, in accordance with school and/or district rules. Awareness of both federal and state laws regarding confidentiality can affect not only a counselor's treatment of information, but also his/her approach to the counseling relationship, including informing both students and parents of these rulings.

School system policy and procedures

Each school system will have particular nuances and interpretations with respect to issues of confidentiality and parental rights. Counselors should be cognizant of these policies/procedures when working with students in order to know:

- When and how to notify parents of student participation in counseling.
- How to respond to suspicion of child abuse.
- Issues of confidentiality in the therapeutic environment, e.g. when and how to report severely at risk behavior, when and how to recognize and report students who may be at risk of harming others.
- When and how to open up the counseling strategies to include collaborative consultation.
- When to involve teachers and other school staff in intervention strategies.

- Understanding the policies and procedures includes not only reading them but also understanding how these policies are implemented in a particular school environment.

Open communication and cultivating relationships with school staff will be beneficial to the counselor in developing an understanding of school policies and procedures.

Goal setting

Collaboration and flexibility
Although it is important for each session with each student to be guided by clearly defined therapeutic goals, it is also important to recognize that reaching those goals is often a result of collaboration with the student, and some degree of flexibility on the part of the counselor. The counseling relationship is inherently a dynamic one, which is most successful when there is a partnership involving the counselor and the student. Setting and realizing goals in counseling should include the following considerations: What is particular about this student or this situation that needs to be incorporated in the strategy for intervention? What are the student's goals for this situation? Including these considerations will enable the counselor to develop and refine goals, timelines, best approaches to each phase of the goals, and possibly even adjustments to the physical counseling environment. All of these and other interactive, collaborative considerations will contribute to the success and efficacy of the counseling session and relationship.

The dynamics of creating positive goals incorporates the capacity to envision oneself realizing those goals. Some of the strategies that counselors can use to facilitate this process include:

- Asking the student how he or she would feel and react if his/her situation were suddenly resolved.

- Asking the student to identify instances where the current situation was not problematic, or when there were exceptions to the situation. This can be a very powerful step in that it may recall a recent instance of resolution that the student can recognize and respond to.
- Asking the student what actions or behaviors led to some resolution, or mitigation, of the situation. Encourage positive actions and results.
- Asking the student to rate their feelings about their behavior or the situation on a scale of 1 to 10.
- Anticipating possible obstacles, and work to guide the students around and/or past those obstacles.

Follow-up meetings
Once counselors have met with students for a sequence of sessions, and feel that learning objectives have been met, it is nonetheless a good idea to schedule follow-up meetings with the students. It is important to realize that students may have effectively mastered particular objectives within the insulated environment of the facilitated classroom sessions, but that they may be inclined to revert to prior behaviors once they are in their familiar milieu. Follow-up sessions can serve as reminders to students of their progress in the classroom, as well as strategies that were successful for them. They can also give students an additional opportunity to assimilate the lessons and imprint them in their everyday lives. Counselors can use some discretion in determining the best timing for scheduling follow-up meetings, but they generally occur within days or weeks of the final session of the sequence.

Follow-up meetings with students who have completed a sequence of counseling lessons are beneficial to the counselor, and more importantly to the students and the overall success of the program. Counselors who meet with students shortly after the final session in a sequence can continue to assess the effectiveness of strategies employed. As with intra-lesson assessment, follow-up assessment may identify particular areas that may need to be targeted more or differently in future sessions about the same topics. Additionally, and more importantly, follow-up sessions can provide counselors with the opportunity to reinforce lessons and strategies employed in the sequence of sessions. This benefits the students and the program exponentially, in that it decreases the chances of repeated negative behaviors, and mitigates the need for redundant sessions targeting objectives that had been previously met. All of this contributes to the overall effectiveness of the program.

Ending the counseling relationship
The academic counseling relationship is perhaps more susceptible to difficulties in closure than the professional relationship, for the mere fact that the student and counselor may have met several days a week, or even several times a day, so the termination of the relationship needs to be approached carefully and methodically. Although there is no definitive research regarding this process, there are some agreed-upon practices regarding this process. Termination can be an abrupt or a gradual process, but it is nonetheless recommended that the counselor use his or her discretion in choosing a time to prepare the student to anticipate the last session. It is a good idea for the counselor to take this time to reinforce with the student the success of the counseling session, including the progress and improvements made by the student during and as a result of the counseling sessions. Counselors should be attentive to student feelings and responses, and recommend outside resources as appropriate.

At risk student guidelines

It is important for counselors to be cognizant of the events and influences contributing to at-risk students, as well as the potential ramifications of their behavior and mental state. Counselors should be aware of changes in student behavior that may signal depression or other mental or emotional fragility. It is worth mentioning that the leading cause of death for young people is suicide, and therefore counselors are in a pivotal position to notice and respond to these symptoms. Some students may need more intensive, outside treatment other than school counseling. Some of the factors that can contribute to emotional vulnerability of at-risk students can include rising levels of poverty, substance abuse of the student or parent(s), domestic violence, and community violence. Other kinds of behavior problems may be a result of ADHD or other behavior disorders and may indicate the need for the student to be referred to special education resources in the school.

Although the factors and behaviors of at-risk students fall within a rather large spectrum, there is an umbrella definition that can be used as part of an overall set of guidelines for identifying these at-risk students. If a student shows decline in any or all of the areas of physical, mental, social, spiritual or economic health, then the student is considered at risk. In addition, community and social circumstances may contribute to a student's sense of isolation, increasing the possibility of deterioration in one or all of these areas. Students who are at risk in any or all of these areas often face a diminished likelihood of becoming productive members of society. Counselors are encouraged to refer to guidelines from professional organizations or literature to identify and appropriately respond to at-risk students. Counselors can provide the support, resources and encouragement that can significantly mitigate deteriorating factors.

There are five key areas of caution to consider when identifying a student as at-risk:

1. Students who fall within the guidelines of at-risk may nonetheless be very resilient with strong coping skills, and

therefore at-risk may be a temporary status for that student.

2. If a student is overtly and obviously treated differently than other students because of the at-risk category, this may have the reverse effect of discouraging any creativity or confidence that student may have otherwise displayed.
3. The term at-risk can easily become a label rather than a status, and therefore there is no mechanism to identify when the student is no longer at risk.
4. The term by itself encompasses so many situations and behaviors, the responsive strategies may be also very generalized and not address the issues specific to a particular student.
5. Cultural factors should always be considered, as possibly contributing to or masking an underlying issue.

Adolescent students between the ages of 14 and 17 are particularly at risk for peer association and influence. Youth in this age group generally gravitate to groups that they can join and belong to, other than their family. Often, young people join groups that are formed around a common ethnicity. Unfortunately, if a good portion of the members of the group engage in violent or illegal activities, those who join the group often mimic this activity in order to be accepted. Consequently, students who participate in violent behavior or drug use engage in a lifestyle that leads to the decline of their physical, mental, social, spiritual and/or economic health, which places them clearly at risk. Although counselors need to refrain from making assumptions based on associations, they nonetheless should be aware of student's association, particularly as it relates to at-risk behaviors and attitudes.

Trends in behaviors

Within a large student body, there will be a small percentage of students engaging in at-risk behaviors, for which counselors should be on alert. At-risk youth commit various crimes after school, generally between the hours of 3 and 8, in fact closer to 3, right after school. Robberies are sometimes committed by youth, usually during the week and usually after 9 p.m. Today's students still face problems with premarital sex and unwanted pregnancies, which can significantly put them at risk for poor academic performance. However, the incidences of student suicides are on the decline, as are those of students riding with drunk drivers, and students carrying weapons to school. Although these activities and behaviors still occur, counselors should be aware of rising and declining trends in at-risk behavior in order to be aware of the signs and symptoms associated with them.

Needs

Counselors are generally responsible for addressing the academic as well as career and social development needs of students. To that end, they should be well versed in the areas of leadership, advocacy, systemic change, and collaboration. Also, they should develop and continually refine the skills to teach in these areas to diverse groups of students which include not only cultural differences but also at-risk students. Within the category of at-risk students are included those students whose behavior and performance are a result of family or socioeconomic factors, as well as students who come from a more stable background but suffer from physiological disabilities. Although the scope of the necessary preparation may be daunting, it can be more generalized to say that counselors should be cognizant of the subject matter, as well as the perspectives of the students, and choose a framework or frameworks for the curriculum delivery accordingly.

Many educators have not addressed the needs of at-risk youth for some or all of the following five reasons:

1. Funding has not been allocated for programs focusing on at-risk youth. Counselors can assist appropriate

entitles in reevaluating the need for programs to address the needs of these students.

2. Existing systems and programs do not include strategies for at-risk students, and changing the systems can be very challenging. Counselors can work with educators to broach this challenge.
3. There is a stigma associated with at-risk youth that presupposes they will always be at-risk. Counselors can implement goal-setting strategies that guide and encourage at-risk students to productive behaviors.
4. Social and community groups usually do not have programs that focus on at-risk students. Counselors can increase awareness for the need to do so.
5. Graduate programs do not always include pedagogy focusing on at-risk youth. Counselors can collaborate with their peers by educating each other about at-risk youth.

Funding assistance

Funding resources and governmental mandates to assist at-risk youth exist at both the state and national level, although this assistance may be found under the auspices of umbrella categories. Program initiatives from the federal and state levels through federal or state departments of education or mental health have developed the 1967 Elementary and Secondary Education Act (ESEA) that provides for continuing public education through grade 12. There is also funding allocation for disadvantaged children, focused on the goal of drug-free schools and the availability of after-school care. The National Defense Education Act (NDEA) of 1958 authorized schools to hire counselors who encouraged students in the areas of math and science and other related areas. Counselors and other educators who are committed to assisting at-risk youth can find government support that relates to a guaranteed education for all youth, safer schools, and improved academic performance.

Community programs

Since schools are the primary focal point for issues relating to adolescents, often counselors and educators work with other community entities in discussing and developing strategies for addressing the needs of youth. Some of these entities include libraries, police departments, private schools, recreation centers, and other community-based programs as well as national- and state-based organizations. One of the ways that counselors can work as liaison between students and these entities is by dispelling the idea that the onus of at-risk behavior lies with the student. They can work with community representatives who feel that students are solely or primarily to blame for their behavior. Counselors can collaborate with educators to develop programs that are designed to address the needs of not only mainstream students, but also at-risk students. These programs can incorporate the needs and concerns of the larger community as well as academic goals identified for the student population.

Rejection by the school system

Students who are displaying at-risk behavior often pose a challenge to educators who are striving for academic objectives and good classroom management. The at-risk behavior can cause a disruption on both fronts. This can be compounded by multiple at-risk students in multiple class periods. Teachers and school counselors faced with this disruptive activity will first attempt to remedy the behavior, using known strategies. However, if this proves unsuccessful and the disruptive, at-risk behavior continues, teachers in particular can become discouraged and begin to develop an attitude of complacency about the behavior that can grow into complacency about teaching in general. Consequently, faced with this possibility, counselors will sometimes make the decision to remove a student or students from the school. Unfortunately, the short-term problem is solved in this case, but a

- 120 -

longer-term issue arises of underserved youth becoming unproductive adults. Counselors can provide a valuable service in preventing this downhill slide in at-risk youth.

Culturally diverse at-risk students

Counselors who work with at-risk youth from diverse cultures are in a pivotal position that both allows and calls them to reduce the gap between intervention strategies designed for the dominant culture, and those that address the needs of minorities. Counselors need to be aware and communicate to school officials that under the umbrella of at-risk students may be ethnic groups whose problems are defined or exacerbated by their marginalized status. Counselors can consider cultural differences of at-risk students and how they will interpret different activities when creating preventative and intervention programs. If necessary and when appropriate, counselors can act as a liaison on behalf of students from diverse cultures, by making recommendations for program changes to better accommodate cultural diversity. Counselors can make significant and important changes in the school system, to the benefit of present and future students.

Individualizing interventions

<u>Determining appropriate interventions</u>
Deciding on an intervention for a student/situation is a multi-faceted approach that should incorporate a number of factors. It is important to remember that there is an array of strategies applicable for most situations, and counselors would be wise to isolate those strategies that would be most effective in an academic setting. It is also important to remember that a particular strategy that might be appropriate and effective for one student and one situation might not be suitable for another student with the same situation. Other factors to consider include:

- Interventions that will serve to develop and maintain a dynamic counseling relationship.
- Strategies that will work in tandem with a student's evolving development.
- Goals that are reasonable within the allotted time frame.
- Flexibility of interventions in relation to individual student circumstances.
- Applicability of intervention to student's overt behavior.
- Considerations of diversity and culture.

General considerations for choosing an intervention for an academic setting include the age and development of the student, as well as the cultural and social background of the student. Cultural and social considerations are particularly pivotal because they can provide the parameters for establishing recognition and context for some interventions. It might be useful to consult the families of students when determining cultural and social relevance of a particular therapeutic method or approach.

Categories of therapy generally fall into broad areas of multimodal counseling, family counseling, direct and indirect play therapy, and expressive art therapy. Common therapy strategies for school-age children include drama, storytelling, music, art, puppetry, use of tactile materials such as clay and sand, and an array of play therapy. Other formalized methods include reality therapy, Gestalt techniques, cognitive-behavioral counseling, and Adlerian counseling. Knowledge of the spectrum of available therapies is particularly valuable for counselors seeking appropriate interventions for students in an academic setting.

Once a counselor has narrowed the choice of appropriate therapies for a particular situation, it is then a good idea to narrow the options to those that would be appropriate for a particular student, with particular overt behaviors or symptoms. For instance, a student with ADHD might benefit most with a

- 121 -

therapy that focuses on impulse control and self-monitoring, while a student who displays difficulty in completing assignments might be better served with a kind of reality therapy that allows him/her to apply abstract thinking to consider the impact of their actions and develop alternative endeavors. Another significant example is that of working with a student who suffers from depression, and may need to first work on thought patterns through cognitive therapy, before or in tandem with other therapies targeting the situation. It is also always appropriate to consider the cultural background and age/developmental level of the student when choosing therapies.

Design and implementation

The procedure for intervention entails setting goals, designing intervention strategies toward achieving those goals, and evaluating the success of the intervention. One of the first considerations in the intervention process is the counselor's consideration of a student's developmental stage, as well as social and environmental settings and context. A counselor will want to make the decision to apply either formal or informal assessment methods, which will in turn affect evaluation procedures. Other factors to consider include informally assessing the level of parent and teacher support available for an intervention, as well as time constraints. Counselors should carefully consider all aspects of a student situation when determining intervention strategies. Another thing to be considered is if resolving a situation may be beyond the scope of the school counseling setting, at which point the student should be referred to an outside resource.

A successful intervention is best preceded by the establishment of a strong relationship between counselor and student. From there, the counselor can recommend an intervention to the student, who in turn will feel empowered by the effect of collaboration. This approach also provides students with validation, encouragement and endorsement of their own desires for resolution. Once the intervention is in place, it may be appropriate for counselors to discuss the progress and goals of the therapy with parents, teachers and possibly others as who are included in the student's support network. Likewise, if the intervening therapy is not progressing as anticipated, it may be appropriate to work with teachers in developing behavioral strategies in the classroom to complement the therapy. This communication and collaboration with teachers and/or parents should be within the context of the counseling sessions, and the counselor's responsibility to the school and the community.

Dropping out

Counselors should be particularly alert and responsive to the plausibility of students dropping out, if they present any or all of the following:

- High rate of absenteeism
- Low or dropping grades
- Low participation in extracurricular activities
- Limited parental support
- Evidence of alcohol or drug problems

Following are recommended intervention strategies for students at risk for dropping out:

- Tutoring services – either peer tutoring or other trained assistance
- Career and skill training for success after high school
- Expressing high but reasonable expectations for students
- Additional general/foundation classes for students with disabilities, or as needed

Continued support and resources are recommended for at-risk students who stay in school, including:

- Relevant curriculum
- Significant support and assistance from teachers and others as appropriate
- Useful and accessible textbooks and other classroom materials

For all interventions with at-risk students, counselors should address interpersonal skill building and self-reflection. It is important for counselors to encourage students to develop strong relationships with peers and school staff/counselors, which often increases their sense of community and belonging. Throughout the intervention, counselors should always assure students that they can discuss personal issues in both individual and group sessions. Often, at-risk students are struggling with numerous issues in several arenas of their lives. There are four key areas that are possibly involved when students are at risk for dropping out:

1. Personal/Affective – Counselors can offer retreats or other groups to encourage interpersonal participation.
2. Academic – Counselors can arrange for tutoring and/or other individualized methods of instruction.
3. Family Outreach – Encompassing increased feedback to parents.
4. School Structure – Possibilities include class size reduction or alternative school options.
5. Work/Career – Vocational training.

Many schools will have ongoing relationships with community groups as a part of a general philosophy of community outreach. However, for at-risk students to receive any direct benefit from these groups or relationships, counselors may have to initiate and coordinate auxiliary relationships for addressing specific needs of at-risk students. Understanding that at-risk students are often overwhelmed by a variety of life challenges, counselors can collaborate with a number of community resources, including:

- Businesses
- Families
- Recreational Centers
- Police Departments
- Universities

Counselors should cultivate these relationships, possibly in tandem with existing school relationships, and coordinate resources available with the complex needs of at-risk students. With the counselor's facilitation and coordination, these resource groups can cooperatively address many of the needs posed by at-risk students. This comprehensive coordination of resources can provide a significant hedge against students dropping out.

Eating disorders

Eating disorders in youth commonly manifest as either bulimia nervosa (BN) or anorexia nervosa (AN), or both. Because both of these disorders result in extremely poor nutrition, and bulimia nervosa can result in esophageal injury, students who are suffering eating disorders are at risk for poor health, poor intellectual and social development, and in some cases death. Counselors can implement intervention strategies through a complete medical assessment and multifaceted therapeutic assessment. In particular, the combination of behavioral therapy and cognitive therapy can be very effective in treating eating disorders. Cognitive therapy can addresses issues of control and self-esteem, while behavioral therapy can promote healthy eating habits and discourage destructive behaviors like purging. Group therapy may also be quite helpful and in some cases, family therapy may be indicated. Medical assessment may also be indicated, to ascertain if the student is in immediate physical danger from an eating disorder.

Tic disorders

Tic disorders are defined by recurrent, non-rhythmic sequences of movements and involuntary sounds from certain muscle groups. These disorders can include Tourette's tic, transient tic, and not-otherwise-specified (NOS) disorders. Counselors should initially garner enough information to accurately diagnose the condition, and educate the student and the parents more fully about the disease. Therapy can include identifying any underlying stressors as well as assessing family interaction and understanding regarding the disease. Various therapeutic strategies can be effectively implemented for tic disorders. Cognitive-behavioral therapies can address stress management. Self-monitoring, relaxation training, and habit-reversal training are effective strategies to consider, once initial data about the tic have been collected. Habit-reversal training is more commonly indicated, which requires the student to relax the affected muscles and introduce a competing response. If students present with frequent or explosive outbursts, counselors should collaborate with a physician to determine if medication is indicated.

Mood disorders

Mood disorders are generally defined as those in which students externalize feelings of depression, sadness, guilt or other negative emotion, possibly including thoughts of suicide. Students with mood disorders may present with somatic complaints. Counselors should be aware of misidentifying a mood disorder when a student may just be experiencing temporary sadness. On the other hand, counselors should be cognizant of the signs of mood disorder, especially symptoms that may signal the risk of suicide. Effective therapeutic strategies for mood disorder include cognitive and behavioral interventions as well as psycho-educational programs that focus on improving social skills and promotion of rewarding activities. Some students suffering from mood disorders have improved with antidepressants. However, studies regarding the efficacy of medicinal treatment of depression are inconclusive, and therefore the use of antidepressants should not be immediately considered, if at all.

Substance-related disorders

One of the initial intervention steps for substance abuse is to identify the abuse, and the substance(s) involved. A strategy is for parents to conduct drug tests at home,

although students may also self-report. An important factor to remember is that students with substance abuse may also have family members with substance abuse, since the correlation is very strong. In addition to individual counseling and education, counselors can conduct school and community workshops that address the benefits of early detection, the risk factors involved, and treatment options available. Based on the type of substance abuse, duration and intensity, treatment models are available, ranging from outpatient therapy to intensive inpatient treatment. The spectrum of treatment options encompasses very restrictive models as well as more participatory models. Treatments include detoxification, contracting, self-help groups, behavior therapy, family therapy, social skills training, as well as nutritional and recreational counseling.

Generalized anxiety disorder

Generalized anxiety disorder (GAD) is defined as a pervasive anxiety that is characterized by excessive, uncontrollable and often irrational worry about everyday things, which is disproportionate to the actual source of worry. Physical, somatic symptoms may include shortness of breath and/or muscle tension in other parts of the body, both of which can be difficult to control. Although GAD is not limited to adolescents, it does present problems particular to students in that the physical symptoms and the irrational worry can overshadow attention to academics, and therefore negatively affect performance. Students who are chronically anxious are unable to focus on their lessons. Counselors can use cognitive-behavioral strategies to mitigate the intensity of the anxiety and the accompanying physical symptoms. Students can be taught coping strategies such as identification, modification of anxious self-talk, education about emotions, modeling, relaxation techniques, and related self-regulating models.

Relationships within the school system

The larger school community is comprised of many subsystems, including but not limited to parents, service staff, librarians, community groups, etc. Even within the teaching staff, there are subsystems comprised of education specialists, resource teachers, etc. Although not necessarily in conflict with each other, often these groups operate quasi-autonomously and are not aware of their contributions to and affect the totality of the larger school community. This is best illustrated within the experiences of the students, who interact with and depend on most or many of these subsystems. Counselors working with students who have complex needs may need to involve several subsystems in order to provide effective treatment for students. It might be beneficial for counselors to form acquaintances with members of the larger school community, in order to better understand the complexities of subsystems in the school, and possibly to facilitate communication between these entities.

When a counselor recognizes that s/he is just one member of a school community, s/he should also recognize that a community contains both formal and informal power structures. Although it is necessary for a counselor to keep open communication with the principal, that line of communication may depend on the counselor's interactions with the principal's secretary or other assistant counselor. School counselors should also be cognizant of the network of communication and influence that exists within the school system, as it does within most communities. Counselors can cultivate relationships with teachers, parents, other counselors, etc. in order to gain an understanding of underlying concerns and agendas within the larger school agenda. These relationships can also provide a vehicle for counselors to inform the school community of his/her concerns for the students and plans for an appropriate counseling program to address those concerns. A healthy environment for a school counseling program includes shared agendas and collaboration.

As with any group dynamic, the interplay of agendas and concerns within a school community may be organic and healthy, may be dysfunctional and conflicting, or may be somewhere in the spectrum between these two extremes. Although it is not necessarily the counselor's role to analyze the dynamics at play in the school setting, s/he nonetheless needs to be cognizant of conflicts between individuals and agendas, particularly if individuals or groups are in opposition to the principal's goals and overall agenda. Counselors should exercise some caution when forming alliances to the benefit of the counseling program that may be in opposition to other groups or the overall agenda of the school principal. It would be better to cultivate relationships with a measure of caution, until a counselor understands the overall interplay of agendas within the school community. Counselors can also strive to facilitate cooperation and collaboration between the parties involved.

When counselors are able to communicate and collaborate with influential and interested members of the school community regarding the counseling program, there are positive far-reaching effects. By recognizing and incorporating the interplay of agendas and concerns in a school community, counselors are able to gain the respect, endorsement, and the contributions of those individuals. When counselors can recognize and utilize the strengths and contributions of individuals working in the school community, the counseling program is able to thrive and grow within the context of the school system. The added benefit is that when the program is working within this context, peripheral individuals and programs will associate the counseling program with the larger agenda(s) of the school community and more readily accept and endorse the program. As these working relationships evolve, the counselor can develop rich alliances and friendships within the school community to the benefit of all the members.

Authority of the principal

The principal of a school administrates the allocation of both monetary and personnel resources. For a school counselor to successfully plan and implement a counseling program at a school, the support and endorsement of the principal is pivotal. In deference to the principal's responsibilities, counselors should keep him/her apprised of the scope of the current counseling program, as well as revisions or plans for future revisions to the program. Not only is this respectful of the principal's/school's agenda; it is also good practice in order to retain the support and endorsement of administration. It is also recommended that counselors meet with principals on a regular basis, at the principal's convenience, and s/he will most likely determine how often these meetings need to occur. Counselors should allow sufficient time to apprise the principal of updates and for discussion as appropriate. Principals may also make suggestions and recommendations for the counseling program, which should be taken into account by the counselor.

Advisory groups

The school counseling advisory committee (SCPAC) is generally comprised of counselors, parents, educators, and other members of the community, all of whom have a stake and influence in the school's decision-making. The school principal should always be included, particularly since s/he will need to be included in the discussion about proposed program improvements or recommendations, and will be instrumental in approving funding for these proposals. The SCPAC can serve as a backboard for decision-making and can assist the counselor in introducing needed program changes or requesting resources. The SCPAC can serve as a liaison committee with the larger community, and can include parent-teacher organizations by invitation or at least by communicating with them regarding relevant impending decisions. By including community input through the liaison SCPAC committee, counselors demonstrate their willingness to consider outside perspectives and additional sources for funding.

A school counseling advisory group can provide guidance counselors with comprehensive expectations of the school community as well as a track record of current and previous school counseling models and strategies. The overall focus of most counseling programs, and therefore their advisory groups, is often the development of curriculum that addresses common and relevant issues such as sexual harassment, bullying, and social relationships. Counselors can refer to past discussions and studies to glean information about strategies that did or did not work, as well as areas that may have arisen as needing particular attention. Advisory groups can inform counselors about pedagogical or counseling approaches that work best in their school environment. It is advisable that counselors maintain ongoing communication with advisory groups and other school community members in order to keep apprised of current needs or problem areas.

Assuming that the SCPAC is active, ongoing, and not undergoing significant changes, it is customary for the group to meet once each semester to discuss the needs and available resources of the counseling program and to provide recommendations and endorsement for proposed improvements. The group can analyze assessment results, propose program modifications, and consider recommendations from staff members. Program proposals are generally based on the results of assessments. The group can identify potential funding sources, but the school principal should always be included in any funding discussions. The group can serve as a valuable resource for demonstrating support among the school community for program enhancement, and potentially for influencing the principal in funding and approval decisions. Counselors should consider the benefits and the potential impact of the SCPAC and focus their attention and time to the group as needed.

Expected student outcomes

Expected student outcomes should reflect the amalgamated input of state and national standards, current literature, as well as formal and informal needs assessments conducted at the school or district level. Advisory groups, when undertaking the task of generating student outcome goals, should first amass the relevant information and resources. This will form the basis for future discussions and collaboration within the group and with the school counselor or counselors. Student outcomes should represent what students should know or be able to do upon graduation from high school. The National Standards for School Counseling Programs delineates 9 standards that incorporate academic, personal, social and career development areas. Student outcome expectations should be broken down into smaller sequential goals. Counselors, working with the district and school community, can develop strategies and rubric for addressing these sequenced student outcome goals.

Community volunteers

Effective counselors know that in order to build a successful school culture, community volunteers need to play a vital role. Asking community members to volunteer their time will help boost their self-esteem and make help them realize they can have a major impact on the student's learning. If there is a strong volunteer program then parents and community members can become actively involved in their child's education and feel their skills are useful and important. This bond will help break down the barriers between teachers and parents. Community volunteers can also have a major impact on the teacher's lives. If volunteers are actively helping to meet the student's needs, then this can give the teachers more time to plan other activities in the lesson plan. Their scheduling can become more flexible.

Emotional objectivity

When counselors join a school community,

they may encounter resistance to their contributions from certain members of that community. Although the school community/system as a whole may endorse and support the counseling program and its inclusion in the larger efforts of the school, the resistance of a few may manifest in covert or overt actions that undermine or impede the counseling program. Counselors need to maintain objectivity when facing these kinds of challenges, and recognize them as symptoms of systemic change. Recognizing this objectively, the counselor can then approach the challenge(s) professionally. Relying on their knowledge of systems change analysis, counselors can objectively isolate and identify the resistance, and openly approach the individuals or entities involved toward a mutual resolution. It is important to remember that, without this objectivity, counselors can become mired in conflict and programs can be rendered ineffectual.

Collaborative group process

Counselors as consultants are in a position to recognize when a student issue could be best addressed by generating dialogue between parents and members of the school community. The initial process should involve bringing the parents together with educators or other school members as appropriate, to discuss and come to an agreed understanding regarding the needs of the student. Through collaboration, parents and school members can recognize that each of their efforts as individual entities would likely not be as effective as the collaborative efforts of the group members, including the parents. Counselors can facilitate the process by helping members to understand each other's roles and prospective contributions. Counselors can guide the group discussions by allowing each of the participants, which may just be a teacher and a parent, to understand their mutual goal of academic success for the student, and to encourage trust in the collaborative process.

After the counselor as consultant has been assigned a role in the group, s/he may have the opportunity to facilitate the process of collaboration. When working within the context of a problem-solving team, counselors can initiate specific practices and procedures toward a collaborative group dynamic. These practices include:

- Noting and encouraging behaviors among the group that contribute to collaboration and cooperation
- Noting and discouraging competitive remarks and behaviors
- Working with the group to establish a collaborative group norm
- Creating an open communication policy that allows the input of all participants to the problem-solving process
- Recognizing and respecting the expertise and contributions of all members of the group

These practices can lay the foundation for collaborative group process. Facilitating a collaborative group dynamic may also occasionally include soliciting the support and endorsement of a school counselor by explaining the value of the collaborative process in a problem-solving group.

When a student's behaviors or problems become such that intervention is necessary, it often provides fertile ground for blaming others for the problems. Parents may harbor blame toward the school for his/her child's problems, and schools may hold parents accountable for student behavior. As consultants, counselors can stress that the student's situation should be viewed as a catalyst for change that will involve the student, the school and the parents/family. Viewed in this way, intervention becomes a collaborative goal rather than an exercise in finding evidence to support blame. Counselors can encourage participants to feel committed to resolution, and to each embrace his/her respective role in its achievement.

The strengths of the teachers and family members should be affirmed and used to bring about the desired objectives. Counselors should remind and encourage participants that change is a process that will take time and the commitment of those involved in the student's life.

When student intervention necessitates a group effort, this usually correlates with a multiplicity and complexity of issues. Consequently, resolution is usually correspondingly complex, and may involve many entities. Sometimes, any change anticipated in the student relies at least in part on changes in family dynamics and/or school systems. Counselors will be well served to remember that student behaviors point to need for change, and to refrain from blatantly identifying any system or individual as a cause for the problem(s). Rather, counselors should use diplomacy in suggesting changes in family or school dynamics, particularly if the respective parties are operating under the assumption that the student's behavioral problems are not connected to other influences in his/her life. This is a situation in which the trust and alliances gained from members of the school community are particularly valuable. Counselors can work separately with a teacher or family member to encourage change as applicable.

The optimum consulting group is one in which the whole is greater than the sum of its parts. Practically speaking, each of the participants comes to the task with particular expertise, a specific set of skills, and a paradigm or perspective regarding the problem and an anticipated resolution. Each member sees himself/herself in a predetermined role. Educators generally approach student problems from an academic perspective; psychologists will tend to be most concerned about the student's mental health. However, in a group setting, with good facilitation, the participants can be encouraged to step beyond their prescribed roles and expectations toward a comprehensive intervention strategy that will bring their collective expertise to a cohesive front. In this setting, counselors may ask a teacher to co-lead the group, or a psychologist to facilitate a discussion about academic goals. This shared crossing over can be most beneficial in a consulting group.

Anticipating action plan change
Counselors understand that any kind of behavioral change is an ongoing process and will often include backsliding or digression. When facilitating a consulting group, counselors can first remind the group that any intervention strategy needs to include plans for protecting the anticipated change. Knowing this initially will enhance the long-term success of intervention strategies. Consultants can assist the group in developing a post-plan for this purpose. This post-plan should include delineation of responsibilities and benchmarks to be used in evaluating progress. It may also include mechanisms that will allow for ongoing communication among the members, as well as support resources. In a school setting, student progress is generally associated with academic achievement, which can provide a clear marker for determining strategy success. Behavioral changes can also be monitored by noting clearly identified actions.

Evaluating plan of action
When an action plan has been developed and implemented, the evaluation process should begin. A component of the action plan should be strategies for evaluation and outcome measurement. It may be appropriate for each member of the consultant group to participate in the evaluation process by monitoring such successes as academic progress, changed behaviors, etc. The evaluation should focus on whether any change has occurred, and to what degree that change can be measured. Participants can develop vehicles for collecting as well as presenting the relevant data. Counselors should provide oversight for this phase of the action plan. They should be attentive to the

degree of change, and determine if it is sufficient to be considered successful. They should also be attentive to any changes that constitute digression, or negative change. If this is the case, they might want to assess possible factors, and meet with the group to develop alternate strategies.

Decision-making

Concepts and steps
Making a decision is a process that takes valued information and opinions from others and in return, you make a choice that you think is best. This whole process follows steps in order to achieve that decision. The first step is defining the situation that needs a decision. This is the time to fully investigate and gain an understanding of what the problem is. The next step is identifying the alternatives that can be used to make a decision. It is important for the counselor to know there can be more than two alternatives. After identifying the alternatives, the next step is to assess them. When the counselor is at this step, they should consider whether they have the resources or power to implement a certain alternative and the kind of reception they will receive. When a desirable alternative has been chosen, then it is time to implement it. A counselor may encounter resistance or complete acceptance. After it has been implemented, the counselor should evaluate the decision and see if any other decisions need to be made.

Assessing effectiveness
Assessing decision-making effectiveness is an important process in order for a counselor to improve as a decision maker. Counselors are extremely busy people and this can be a challenge to complete, therefore, often times this step is overlooked. It can be difficult for a counselor to be objective about their decision, especially since they have invested so much of their time. It might be helpful to involve outsiders who do not have vested interest in the assessment process. There is a chance that the decision's effectiveness could reflect negatively on the counselor. However, if the

counselor wants continued improvement for their school, they should occasionally asses the effectiveness of their decision. Many times there will not be enough time to assess every time a decision is made; however, if he or she wants to improve their decision-making skills, a periodic check will be in their best interest.

Rational model
The rational model for decision-making is viewed as a process that first begins with the counselor admitting they are facing a problem. Then the counselor addresses this issue through a series of steps, which in return comes out with an effective decision. This model focuses on what should be done and requires the counselor to follow certain actions that have already been designed to help achieve the best solution. It is assumed that the counselor is a rational counselor that works in an environment that functions rigidly and in a bureaucratic nature. Obviously, many school counselors do not work in this type of environment. This model does have some advantages; it clearly states the actions a counselor should take in certain situations and forces the counselor to decide which actions are most appropriate. However, this model has also shown that counselors are too quick in making decisions and do not attempt to try to find the true cause of the conflict.

Shared decision-making
Shared decision-making, which is also known as participatory or site-based decision-making, is also built on the idea of choice. This model states that choices are made by the counselor in order to satisfy constraints. The focus of this model is on consensual decision-making that is based on the values of the members in the group. The members of the decision making process also have open communication and everyone's status is equal. The whole idea of a participatory decision-making theory centers on the idea of the way counselors make decisions versus how they should make decisions. Some critics believe this way of making decisions limits

the control of the decision maker and they believe counselors are influenced by other's personalities and values more than their own reason or intelligence.

Strategic decision-making
When a counselor uses this model, they are making a decision based on information they have gathered for their own knowledge and evaluating the internal and external environment. The environment is made up of interest groups, negotiation, and informal power. In order for this model to work, the members need to identify what the obstacles are as well as what challenges may affect the decision choice. A counselor will want to use this model if they are interested in making a plan that has room for change, is flexible and has a long term effect. It is important that the individuals involved with this decision have the same philosophy and purpose in common. There will situations when unexpected events occur and a counselor may find themselves making decisions based on these unexpected events despite trying to strictly use the strategic decision making model.

Situational decision-making model
This decision making model does not follow the traditional way of thinking. The counselor needs to take into consideration a variety of points and each point will affect the decision choice in some way. Certain situational variables can have an impact on how the counselor will make their decision choice. This model recognizes that counselors may need to take a different approach in deciding what is best for the school. A decision can be made regarding the goals of the school itself or just about the whole process. Other factors that counselors should take into consideration are ethical considerations, values, culture and climate. It is important that counselors are prepared that different situations will arise and the need for a decision may be needed immediately. The process will not be the same each time, different situations call for different decision-making processes.

Conflict management among consulting personnel

Any time when leaders of the school are different people, there is a strong potential for conflict. There could be a disagreement on a wide variety of topics, and any type of conflict could make it harder on the counselor to build a unified organizational culture. The important issue a counselor needs to remember is to listen effectively to both sides in order to understand the main issue of the conflict. There should be an opportunity for both the formal and informal leader to be able to voice their opinion and ensure they feel they are important. A counselor can use their influence to persuade one party into the direction that is more suitable to the overall school organizational culture, however this may not work every time. There is not a correct way of handling a situation like this; however, a counselor with strong conflict resolution skills can change a difficult situation.

In most cases, when a counselor is deciding which technique is the most appropriate to resolve conflict, they would choose a contingency approach, which is choosing the technique based on the nature of the situation. However, a counselor should also consider the individual personal needs of the staff in selecting a conflict management technique. Other important factors to consider are the people involved in the conflict, how serious the situation is to them, the type and intensity of the conflict, and the authority that some individuals possess. A counselor is likely to encounter several different types of conflicts and therefore there will be a number of alternative techniques from which to choose. One technique will not be suitable for all situations.

Counselors can choose from four different options about how to deal with conflict. One option is to use the *cooperative approach*, which means to hear other's points of view and show empathy toward that group's feelings. After this has been accomplished then the counselor can attempt to find a compromise that will lead toward a mutual solution. Another approach is *confirming*, which means the counselor communicates to the groups that he or she feels they have a great deal of competency and they are highly respected for it. Another option is to use the *competitive approach*, which views conflict as a win-lose battle. One of the groups at conflict must back down from the conflict and it is only then that the conflict will end. The last option a counselor has is to use the *avoidance approach*. This approach is when the groups stop discussing the situation and end the conflict but do not resolve any issues.

Research has shown that counselors who use both the cooperative and confirming approaches have much more success in resolving conflict. Those who choose to use the competitive or avoidance approaches are less likely to succeed in conflict resolution. The cooperative and confirming approaches are considered to be more successful because when an individual feels they are recognized for their competence they feel a sense of security and value and more likely to want to resolve the conflict. The competitive approach seems to be less effective because many times the counselor will use this approach when he or she thinks they can win the conflict and they use the avoidance approach when they are uncertain of how to handle the situation. The cooperative and confirming approaches requires the counselor to have strong interpersonal skills and if they are lacking these special skills, then it is best for the counselor to designate someone who does posses these skills.

Using groups to resolve conflict can be extremely resourceful to a counselor. Individuals in groups can provide a variety of opinions and offer creative ideas on how to resolve issues. It is important to establish the rule that everyone's opinion will be valued and respected. If there are too many individuals involved, it could become a chaotic situation and nothing will be achieved, therefore, it is important for the counselor to keep order and structure. It may also be wise to keep the amount of people involved to a minimum. Once an idea has been agreed upon on how to solve an issue, it is now time to decide on how to implement the plan. Everyone will have their own opinion but it is important for the group to come to an agreement on which plan best meets the needs of the school.

The *problem-solving approach* is another method of conflict resolution and can be the most effective. However, this method is most likely to be successful if the parties are willing to compromise and an agreement is possible. It is also important that both parties can contribute something valuable and they are reassured and confident that the solution will made that will not exclude their interests. Each group should be allowed the opportunity to state their opinions and their conflicting positions. The group members should also state the opinions and position of the opponents as way of assuring their opponents that their points of view were heard and understood. This way the counselor can also ensure each group is clearly listening to the other. A counselor should then clarify with the groups if there is still conflict. Group members should state why their opinions and views are valid to them. When all members are through stating their viewpoints, the members should be asked if they have anything that needs to be added. There is a possibility that conflict may still be unavoidable.

Alternative resolution methods

Arbitration
There will be many times when conflict cannot be resolved usAltering mediation; it may be necessary to use arbitration. This process involves the parties at conflict explaining their point of view to a third party who is the arbitrator. Each party must agree to accept the third party's decision and they must commit to carry out the arbitrator's decision when they agree to discuss the issue with the arbitrator. The best way to choose the person to be the arbitrator is to base the decision on the type of conflict and the circumstances surrounding it. Using an outside party for arbitration is not common; it is more common to use a superior in the organization. The growing trend of arbitration is a reflection on the fact that traditional means of conflict resolution is failing to achieve results.

Conflict initiation
In most cases, counselors will want to prevent conflict from happening and may find it impossible to prevent conflict. However, if a counselor finds himself in a situation where an individual or group is not performing at the level they should and does not want to change; it may be cause for the counselor to actually initiate conflict. If a counselor is in a situation where he or she observes a problem with a teacher and the teacher disagrees, the avoidance of conflict will not be possible. It is the counselor's responsibility to ensure that all staff members are performing to the best of their abilities, and conflict may be needed in order to bring about improvement. It is important that all possible outcomes be considered before conflict is initiated and that conflict is necessary for improvement.

Power struggle bargaining
Counselors can possibly find themselves in a situation where they feel strongly about their objectives and conflict cannot be avoided, and chances are an agreement is impossible. This situation is called *power struggle bargaining*. The counselor will do everything it takes to resolve this conflict; however, they may be convinced the solution must go their way. This can cause hurt feelings and destroy many personal and professional relationships with individuals that may be involved with this situation. Many times conflict may seem to be resolved, however it will reappear in future situations. However, the advantage to power struggle bargaining is that the conflict may end in complete favor of the counselor. It may be necessary for a counselor to get involved in this power struggle; however, if

they want the conflict to end in their favor they must assess their power and authority accurately or there could be disastrous results.

Conflict avoidance

Other techniques that can be used for conflict resolution are techniques called conflict avoidance methods. One of these techniques is called the withdrawal method in which a counselor will not argue in a certain situation and just accept the outcome. The other method is indifference, this is when a counselor makes it seem as though an issue does not matter to them personally. A counselor can also avoid any circumstances that would cause conflict: this method is called isolation. Using the smooth over method would mean the counselor accepts the situation and minimizes any arguments. The consensus method allows others to discuss their views and try to persuade others. Although these methods avoid conflict, they do not resolve it. These methods may be necessary to use, especially in situations when one group feels powerless in changing the views of the other group.

Resolution groundwork

Fact finding

Once the counselor has heard each party's point of view about the dispute, it is important for the counselor to validate the facts of the situation. Many times individuals will consider their opinions to be the facts and the absolute truth; however, those facts need to be verified. It is very common that a person's emotions can distort their memory and the facts of the situation. The counselor must also recognize that individuals in the conflict can agree on the facts; however, their interpretations are complete opposite. The counselor's goal while in the process of fact finding is to clarify the areas that the parties do agree upon and narrow down the issues that are at disagreement. The counselor is put in the position to act as mediator; this role will be much easier to play if he or she is not one of the parties at conflict. If they are, then

it is best if a neutral person acts as mediator.

Exercising authority

There are numerous reasons why people question and challenge authority. However, if a counselor follows certain guidelines, then this issue can be overcome. Counselors are obviously going to have to make some very difficult decisions and give directives to others. One consideration a counselor should decide on is how and in what style the directive will be given. It is important for a counselor to remember that regardless of how professional the directive was given, if the person who received it does not feel that it is in their best interest, there is going to be an issue of resistance. A counselor should also consider the strengths and weaknesses of the person before giving a directive. Issuing an order for someone who is not motivated will result in failure. They should also explain the rationale behind the directive and remember not everyone may understand the value in it.

When a counselor is faced with a negative reaction to authority, their first reaction may be to become defensive or become upset. However, the appropriate way to handle this situation is to investigate and examine the reasons why others are responding this way. This may be a difficult reaction to have for many counselors. The feelings of hurt and anger are normal, however, an effective counselor knows how to put those feelings behind them and move on to the problem solving stage. The challenging of authority can be a positive situation, especially if the causes are understood. The key to diagnosing the reasons for the negative reaction is to have a discussion with the parties involved. Every effort should be made to avoid putting anyone on the defensive and every attempt should be made to understand the person's point of view.

Effective communication

If a counselor can communicate in a certain manner, this can create a more encouraging environment. If a counselor can open a meeting by just stating their true feeling or their reaction to a certain situation, then this can create a more secure environment. Opening with these kinds of statements can put a staff at ease because they know there is a common ground that has just been developed. It is always crucial that a counselor talk to the staff in a non-threatening manner; nothing will cause a person to become defensive faster than if they are under the assumption they are being attacked personally. A counselor must also learn how to become accepting of others and that includes their personality, opinions and approaches. Another important consideration is to remember that a counselor can control the attitude of the group. If he or she comes in and is positive about a situation, then the chances are the group will be more positive.

Every message a counselor sends out will be interpreted in different ways from every person who receives it. Many times the message will not be successfully communicated simply because of factors that are not in the control of the counselor. Many times a counselor will send out a message they believe is extremely important and the persons receiving it do not share that same opinion. Many times the person receiving it may have a lack of interest of what is being said. Another factor is the person receiving the message lacks the background knowledge needed to understand the content of the message. Certain phrases or words require a certain degree of knowledge in order to understand it. Understanding the group who will be receiving the message can help the counselor with how the nature of the message should be written in order to help reduce the misunderstanding.

Social barriers the may deter from a message include factors such as age, sex and position in the hierarchy. Teachers who teach different subjects or grade levels may misinterpret the message. The same is true for men and women teachers as well as new and experienced teachers; each one will develop their own interpretation of what the counselor was trying to say. Men and women each have their own way of communicating with others. Males can often be misinterpreted as arrogant or harsh whereas females can come across as weak and lack leadership. Different communication styles carry into the different cultures. Counselors should be aware of the different ways of communicating that may be inappropriate. Certain cultures may find it inappropriate to stand too close or to use a certain voice tone.

Identifying goals and outcomes
It is important to remember the initial process of problem solving is that of comprehensive problem identification. This identification should include the scope of the problem, specifically if it is isolated to a particular student and/or the student's family dynamic, or more generalized within a group of students, or throughout the school system as a whole. Once the problem is identified, the problem-solving team should clearly identify goals for the student or the particular group, as well as anticipated outcomes. Academic goals for students should fall within the academic parameters and mission of the school. Inherent in the process is the need for developing viable outcome assessment measures, which will be made easier with clearly stated objectives. When the group can articulate the objectives, as well as measurements of outcome, they can best formulate goals that are reasonable and achievable.

Outside consultation

School districts may employ or call upon numerous professionals in the endeavor to provide mental health services to students. These may include psychologists, school nurses, social workers, crisis intervention counselors, as well as staff educators and counselors. School counselors often form a part of this larger network of mental counselors on the school campus, working with the same population of students. It is in the counselor's and program's best interest that school counselors develop and maintain a spirit of cooperation when working with these diverse groups of mental counselors. It is not advisable, nor is it generally successful, to generate an attitude of superiority or a hierarchical stance when working with other professionals. Remember that all of the groups and individuals involved are striving for the same goal: the mental health of the students. By working cooperatively and inclusively, counselors can benefit from the support and expertise of those in peripheral professional positions.

It may be the case that a student is already interacting with other professionals/professional groups outside of the school community. Often this is the case if students present a complexity of issues. In order to approach the student holistically, counselors may want to include these individuals in a consulting group, or as part of the school-based consulting group. Through collaborative consultation, the individual members should endeavor to adopt an integrative approach that will result in shared input and shared responsibility. It is generally recommended that each member's interaction with the student should be suspended or altered in deference to the participant's involvement in the collaborative consultation model. Counselors as consultants should become familiar with the expertise and scope of each professional/group, and possibly involve the parents in the consultation. Overall, the collaborative consultation model can prove much more effective than if counselors were to meet individually with respective professionals/groups.

Problem solving
Once a consultant is in the school system, s/he is in a position to initiate problem solving. Regardless of the problem, or the complexity of the problem, the initial stage of problem solving is generally that of identifying the problem to be addressed. This involves collecting information necessary to comprehensively assess the issue at hand. If the difficulty relates to a student, the information collecting may involve parents,

teachers, and/or the student directly. The problem-solving process can also engage other educators or family members to form a collaborative problem-solving team. Problems to be addressed might also be more macrocosmic, involving several students with violent behavior, or possibly system-wide issues affecting the entire school. Counselors can be most successful in tackling large or small issues by first identifying the problem to be addressed. Once the problem has been comprehensively isolated, counselors can then progress to determining the most appropriate consultation model for working toward resolution.

The counselor as facilitator can work with members of the group to set goals and create a viable action plan. It is important that the parameters of this action plan fall within the capabilities and contributions of the group members. Individuals in the group should be able to recognize and embrace their role in facilitating change in the student(s). Specific steps in the process of developing an action plan include:

- Identify the goal and the action plan for achieving it.
- Determine an appropriate and reasonable measurement of outcome.
- Empower group members to act as change agents.
- Identify the individual and group strengths applicable to the action plan.
- Encourage flexibility of roles and expanded boundaries as appropriate.
- Encourage collaboration within the group and with other entities as appropriate.
- Develop a plan to implement and retain the changes.

School teams brought together to resolve an issue are often task-oriented, and generally not focused on process. Without some attention paid to process, the collaborative effect of the team can be much diffused and the efficacy of the group diminished. The counselor as consultant can contribute to the group discussion with not only knowledge about a particular issue, but also specific expertise in group dynamics. As facilitator, s/he can encourage the group process necessary for completing the problem-solving task. As with any interaction with other professionals, counselors will do well to remember they are a part of a larger whole and to maintain an openness to the strengths of the group and the individual members. If approached well, a successful collaborative process will significantly contribute to the overall success of the task team, as well as establish the counselor as a valuable member of the school community.

Ad hoc consultation closure
If the consultant is not a regular member of the school community, closure may be more definitive than if the counselor as consultant is a part of the school staff. In that situation, counselors can maintain communication with the participants and provide validation of successful completion. The counselor can also conduct debriefings with the participants to reflect on the process, the success(es), and the value of collaboration. Counselors can also maintain communication with school counselors and peripheral professionals as a follow-up to a successful intervention, as appropriate. If, on the other hand, the counselor as consultant is a regular member of the school staff, it is important to be attentive to sensitivities that the student might have regarding regular proximity to the participants of the consulting group, including the counselor. In that event, formal follow-up might be less appropriate than if the consultant is regularly not on campus.

Cross-cultural consultation
When working with consultees from diverse cultural backgrounds, counselors should refer to their knowledge of cross-cultural counseling in order to facilitate the group with confidence and skill. Multicultural participants in a consulting group will inherently present certain considerations regarding diversity of culture:

- Impact of culture: How do diverse cultural paradigms affect the consultation process?
- Recognition of culture: Understand the richness of contributions from diversity of culture.
- Be sensitive to cultural differences when developing rapport within the group.
- Be cognizant of cultural factors within the group as well as between the group and the student.
- Develop appropriate interventions with these cultural considerations in mind, if indicated.
- Respond objectively to diverse circumstances.
- Identify and emphasize similarities between the represented cultures, as appropriate.
- Address balance of power issues.
- Endorse success of student and consultees.

Collaborative style of consultation
The collaborative style of consultation is distinguished by five key features:

1. Voluntary participation of members toward resolution of a problem, as opposed to hierarchical direction from a counselor.
2. Shared input for decision-making. This is opposed to a model whereby outcome is decided before the group convenes, or presupposed assumptions color the outcome.
3. Shared responsibility for decision-making. This implies both an expectation and a privilege for addressing the issue at hand. All parties participate in identifying the problem, developing objectives, implementing strategies, and evaluating outcomes.

4. Shared investment and ownership of the problem as well as the solution for all parties, potentially including family, school, and community. All parties recognize what needs to be accomplished and are committed to contributing their particular expertise.
5. Shared resources. This implies less ownership so that the group decides how the resources will be utilized.

The role of the counselor in the collaboration consultation format is that of both facilitator and role model for the consultation. The distinguishing advantage of the collaborative format is that of shared and interactive input regarding the student. Each person's perspective, each person's expertise, each person's knowledge of the student and the situation, is valuable and contributes to a whole that is often greater than its parts. Counselors can model this format by encouraging input from all the members, and can facilitate the group by maintaining the guidelines that allow for interactive sharing. The counselor's role in the collaborative model is not that of leader, but more of guide and facilitator. Some of the key points to address in collaborative consultation include:

- Open consideration of other perspectives. Willingness to revise one's perspective
- Integration of others' ideas in intervention
- Flexibility of counselor to de-emphasize his/her role as leader
- Guiding the group in a manner that encourages collaboration

Triadic-dependent consultation model

The triadic-dependent consultation model is essentially a partnership formed between the counselor, parents and/or school staff to provide indirect services to a student. It provides a problem-solving solution for some students and situations in which strategies

implemented at home or in the classroom can augment strategies implemented in the counseling sessions. In this model, the counselor works directly with the student, but augments that work by consulting with parents, schoolteachers, and school counselors. Those third parties are identified as the consultees, and the counselor as consultant can provide information and advice toward the goal of improving relations with the student. The triadic-dependent consultation model does not exist for the benefit of the student, but rather for the parents and/or school personnel to develop strategies to improve the student's academic or personal situation.

In the triadic-dependent consultation model, counselors can initially meet with family and/or school personnel to discuss the student's problems and goals, within confidentiality guidelines. In these meetings, counselors can glean additional information about the student that will help in the individual sessions. Since many student problems can both affect and/or be exacerbated by their social and family network, this model can address the interrelations of various dynamics in the student's life. Counselors may also want to include other members of the student's network, such as peers or other family members, as appropriate, in the process of developing a more comprehensive profile of the student. After assessing the student more comprehensively, counselors can then recommend particular prevention or intervention strategies to the family and/or school personnel. Counselors may recommend interventions focusing on changes for the student, consultee, and/or the school system.

Counselors can apply the principles of behaviorism to a triadic-dependent consultation format very successfully. Using these principles, counselors can meet with parents/school personnel to identify and define the student's problems as well as any peripheral circumstances that could be contributing factors. Once the counselor has developed a comprehensive profile of the student's problem(s) in the context of his/her surrounding circumstances, s/he can the create strategies for changing the student's behavior, and possibly the consultee's behavior or actions. Counselors can also work to modify the social context of the interrelationship between the student and the consultee. Possible therapeutic strategies include behavioral contracting, positive reinforcement, and response cost.

The behavioral consultation model can be represented by the following four areas of focus:

1. Initial assessment: Identify problems, circumstantial contributors.
2. Analysis: Develop comprehensive profile of student needs.
3. Implementation: Develop and implement behavior modification strategies.
4. Evaluation: Evaluate efficacy of strategies and revise as appropriate.

Counselors meeting with parents/school personnel should strive to make the environment and the dynamics comfortable yet professional. This is particularly important for meeting with parents. Initially, counselors can restate the purpose of the consultation, identify the student and define the issues of concern. Initial interaction can serve to ease any anxieties and continue to establish the professional but comfortable dynamic. The student's behaviors should be the focus of the meeting, and counselors should redirect the conversation within those boundaries if needed. Nonetheless, consultees should be given the opportunity to give input, as with any therapeutic group. Counselors should probe for any relevant conditions that would affect the treatment planning, and glean any additional information about the student from classroom observations. Counselors may also want to provide reference materials to the consultee(s) to offer a better understanding of the issues and behaviors involved. All consultant/consultee interactions should be in writing, and follow-up actions should be scheduled during the initial consultation.

Collaborative-dependent consultation model

The collaborative/dependent consultation model is also a partnership, but one in which the counselor/consultant may play more of a role as participant rather than facilitator. The counselor is expected to contribute to problem-solving expertise, but is not the sole expert. The consultee in this model may have a more in-depth knowledge of the student or the system on which the consultation is focused. In this model, the consultant and the consultee can be educated on both the problem-solving process for the student and the response of the student. Both consultant and consultee may have working knowledge of normal and abnormal student development. The consultee may be able to contribute knowledge about the efficacy of previous interventions, and/or the impact of peripheral factors. In the collaborative/dependent consultation model, the partnership collaborates to develop an intervention plan that will be based on the counselor defining the problem and completing any evaluation and follow-up services, while the consultee implements the intervention plan.

When the collaborative-dependent model is applied to an organizational system, the focus can be on the student, on the consultee, or on initiating change within the system. Family dynamics, or a family system, can also be included in this paradigm. In the system application of the collaborative-dependent model, the counselor participates as process consultant to address problem-solving within the context of the system. S/he can contribute his or her expertise on the assessment and interventions that are related to system change.

This application should address the following six variables:

1. Communication patterns within the group
2. Roles and functions of the various group members
3. Processes and procedures involved in group decision-making or problem-solving
4. Normal group performance and expected growth
5. Leadership and authority within the group
6. Intra-group cooperation and competition

Collaborative-interdependent consultation model

The collaborative-interdependent consultation model is one that is more complex and comprehensive and is most applicable for addressing the multiplicity of issues related to at-risk youth. In this model, the partnership may be comprised of family, counselor, students, school personnel, and/or community members, and all may act as equal partners. This model is a collaborative, dynamic one in which the combined input and efforts of its members sharing their knowledge expertise enable the group as a whole to develop and implement a comprehensive plan. The counselor is not expected to be the sole expert or the central source of information. The onus does not lie on the counselor to develop and implement a plan. The collaboratively developed plan may include change for an individual student, additional knowledge and skills for the team, and/or a change to the system.

There can be inherent difficulties in the collaborative-interdependent model, relating to the fact that its members are included in the partnership because of their knowledge or perspective of the issue at hand, and not necessarily because they are good collaborators. The collaborative-interdependent partnership can be comprised of parents, school counselors, community members, etc., who may each be operating within a different paradigm to address the student issue(s). This can be particularly problematic if the members are each implementing a portion of the solution strategy, and not working together to do so. The ability to work effectively presupposes the ability to work collaboratively. Counselors should stress the importance of collaboration to all members of the group, and as facilitator of the group as a whole. This should be done at all levels of interaction: identifying the problem, determining the necessary goals, creating strategies, implementing procedures, and evaluating outcomes.

Professional Issues

Legal and Ethical Considerations

Legal and ethical obligations
Counselors are obligated both explicitly and implicitly to treat each of their clients ethically and within legal boundaries. Counselors need to be aware of all federal, state, district and other institutional laws and mandates regarding school counseling. Counselors also should recognize the ethical obligation to be cognizant of current research and resources pertaining to issues that students will be dealing with in the counseling sessions. Although it is understandable that no one can know resources for all the possible situations facing students, it is nonetheless ethically required of counselors to endeavor to add to his/her knowledge as is reasonable, to best serve the students. Counselors who are beginning their careers may spend more time researching specific issues, but will become more increasingly more knowledgeable about issues affecting students. Professional associations provide guidelines and sources for counselors regarding this aspect.

Ethics

Standards
Ethical standards are developed by most professional organizations, and are designed to direct the behavior of its members. The ethical standards for school counselors are frequently updated to reflect changes in the school system, usually at the federal level. These updated standards are revised in order to be relevant and appropriate for the school counseling profession. Ethical standards generally address the following three purposes:

1. To educate members about sound ethical conduct.

2. To provide a mechanism for accountability.
3. To provide a mechanism for improvement of professional practices.

The ACA's Code of Ethics is based on the following five moral principles:

1. Autonomy – the ability to make independent decision.
2. Justice – treatment that is fair and appropriate.
3. Beneficence – services and actions that are in the students' best interests.
4. Fidelity – commitment to the student regarding honor, loyalty and faithfulness.
5. Nonmaleficence – avoidance of actions or services that would cause harm to others.

Codes of ethics
Codes of ethics for the counseling profession generally apply to and are designed for actions and behavior that are best for the student, the situation, and the profession. These codes are reviewed and revised as appropriate. The most current revision in August 2005 addresses the following key areas:

- The Association asks for clarity regarding all ethical responsibilities for current members.
- The Association and its Codes support the mission of the membership.
- The Association endeavors to establish principles by which ethical behavior is identified, and the practices of its members are delineated.
- The Association assists its members in generating a course of action that will utilize counseling services and promote the overall values of the counseling profession.
- The Association establishes the manner in which ethical complaints should be processed, and inquiries against its members should be initiated.

Since the ASCA falls under the organizational umbrella of the ACA, its Code of Ethics parallels that of the ACA in general scope of benefit to the student, the situation, and the profession. The ASCA Code is delineated more specifically through its eight major sections:

1. Duties to Students
2. Duties to Parents
3. Duties to Colleagues and Professional Associates
4. Duties to the School and Region
5. Duties to Self
6. Duties to the Profession
7. Adherence to Standards
8. Resource Materials

Counselors should treat each student with respect and consider the student's best interest. They should involve the parents when possible, and exhibit professional and ethical behavior. They should also maintain their expertise through continued learning and development. School counselors should be well versed on both the ACA Code of Ethics, and the ASCA Code of Ethics. They should endeavor to incorporate the tenets of both in their professional life, and carefully research both in the event of an ethical dilemma.

There is some responsibility on the part of the school counselor to critically apply codes of ethics in his/her professional life. It is worth noting that there are minor differences in the codes of ethics published by different professional organizations, for instance between those published by the ACA for counselors in general, and by the ASCA for school counselors in particular. Counselors should be cognizant of the codes and any relevant disparities, and be prepared to apply the appropriate code based on both the counseling setting, and in what capacity the counselor is operating. There are also, on occasion, ethical codes regarding a particular situation or relationship that seem to conflict with laws governing the same relationship or situation. Counselors are, within reason, obligated to adhere to the applicable law.

However, counselors are encouraged to participate in the dynamics of setting ethical standards by initiating changes to mandates as appropriate.

Determining ethical problems
There are prescribed steps to take in the process of identifying and addressing an ethical problem in the counseling profession. Both the ACA and the ASCA delineate these steps, with those generated by the ASCA tailored to the school counseling profession. The ACA model is comprised of the following steps:

1. Recognize the issue.
2. Consult direction from the ACA Code of Ethics.
3. Identify the type of issue and its components.
4. Consider possible courses of action.
5. Identify the potential consequences of each course, and choose the most appropriate action.
6. Assess the results of the course of action.
7. Implement the course of action.

The ASCA model specifies:

1. Identify the issue both realistically and philosophically.
2. Consult direction from the law, the ACA Code of Ethics, and the ASCA Code of Ethics.
3. Factor in the developmental and chronological age of the student.
4. Assess the student rights, parental rights, and circumstances.
5. Adhere to ethical and moral principles.
6. Identify the potential courses of action and consequences.
7. Assess the results of the selected action.
8. Consult.
9. Implement the action.

Laws

Although laws are based on generally

accepted norms, customs, values and beliefs, they are more binding and carry more severe penalties than ethical standards. Laws are codified into written governing documents. Laws are more prescriptive and require that counselors comply or be penalized. Both laws and ethical standards are designed to ensure that professionals following appropriate behavior patterns and act in the best interests of the student(s). Laws and ethical standards should adhere to the same patterns and expectations, but if on occasion a law conflicts with an ethical standard, the counselor is encouraged to comply with the law. Counselors must advise the student if they encounter a situation where the laws and ethical standards are in conflict, and inform the student that they will follow the legal course of action, provided there is no harm to the student as a result.

Counseling behavior
There are numerous laws and levels of law governing the behaviors, expectations and limitations of school counselors. Counselors are obligated to follow the laws of their state, and those of the federal government. However, these laws may be further tempered by statutory laws, common laws and/or appellate decisions. Although counselors are not expected to be legal experts, they should nonetheless be cognizant of the federal and state laws governing their scope of responsibility. As needed, they should critically analyze relevant interpretations of the law, such as in common law. They should also refer to peripheral mandates and appellate decisions if a particular situation warrants the time and clarification of researching it to this extent. If counselors are researching appellate decisions, they should have a working knowledge of the appeal process in their particular state, and any relevant appeal procedures in other states, should the situation call for reference to precedent.

Statutory law
Federal law serves to enact the Constitution. Under this umbrella, state laws generally address education, health, and other comparable programs through mandates. These state mandates, the body of which is referred to as statutory law, are created through legislation passed by state legislatures and the U.S. Congress. State mandates generally are more specific and more prescribed than federal laws, although they cannot be more restrictive than federal law. State legislatures create state laws that implement federal legislation, as well as laws specific to the state. The federal government has also passed several laws, within the parameters of the Constitution, that affect professional school counselors and others in comparable fields. Because statutory law generally addresses issues related to health and education, school counselors should be well versed in relevant state law, but should also be aware of federal laws that can affect their profession.

In the broadest sense, governance is the interpretation and implementation of codified laws. Tailored to the school counseling profession, the state legislatures as a rule create legislation that addresses the field of education, from which state and local agencies interpret and implement rules and guidelines. The state boards of education generally enact regulations at the school district level that either address areas not specifically addressed in state legislation, or interpret it more specifically to that arena. These regulations or guidelines are not legally binding like legislation, but are representative of how agencies view certain circumstances. This interpretation is subject to the oversight of the state attorney general, particularly if a regulation is challenged. Local school systems may also develop guidelines and policies, tailoring state regulations to the local environs. Individual schools may further refine these policies addressing the professional behavior of school counselors.

Incorporating knowledge of law
For school counselors to act professionally and ethically, a basic knowledge of the laws governing their profession is expected.

Beyond that, counselors should avail themselves of information regarding updates or interpretations of relevant law, and other pertinent data. Sources for this information can include on-site supervisors, ACA newsletters, professional journals, commercially available newsletters, the internet, etc. Counselors should recognize that the law and its interpretation are not static, and knowledge of the law needs to be maintained on an ongoing basis. Counselors also have the responsibility to implement and interpret the law reasonably. If state mandates appear to be in conflict with other regulations or ethical standards, counselors should apply common sense and critical thinking to the interpretation or application of the ruling. If this should occur, any decisions or actions should be documented carefully, and counselors should bring the conflict to the attention of appropriate parties as soon as possible.

Subpoenas
Counselors may be served with subpoenas, relating to allegations of child abuse, neglect, custody disputes, etc. Counselors should recognize that subpoenas are legal documents, but should respond within the context of his/her obligation to the student and the school guidelines. Counselors should not violate a student's confidentiality beyond that mandated in the school guidelines. The subpoena should always be discussed with the student or the student's attorney, and in some cases the school attorney, before any information is provided to a legal entity. Once the appropriate counsel approves compliance with the subpoena, school counselors should then discuss how the release of information will affect all parties, and should obtain a signed informed-consent form in order to release necessary records. If, on the other hand, the attorneys do not approve the release of information, they should file a motion to quash, which will release the counselor from the obligation to respond. All actions should be clear and documented.

HIPAA and FERPA regulations
There are three key federal acts governing the disclosure of student records. The most significant is the Family Educational Rights and Privacy Act (FERPA) of 1974, which limits the disclosure of student records. The Privacy Rule of 2001 established national rights for privacy and security regarding health information, which rights were in concert with FERPA. The Health Insurance Portability and Accountability Act (HIPAA) of 1996 generated national standards regarding the privacy of individually identified health information, set criteria for health records, and delineated patients' rights. Any school records, including health records, that are protected under FERPA are not subject to HIPAA regulations, however educators in special education may be required to obtain the services of outside professionals whose services are governed by HIPAA. Counselors should be knowledgeable and aware of regulations regarding the exchange of student information and when exceptions to FERPA are warranted by HIPAA or other law.

Suspicion of child abuse

Counselors are required by federal mandate to report any cases of child abuse or neglect. This is mandated by the Keeping Children and Families Safe Act of 2003. If a counselor or other professional has reason to believe that abuse or neglect has occurred within 24 to 72 hours, s/he is obligated to call Child Protective Services (CPS) and report orally and in writing their suspicions within a time frame specified by the state. Note that if a report proves false, the counselor/professional is not liable unless the report was made with malicious intent. Child abuse can include physical abuse, mental injury, sexual abuse or exploitation, maltreatment of a child under 18 or the age specified by the state child protection law, and negligent treatment. Counselors should be knowledgeable of state and other mandates regarding the report of child abuse.

Counselors who suspect child abuse and do not report it could lose their license or certification, face disciplinary action, and/or have their employment terminated. It is also significant to remember that an individual who reports reasonable suspicion of child abuse is not required to prove the abuse, but rather just to report suspicion. The law protects the individual who reasonably suspects child abuse. Also notable is that parents and guardians are not granted rights to information during this process, and should not be informed regarding the report. The department of social services and/or law enforcement agencies will contact the parents as appropriate, and will conduct the investigation. Counselors should be knowledgeable about laws regarding child abuse, as well as school, district and other applicable procedures.

Confidentiality

Counselors are both legally and professionally committed to respect and protect students' confidentiality. The primary professional consideration relates to the establishment of trust with the student. Confidentiality essentially belongs to the student. It is his or her right and choice to disclose information. Counselors who respect this contribute to the cultivation of trust that is vital to the counselor-client relationship. However, if students who are under 18, this legal right expands to the students' parents. In the case of counselors working with students under the age of 18, they can request that parents respect the student's confidentiality, but parents of minors are allowed to be present during the session(s). Nonetheless, whether a student is a minor or over 18, counselors can communicate with the students regarding their rights and responsibilities relating to confidentiality, such as whether it is optional or not that parents be informed.
There are certain circumstances, as outlined in the ACA Code of Ethics, whereby a counselor may break, and in some cases is obligated to break, student confidentiality.

Generally, counselors may break confidentiality if a student is in danger of harming his/herself or others, if there is indication of abuse, or if there is any other life-threatening situation. There are other circumstances for which confidentiality may be breached:

- Counselors may disclose confidential documents with subordinates in the regular course of business.
- Members of treatment teams, consultation groups, families, and third-party players may break confidentiality through regular verbal interaction.
- Parents may be legally informed of the counseling discussions held with their minor children.
- Parents or family members may be justifiably informed if they could contact a life-threatening disease through association with the student.
- Court-ordered disclosure by way of a subpoena may require the counselor to share information, although that information can be restricted to what is necessary.

Minor consent laws are mandated at the state level and define the circumstances under which counselors may protect the confidentiality of a minor student. These laws fall under the federal regulation that prohibits the breaking of confidentiality for patient recovery, regardless of the patient's minor status. Generally, minor consent laws allow confidentiality regarding issues such as substance abuse, mental health, and reproductive health areas, without releasing information to parents or guardians. There is some controversy regarding the interpretation of these laws, but a common implementation is a school-based student assistant program (SAP) comprised of teams that include a counselor, a counselor or a nurse, a teacher and possibly substance abuse assessors from local agencies. School staff can refer students to the SAP team who will collaboratively determine best action for the student. Counselors should be well informed about the state mandates and local interpretations of the minor consent law.

Counseling minors

The ideal situation regarding a minor student is if a student readily accepts and invites his/her parents to participate in the session(s). However, if this is not the case, there are steps counselors can take to ease the disclosure. Counselors should discuss confidentiality with students at the initial session, and let them know the legal parameters. Students may be hesitant to let parents know about their problems, for fear of the parents' reactions. Also, when broaching the subject of disclosure, counselors should be sensitive to the possibility of family secrets, sensitive information, cultural issues and other factors that could be problematic when including parents in counseling session. Counselors can work students to get them comfortable with the idea of including their parents, and can discuss reasonable boundaries before the parents are invited to participate. However, if minor students refuse to include their parents or to give permission to disclose information, counselors may be obligated to inform the parents without the student's permission.

Providing competence

In addition to keeping abreast of laws and guidelines, counselors should include the following practices in order to provide current, optimum competence to their clients:

- Pursue opportunities for professional development. Most national and state credentials even require counselors to complete continuing educations training in order to stay current on theories, trends, and new data in the field.

- Remain current within the counselor's area of responsibility by reading, consulting, networking, and otherwise bringing new research, trends, and information as added resources for serving the clients.
- Represent credentials accurately. Only earned and applicable credentials should be listed.
- Provide only those services for which the counselor is trained and qualified. Counselors should have training in a particular technique before they practice it and should not try to work with students who have conditions beyond the counselor's realm of knowledge.

Changing behavior

Achieving goals is never an easy thing to do. Counselors assert that recognizing a negative behavior is the first step towards change. Many individuals will undergo a period of self-observation before they decide that they need to alter their behavior. During this period, they may identify the triggers for the particular behavior, and they may try to discover the underlying psychological reasons for the behavior. Oftentimes, a change is more successful if the individual makes his or her goals known, or even signs a contract pledging the change. The most important factor in achieving a long-term change, however, is confidence. Study after study shows that individuals who are optimistic about their chances for permanent positive change are very likely to achieve it.

Locus of control
One of the factors counselors have identified as being crucial to an individual's ability to change his or her behavior is the locus of control. When an individual believes that he or she can positively influence his or her own behavior, he or she is said to have an internal locus of control. Individuals who believe external forces (like their friends, their neighborhood, or the society as a whole) will

determine their behavior are said to have an external locus of control. Studies have shown time and again that individuals with an internal locus of control are far more likely to make long-lasting positive changes. Individuals who have an external locus of control are less likely to seek help and rate their behavior more poorly overall.

Reinforcements and self-talk
Individuals can improve their chances of reaching their goals if they implement a program of reinforcement. In such a program, an individual gives him or herself a reward for clear progress towards the goal, or gives him or herself a punishment for negative or counterproductive behavior. Research has also shown that an individual can influence their chances of success with their self-talk, or the messages they send themselves. In other words, an individual who consistently praises him or herself for a job well done is more likely to repeat a positive behavior, while individuals who beat themselves up over every minor mistake or relapse into a negative behavior are more likely to commit that behavior in the future.

Intellectual health

When counselors consider a person's intellectual health, they are considering his or her ability to gather and process information, to make decisions, to set goals, and to solve problems. Intellectual health also means being able to learn from experience, being open to new ideas, and being able to question and evaluate new information. This ability to think critically about new information will be crucial to success in every area of life: for instance, achieving social health means choosing one's friends carefully, and achieving physical health means making the right decisions for one's body. One aspect of intellectual intelligence that has become increasingly discussed in the counseling community is emotional intelligence, the ability to manage one's moods.

Substance abuse

Alcohol and alcohol abuse
Any liquid that contains sugar and is fermented will produce the colorless liquid known as alcohol. The kind of alcohol found in alcoholic beverages is ethyl alcohol. Since different alcoholic beverages contain different amounts of alcohol, a standard measurement for one drink has been created. In health literature, a single drink may be 12 ounces of beer (assumed to be 5% alcohol), 4 ounces of table wine (12% alcohol), 2.5 ounces of fortified wine (20%), or one ounce of distilled spirits (50% alcohol). Each of these drinks contains approximately half an ounce of ethyl alcohol. The amount of alcohol may also be measured in terms of proof, which is derived by multiplying the percentage of alcohol by 2. Thus, a bottle of whiskey that is 40% alcohol will be marked as 80 proof.

Alcohol has been popular throughout history because it depresses the central nervous system and makes people feel more relaxed. People also often drink in celebration, or when meeting with friends, as alcohol tends to reduce inhibitions and male conversation easier. People who drink alcohol often report feeling smarter, sexier, or stronger, even if studies indicate the opposite. Alcohol is also used by many people as a way to escape personal problems or a bad mood. Many people drink because they are swayed by the massive advertising campaigns launched by brewers; indeed, there is often controversy over the effects of alcohol advertising on underage consumers. Finally, many people drink in order to emulate people they admire, whether famous figures, family members, or peers.

The individuals who are at great risk of developing health problems from alcohol are those who follow the patterns known as problem drinking and binge drinking. Problem drinking is defined as any amount of drinking that interferes with a major part of the individual's life, whether safety, sleep, energy, family relationships, sexual activity, or health. Although some of the negative consequences associated with problem drinking are immediate (like bad judgment and physical impairment), other effects of consistent alcohol abuse may only be evident over the long term. Binge drinking is defined for a man as having five or more drinks in a sitting (the amount is four for a woman).Binge drinking is most common among young, single men.

Alcohol abuse is defined by the American Psychiatric Association as the continued use of alcohol despite an awareness of any social, physical, psychological, or professional problems it is causing. Alcohol abuse can also entail drinking in dangerous situations, for instance before driving a car. An individual who is diagnosed as an alcohol abuser usually has trouble fulfilling one of his or her major roles at work, school, or home, and may have legal problems related to alcohol. He or she may frequently abuse alcohol at inappropriate or dangerous times, like at work or before driving. Also, an individual may be diagnosed as having a problem with alcohol abuse if he or she continues to drink despite persistent relation trouble caused by drinking.

The National Council on Alcoholism and Drug Dependence consider alcoholism as a disease that is influenced by social, environmental, and genetic factors. The common features of alcoholism are the inability to control consumption, continued drinking despite negative consequences, and distorted thinking patterns (like irrational denial). It is important to note that alcoholism is not simply the result of a weak will, but is a physiological state that may require medical treatment to be corrected. Many individuals may have a problem with alcoholism and not realize it if they are still functional in the rest of their life and if they only drink in social situations. Alcoholics tend to be those who, even when they are not drinking, place an undue amount of psychological emphasis on alcohol.

Although there is not yet any hard evidence, there is plenty of anecdotal material to suggest that individuals can inherit a predisposition to alcoholism. For instance, the son of an alcoholic white male is four times as likely to develop alcoholism, even if he was adopted by another family at birth. Interestingly, the identical twin of an alcoholic is twice as likely as a fraternal twin to develop a disorder related to alcoholism. Brain scans have shown that the sons of alcoholic fathers have a characteristic pattern of brain wave activity. Still, despite all of this fascinating data, it should be noted that scientists have not yet been able to identify the specific gene that makes an individual more susceptible to alcoholism.

In order to figure out what amount of alcohol a person may consume at a time, it is important to determine their blood-alcohol concentration. BAC is the measure taken by breath or urine samples, including those administered to drivers suspected of being under the influence. According to the Federal Department of Transportation, a person should be considered unfit to drive if he or she has a BAC of 0.08% or higher. This is approximately the BAC that a 150-pound man will have after consuming three drinks in an hour. A BAC of 0.05% or higher will cause a person to experience many of the problems associated with intoxication; a BAC of 0.2% will probably result in the person losing consciousness; a BAC of 0.03% can result in a coma; and a BAC of 0.4% generally means death.

There are a few things that will determine the severity of an individual's response to alcohol. Obviously, the more alcohol that is consumed, the higher the individual's blood-alcohol concentration will be. Also, since the liver can only process half an ounce of alcohol every hour, drinking quickly will result in a higher level of intoxication. More potent forms of alcohol, like liquor and fortified wine, get into the bloodstream more quickly, especially if they are accompanied by carbonated beverages. Heavy individuals tend

Copyright © Mometrix Media. You have been licensed one copy of this document for personal use only.
Any other reproduction or redistribution is strictly prohibited. All rights reserved.

to get drunk more slowly, as they have an excess of water with which to dilute the incoming alcohol. Women typically can drink less than men, because they have less of the stomach enzyme that neutralizes alcohol. Older individuals tend to have less water; therefore, they are more affected by alcohol. If an individual has an empty stomach, does not regularly consume alcohol, or has taken some prescription medicines, he or she will be more quickly intoxicated.

The immediate consequence of alcohol consumption is intoxication. Individuals who become intoxicated from alcohol will exhibit negative behavioral and psychological changes, which may include aggressive behavior, inappropriate sexual conduct, mood changes, or impaired judgment. Intoxication is generally manifested in the following: slurred speech, poor coordination, unsteady walking, abnormal eye movements, impaired concentration and memory, and a general stupor. Severe intoxication may cause a loss of concentration, coma, and even death. Intoxicated individuals are also at greater risk of infection, as alcohol suppresses the work of the immune system. Severely intoxicated individuals may be at risk of shock, particularly if they lose consciousness.

From the moment it is consumed, and even before the individual notices any of the psychological effects, alcohol is at work in the human body. It is almost immediately absorbed into the bloodstream through the walls of the stomach and the upper intestine. Typically, it takes about fifteen minutes for the alcohol in a drink to reach the bloodstream, and usually about an hour for the amount of alcohol to reach its peak. Once in the bloodstream, alcohol is carried to the liver, heart, and brain. Although alcohol cannot leave the body until it is metabolized by the liver, it is a diuretic, which accelerates the removal of other liquids from the body; thus, alcohol has a dehydrating effect. Alcohol also lowers the temperature of the body.

Alcohol has a number of effects on behavior and judgment. For one thing, it is known to impair sensory perceptions: the eye is less able to adjust to bright lights, and the ear has difficulty distinguishing sounds. The senses of smell and taste are also diminished by excessive consumption of alcohol. Alcohol will decrease sensitivity in general, making it possible for individuals to feel comfortable in extreme temperatures that may be hazardous to their health. Intoxication typically causes an impairment of motor skills, meaning that activities performed with the muscles cannot be done with any precision or coordination. Finally, intoxication usually has a negative effect on sexual performance, even though it may increase interest in sexual activity.

Drug abuse
In recent years, medical professionals have shifted from viewing drug addiction as a sign of immorality to seeing it as a legitimate physiological disorder, which can be treated by medicine and psychological therapy. Scientists believe that prolonged use of drugs can cause chemical changes in the brain that create addiction, and can endure for the entirety of the person's life. The most common traits of chemical dependency are loss of control over dosage and frequency of use, and continued use despite harmful consequences. Unfortunately, one of the other common characteristics of drug addiction is the refusal to admit that it exists. Many doctors believe that only by removing the stigma of drug addiction will it be possible to treat all those who need help.

A drug is any chemical substance that changes the way a person acts or feels. Drugs may affect a person's mental, physical, and emotional state. Though many drugs are taken to improve the condition of the body, or to remedy personal problems, drugs can also undermine health by distorting a person's mind and weakening a person's body. According to the World Health Organization, drug abuse is any excessive drug use that is not approved by the medical profession. The use of some drugs in any quantity is considered abuse; other drugs must be taken in large quantities before they are considered to have been abused. There are health risks involved with the use of any drug, legal or illegal, insofar as they introduce a foreign substance into the balanced system of physical health.

In the United States, there are more than half a million health products that can be purchased without the approval of a doctor. Many of these products (aspirin, for example) can have serious side effects. Some drugs that could formerly only be obtained with a doctor's permission are now available for immediate purchase, though consumers should be aware of their possible dangers. Nasal sprays, for instance, can have the opposite effect than they intend if they are used too often. Laxatives can also do permanent damage to the body if they are taken too regularly. Eye drops may eventually make eyes redder if they are used habitually. Lastly, over-the-counter sleep aids have not yet been adequately researched, and some doctors suspect they may have negative consequences for mental health.

The particular effects experienced by a drug user depend on a few different variables: dosage, individual characteristics, and setting. For most drugs, an increase in dosage will intensify the effects of the drug. There may also be a change in the effect experienced from a drug at low dosage than from that same drug at a higher dosage. Every person will respond differently to a drug as well, depending on his or her psychological and physical state. The enzymes in the bloodstream play a major role in reducing drug levels in the blood, so an individual's drug experience will largely depend on the quality and quantity of his or her enzymes. Many people report a change in the effects of a drug related to their setting; a stressful situation, for instance, may cause the effects of some drugs to be more intense.

In clinical terms, intoxication is the behavioral, psychological, and physiological changes that occur in a drug user. In the beginning stages of drug addiction, the goal is usually intoxication. Later in the addiction process, however, the goal of use tends to be avoiding withdrawal symptoms. Withdrawal is any physiological distress that occurs because a drug is not taken. Many drug abusers take several different drugs, though they may prefer only one; this condition is known as polyabuse. Studies have also shown that there is a significant overlap between people with chemical dependencies and people with psychological disorders. This overlap is known as comorbidity, and in part, accounts for the profound problems that many drug abusers face in trying to escape their addictions.

Scientists have recently made great progress in understanding the biology of addiction by observing that many abused substances (alcohol, marijuana, and cocaine, for instance) trigger the release of dopamine in the brain. Dopamine is a neurochemical associated with the feeling of satisfaction and pleasure. Not only do many addictive substances raise the level of dopamine in the brain, they also alter the pathways through which dopamine is released and accessed in the brain, so that it becomes possible for the user to enjoy these feelings only when the particular substance is used. There is also evidence to suggest that individual born with especially low levels of dopamine may be more susceptible to drug addiction.

Some individuals are at a higher risk of addiction because they lack self-control, have no moral opposition to drugs, have low self-esteem, or are depressed. Research has also shown that individuals who live in isolation or in poverty are more likely to become addicted to drugs. People who associate with drug users are more likely to become users themselves. Drugs that produce a short-lived but intense state of intoxication (cocaine, for instance) are more likely to be addictive, as are those that have especially painful withdrawal symptoms. Most of the people who will experiment with drugs do so during adolescence. Although many have suggested that drugs like alcohol, tobacco, and marijuana lead to use of harder drugs, most research on this subject has been inconclusive.

For most drug users, the most difficult part of the recovery process is admitting that they have a problem. Sometimes, it is necessary for friends and family to intervene in order to get the user to realize the dangers of his or her behavior. Once this is accomplished, treatment can take place in an outpatient facility, a residential facility, or a hospital. Many individuals receive both physical and psychological therapy to help them break the addiction in its every form. For drugs that have painful withdrawal effects, it is recommended that the user be supervised closely by a professional. One of the key parts of any rehabilitation effort is continued contact with the patient after the period of therapy, as most addicts will relapse into their former behaviors after release.

Smoking
One of the most important factors associated with smoking appears to be education; for instance, about 90% of white males with less than a high school education are current or former smokers. Most scientists also believe that heredity plays a part in the development of a smoking habit. Studies have shown that identical twins (who have the same genes) are more likely to have similar smoking habits than fraternal twins. Young smokers are also very likely to have a parent, especially a mother, who smokes. Many youths will begin smoking either as a form of rebellion or simply to see if they like it. Unfortunately, young smokers rarely acknowledge the tremendous addictive power of cigarettes; most of them state that they are able to quit at any time, yet few actually do.

Nicotine is consistently shown to be far more addictive than alcohol; whereas only one in ten users of alcohol will eventually become alcoholics, approximately eight of ten heavy smokers will attempt and fail to quit. The method that nicotine uses is similar to that of other addictive substances: it creates an immediate positive feeling when taken; it will cause painful withdrawal symptoms if it is not taken; and it stimulates powerful cravings in the user even after it is removed from the system. Nicotine addiction can become so string that a heavy smoker will experience withdrawal symptoms a mere two hours after smoking. Persistent tobacco use will also lead to an increased tolerance for nicotine, and so the user will have to consume more and more to achieve the pleasure or avoid the pain.

Tobacco creates in the user certain psychological changes that may become addictive over time. For instance, nicotine is known to stimulate the part of the brain that generates feelings of satisfaction or well-being. Nicotine is also known to enhance memory temporarily, the performance of repetitive tasks, and the tolerance of pain. It is also credited with reducing hunger and anxiety. Individuals suffering from depression may also seek relief through tobacco. Studies have consistently shown that depressed individuals are far more likely than others to develop a smoking habit. Even more troubling, the effects of depression make it much more difficult to quit smoking, so the interdependent relation between tobacco use and depression is likely to continue for a long time.

Quitting: Nicotine patches, formally known as nicotine transdermal delivery systems, are affixed to the skin and slowly provide a low level of nicotine to the body. Typically, patches are worn for between 6 and 16 weeks. Although the patch is known to minimize withdrawal symptoms, it has been most successful only with those individuals who are highly motivated to quit, are enrolled in some kind of counseling program, and were smoking more than a pack of cigarettes every day. Doctors caution those who use the patch that, although it can help diminish the physical dependency on nicotine, it does not reduce the psychological addiction. Pregnant

- 150 -

women and individuals with heart disease should not use the patch, and under no circumstances should any individual wear more than one patch at a time.

Many individuals who have tried unsuccessfully to quit smoking in the past will explore hypnosis and acupuncture therapy. When hypnosis is used, the individual is put into a mild trance state and given suggestions that will hopefully persuade them to quit smoking. Hypnosis may not affect the physical dependence on nicotine, but it can create a good attitude for quitting successfully. When acupuncture therapy is given, the individual has a circular needle or staple inserted into the flap in front of his or her ear hole. This therapy is meant to stimulate the production of calming chemicals in the brain, and those who are given the therapy are encouraged to move the needle or staple gently when they feel a temptation to smoke.

Phobias

The most common kind of anxiety disorder is a phobia, an irrational and intense fear of some object or situation. About one in ten adults will develop some kind of intense phobia at some point in his or her life. Although many prescription medications have been used to treat phobias, none seem to be very effective unless they are taken along with behavior therapy, in which the individual is subjected to gradually increasing levels of the feared object or situation. Medical hypnosis therapy has also proved effective in combating phobias. An individual may have developed a phobia if he or she recognizes that the fear is excessive or irrational, and is unable to function because of fear.

Mental disorders

Panic attacks and panic disorder
Panic attacks are massive feelings of anxiety, often accompanied by hyperventilation, racing pulse, and dizziness. The victim of a panic attack may become numb in some of their extremities, and will usually feel a string sense of impending doom. Most of these attacks climax after about ten minutes. If an individual has frequent panic attacks, he or she may be said to have panic disorder. About one-third of all individuals will experience a panic attack before the age of 35. There are two common treatments for panic disorder: cognitive-behavioral therapy, in which the individual learns specific strategies for dealing with a panic attack; and anti-anxiety medication, which only seems to work well when it is combined with behavioral therapy.

Obsessive-compulsive disorder
One extreme kind of anxiety disorder is obsessive-compulsive disorder, in which the individual is plagued by a recurring thought that they cannot escape, and may display repetitive, rigidly formalized behavior. Individuals who suffer from OCD are most often plagued by thoughts of violence, contamination (for instance, being concerned that they are infected), or doubt. The most common compulsions among individuals with OCD are hand washing, cleaning, counting, or checking locks. Individuals suffering from OCD probably recognize that their behavior is irrational but feel powerless to stop it. OCD will eventually get in the way of the person's functioning in other areas of life, and will require treatment. Though OCD is thought to have biological origins, it can be treated with a combination of medication and behavioral therapy.

Major depression
A major depression is an overwhelming feeling of sadness that extends over a long period of time. Though about one in ten Americans will experience a major depression in any given year, only about one in every three of these will seek treatment. Most cases of depression can be helped with psychotherapy, medication, or both. An individual may be depressed of he or she feels sad or discouraged for a long period, lacks energy, has difficulty concentrating, continually thinks of death or suicide,

withdraws from his or her social life, has no interest in sex, or has a major change in his or her eating or sleeping habits. Some individuals who do not respond to therapy or medication may receive electroconvulsive therapy, the administration of electrical current through electrodes placed on the scalp.

Manic depression (bipolar disorder)
Individuals suffering from manic depression will have violent mood swings, ranging from unbridled euphoria to crushing despair. An individual with this form of mental illness may also have wild, uncontrollable thoughts, unrealistic self-confidence, difficulty concentrating, delusions, hallucinations, and odd changes in behavior. During a "high," such an individual may make unrealistic and grandiose plans, or take dangerous risks. During a "low" period, the same individual will feel hopeless, and may contemplate suicide. Manic depression, otherwise known as bipolar disorder, is a very serious disorder that requires immediate medical treatment. Anti-convulsants and lithium carbonate are the most common drugs prescribed to treat this illness.

Suicide
Although suicide is not considered in itself to be a psychiatric disorder, it is the unfortunate result of many of these conditions. Every year about 30,000 Americans will take their own lives, and about ten times this number will make a serious attempt. The rate of suicide among citizens between the ages of 15 and 24 has tripled over the past thirty years. Men are about three times as likely to commit suicide as women, though women make the attempt far more often. The majority of suicides, especially those committed by young people, involve firearms. Suicide is more common among whites, though it appears to be rising quickly among African-American males. Counselors believe that as many as 80% of those who are at risk of suicide can be helped with immediate therapy.

There are a number of factors that can make an individual consider taking his or her own life. About 95% of those who commit suicide have some form of mental illness, most commonly depression or alcoholism. Individuals who for whatever reason have lost hope that their life will improve are at a high risk of suicide. There appears to be some hereditary influence, as well: about one in four who tries suicide has a family member who has killed him or herself. Autopsies have shown that suicidal individuals often have a low level of the neurotransmitter serotonin. Finally, it is well documented that individuals who have easy access to firearms are far more likely to commit suicide.

Schizophrenia
Schizophrenia, one of the most crippling forms of mental illness, exists when an individual loses the unity of his or her mind, and suffers impaired function in almost every mental area. An individual suffering from schizophrenia may see or hear things that do not exist, may believe that an external force is putting thoughts into their head or controlling their behavior, or may suffer delusions about their identity. Many schizophrenics will develop severe anxieties and will become obsessive about protecting themselves. For most individuals, antipsychotic drugs can help to restore mental control and minimize delusional episodes. However, these drugs can cause a person to become apathetic, and many impoverished individuals will lack the resources to receive treatment at all.

Eating disorders
Eating disorders have only been acknowledged and treated in the past few decades. The most common eating disorders are anorexia nervosa and bulimia nervosa. Typically, eating disorders have to do not only with food, but also with a person's overall self-esteem and body image. They are a threat to physical, psychological, and mental health. Some of the medical problems that stem from eating disorders are an increased susceptibility to cold, irregular heartbeat, bloating, constipation, and osteoporosis, the

growth of fine hair all over the body, depression, severe abdominal pain, and even sudden death. Individuals who have an eating disorder or who suspect that someone they know may have one should immediately see a doctor.

Many Americans are causing themselves serious harm by pursuing unhealthy dietary plans, often unnecessarily. Indeed, it has been observed that most people who are dieting should not be, and most people who should be are not succeeding. Few people actually diet for health reasons; most do so to improve their appearance. Extreme dieters are those who lose enough weight quickly to cause physical symptoms, such as vulnerability to cold and weakness. Extreme dieters tend to consume only a narrow range of foods, and may focus obsessively on diet as a remedy for all of their problems. Although extreme dieting is not technically anorexic behavior, it is considered dangerous and should be immediately stopped in consultation with a counselor.

Compulsive overeating

If an individual cannot stop him or herself from eating, if he or she eats a great deal or very quickly, then he or she may be considered a compulsive overeater. Compulsive overeaters eat even when they are full, and they often eat alone if they know that their consumption of food is worthy of shame. Most doctors agree that compulsive overeating is more likely to occur in women, especially those who suffer from low-self esteem or a sense of abandonment. It can be difficult to recover from compulsive overeating because, unlike other abused substances, food is a habit that cannot be completely kicked. A person should seek medical advice if they are constantly eating when depressed, if they get no satisfaction from food, or if they have the fear of not being able to stop eating once they start.

Binge eating

Closely related to compulsive overeating, binge eating is the swift consumption of an abnormally large amount of food. Individuals who have a problem with binge eating often feel they have no control over their eating, and typically binge at least twice a week over a period of six months. A particular binge often lasts for more than an hour, and may include the consumption of more than 2000 calories. Binge eaters do not use vomiting or laxatives to control their weight; instead, they simply become fat. This tends to lead to contributing symptoms like depression, anxiety, and low self-esteem. Some five million Americans may be binge eaters; it is most common in college-age women. People with a binge-eating problem should immediately seek medical attention.

Anorexia nervosa

People who suffer from anorexia nervosa believe that they are fat and seek to avoid eating at all costs. Even individuals with body weight far below normal tend to consider themselves unattractively overweight. In the restricting type of anorexia, the individual seeks to lower his or her weight by dieting, fasting, and exercising. In the binging/purging type of anorexia, the individual tries to limit his or her weight by ingesting huge amounts of food and then forcing him or herself to vomit or defecate. There is any number of possible causes of anorexia; it may be genetic, physiological, or social in origin. In any case, it is extremely destructive to the body and must be stopped as soon as possible.

Bulimia nervosa

Individuals who suffer from bulimia nervosa go on extended eating binges and then take drastic steps to reverse their effects. People with purging bulimia make themselves vomit or take massive doses of laxatives to remove food from their system; people with non-purging bulimia either fast or exercise excessively in an effort to lose weight gained during binges. Bulimia often develops after an extreme diet has reconfigured the brain to become obsessive about consumption and weight loss. Breaking the diet leads the individual to feel guilty and overcompensate

- 153 -

by purging. Bulimia, like anorexia, poses major risks to health and should be treated as soon as possible. It can cause dehydration, tooth decay, erosion of the esophagus, and eventually death.

Obesity
Obesity is defined by counselors as the state of an individual who is 20% or more than their ideal weight. Mild obesity means the person is between 20% and 40% higher; moderate obesity means the person is from 41% to 100% heavier than they should be; and severe obesity indicates a body weight more than 100% higher than the ideal. Every segment of American society has cases of obesity, although it is especially high among African-American and Mexican-American women. Of particular concern is child obesity, which has increased by about 50% in the last twenty years. Obesity in children increases the risk of heart disease, diabetes, and osteoporosis later in life. Obesity is often the result of slow and steady weight gain over a number of years rather than sudden change in lifestyle, so individuals should be on guard against developing obesity.

When obese individuals claim they have no control over their weight, they may be somewhat correct. There is a protein in the brain responsible for limiting food intake and signaling satiety; if this gene is defective, obesity can be the result. However, obesity may also be caused by the individual's failure to eat properly or get enough exercise. Impoverished people are more likely to be obese, partly because they are not taught about nutrition, and because a diet rich in fruits and vegetables can be expensive. Some individuals may be predisposed to obesity by overfeeding in childhood; their fat cells are large and numerous, and more likely to contribute to obesity. People who suffer from psychological disorders like depression and chronic anxiety are also more inclined to obesity.

There are numerous dangers to health associated with obesity. For one thing, obese individuals are almost three times as likely as their fellows to have diabetes or high blood pressure. For women, obesity can lead to heart attacks, chronic chest pain, higher blood pressure, ovarian cancer, and breast cancer. For men, obesity may contribute to heart disease and to cancer of the colon, rectum, and prostate. More generally, obesity is often at the root of psychological problems like depression, guilt, and anxiety. However, it has been noted in many studies that the differences in health between obese and non-obese individuals seem to decline with age, raising the question of whether mild or moderate obesity can be condemned entirely.

Learning disabilities

Learning disabilities are physiological disorders that may damage a person's ability to store, process, and retrieve information. For the most part, learning disabilities affect reading and language skills. It is important to note that learning disabilities do not indicate that a student has a lower level of intelligence, or is more likely to be emotionally disturbed. Teachers should be aware of their students with learning disabilities, so that they can avoid discriminating against them for their handicaps. The most common learning disability is dyslexia. One reason why learning disabilities can be so frustrating is that they are so specific, so that a student who excels in almost every area of school may be terrible in one particular area.
There are a few common ways for teachers to minimize the problems their learning-disabled students face in a normal classroom. One way is to break complicated tasks down into a series of small steps; often, students with learning disabilities have a difficult time imagining the chain of tasks they will need to perform to accomplish some larger goal. Establishing a regular routine is also a good way to keep students involved in class. Learning-disabled students may need to learn abstract concepts through drawing, movement, or conversation. Finally, teachers can help remove some of the anxiety

- 154 -

associated with having a learning disability by assuring their students that it is all right to make mistakes, as long as the best effort is given.

Apraxia, dysgraphia, dyslexia, dyssemia, auditory discrimination, and visual perception

There are a few common learning disabilities that teachers are likely to encounter. *Apraxia* is the inability to plan motor activity; that is, the inability to move correctly to accomplish a particular task. *Dysgraphia* is difficulty in writing, and difficulty with spelling. *Dyslexia* is difficulty with language that extends beyond just reading. *Dyssemia* is any difficulty an individual may have distinguishing social cues and signals. Problems with *auditory discrimination* mean that a student has a hard time telling the differences between sounds and their sequence. Problems with *visual perception* are those in which a student has trouble identifying and assigning meaning to the things that he or she sees.

ADHD

Attention deficit/ hyperactivity disorder is the diagnosis given to a range of conditions in which the individual has a hard time controlling motion or sustaining attention. Although ADHD is typically thought of as a disorder that affects children, new research suggests that it is not outgrown, and that adults may be just as likely to suffer from it. Individuals suffering from ADHD are impulsive, constantly in motion, and easily distracted. They may feel perpetually restless, may be unusually forgetful, and are likely to be socially immature. Although there is no specific test to determine whether someone has ADHD, most doctors are trained to recognize the condition. Most of those who suffer from ADHD are benefited by behavioral therapy and medication.

Teachers should have little trouble identifying those students who may be suffering from attention deficit disorder, as the behavior of these students will probably be disruptive. Students with ADD usually make careless mistakes in their work and have a hard time sustaining their attention during long lecture periods. They are typically disorganized and often lose things. They may fidget a great deal with their hands, and just seem to have a great deal of nervous energy. They often talk too much and out of turn. They often have a difficult time working quietly and keeping their hands off of the other students. Many students are so afflicted by attention deficit disorder that they almost seem to be possessed, or driven by some internal motor.

Recognizing disabilities

Some students may struggle for years without ever realizing that they have a natural learning disability. For this reason, secondary school teachers should be familiar with the signs that a student may be learning disabled. One sign of a disability is spelling the same word several different ways in the same document. A teacher may also become alarmed if a student is unable to answer open-ended questions, or accomplish basic reading and writing tasks. If students seem to be consistently misreading information, or having a hard time grasping abstract concepts, they may be battling an undiagnosed learning disability. Finally, students with learning disabilities frequently have a hard time focusing on details and working at a fast pace.

Decision-making

The primary reason that the decision-making process is important is because understanding the process can aid in the discovery of a future rational and reasonable course of action when presented with a decision that needs to be made. Each individual has a different perspective and therefore a different way of coming to a particular decision, but through a combination of intuition, knowledge, and an understanding of how the process works, a decision that is more suited for the goals of a particular individual or group can be made. A well thought out method of decision-making consists of identifying the decision that needs to be made, identifying the benefits of each choice relating to that decision, identifying the potential drawbacks of making each choice relating to that decision, and finally actually making a choice. An individual or organization by understanding what needs to be identified at each stage of the decision-making process will be able to make a more informed decision that will be more likely to lead towards a particular goal.

Basic techniques

An individual that is attempting to make a well-informed decision will often attempt to gather as much information as possible from as many reliable sources as possible, list the advantages and disadvantages of each choice, and then compare each choice with each other. In an employment or business situation where finances are involved, an individual may use a mathematical approach and calculate exactly how much money each job choice or each potential new product could offer and how much it might cost the individual if something goes wrong. A mathematical approach, when it is possible to use one, can be an extremely sound strategy when attempting to determine which choice is more appropriate. However, many individuals do not make well-informed decisions and they may rely on random chance such as flipping a coin, on the opinions or pressure of the individual's peers, or rely heavily on information from unreliable sources such as a high school student's web page.

Actions to avoid

Some of the most common pitfalls that need to be avoided when attempting to make a well-informed decision are entering the decision-making process with a preconceived notion that the individual is unwilling to abandon, allowing peer pressure to influence a decision, and over-generalizing. Entering the decision-making process with a prejudice against a particular idea or source of information or with an inappropriate bias towards a particular choice will often lead to

the individual or group choosing an option that is not the best or most logical of the choices available. Outside sources should be used to gather information about the decision that needs to be made, but no single source should be allowed to force or pressure the individuals involved in making the decision into choosing a particular choice. Finally, the overuse of generalizations, stereotypes, and attempts to attribute effects to causes that may not have any logical link will often lead to a decision being made that may not be the best course of action.

Professional Development

Multicultural and anti-oppression training

As with developing counseling programs, counselors who conduct individual counseling sessions can sometimes suffer from a dearth of multicultural knowledge, at least in part because of the limited scope of their training. This can affect counselors' interactions with students as well as strategies for addressing problems. Many graduate programs fail to address cultures other than those with a Western European perspective. This can be a handicap for counselors working with a diverse student body, since they would lack a multicultural understanding of beliefs, terminology, historical oppression and other factors. Understandably, their approach in counseling at best would be irrelevant, and at worst offensive. Counselors working with a diverse student body would be well served to obtain multicultural training, develop relevant strategies for individual counseling, and collaborate with other counselors or school staff as appropriate for working with diverse cultures.

Traditional school counseling programs reflect long-practiced curricular parameters based on Caucasian/Western European culture and history. Consequently, practice and discussions tend to be non-inclusive of other cultures, and particularly diversity and multicultural counseling issues. Counselors who have been trained in a traditional Western European program are usually not adequately prepared to address issues associated with multicultural identities, including practices and environments of oppression. Without infusing additional multicultural training into a counseling program, counselors often unknowingly perpetuate the Western paradigm. The counselors and the programs they create will then lack an understanding of oppression, cultural histories, cultural identity, and how to strive for and assess multicultural competency. This is why the onus is usually on the counselor to obtain ongoing multicultural training, and to invest in research about multiculturalism and oppression, in order to bring a more comprehensive perspective into the school environment.

There are many resources available for teachers who would like to improve their sensitivity to differences in culture. The Center for Multicultural Education at the University of Washington maintains a comprehensive on-line library of multi-cultural information at http://depts.washington.edu/centerme/home.htm. Brigham Young University publishes Culturegrams, a series of summary descriptions of various cultural beliefs and practices. Teaching Tolerance is a biannual publication designed especially for teachers, and includes projects and activities that will encourage cultural literacy and appreciation. The International Multicultural Education Association publishes the Multicultural Messenger, with reviews of multicultural resources and news updates.

ACA

The American Counseling Association (ACA) is a professional organization that purposes to promote the development of counselors, advance the counseling profession, and promote social justice within the profession. Their scope is all professional counselors. The ACA seeks to apply the profession and practice of counseling to the purpose of promoting and respecting cultural diversity, while enhancing the overall quality of life in society. The ACA includes 18 divisions that focus on particular areas or work settings within the counseling profession, four geographic regions and 56 affiliate branches. It actually is comprised of a partnership of associations. The Association influences many aspects of professional counseling including credentialing of counselors, accreditation of counselor education programs, public policy and legislation, and professional resources and services. The Association operating in part through committees, holds functions and develops specific programs for the advancement of the profession.

The following are the 15 standing committees of the ACA, identified by the professional issues addressed by each:

1. Ethics
2. Awards
3. By-laws and Policies
4. Cyber-Technology
5. Financial Affairs
6. Human Rights
7. International
8. Interprofessional
9. Nominations and Elections
10. Professional Standards
11. Public Awareness and Support
12. Public Policy and Legislation
13. Publications
14. Research and Knowledge
15. Strategic Planning

Ad hoc task forces are created annually to address current concerns and relevant business issues. Most task forces are brought together for a year only, but can stay together if additional time is needed for the purposes at hand. In that case, members must be re-appointed. The ACA, with its affiliates, offers training workshops, professional development conferences, and learning institutes. ACA publications address current research and other relevant information.

Many ACA books are used as textbooks in counseling courses.

ASCA, NBCC, and CACREP

A subgroup of the ACA, the *American School Counselor Association* (ASCA) addresses those issues in professional counseling that pertain to students, with a focus on academic, personal-social, and career development issues. School counselors are particularly pivotal in the lives of students in that long-term life success patterns are often closely tied to academic success and a positive school experience. The ASCA provides additional information to school counselors through professional development, research and advocacy. The NBCC, *the National Board for Certified Counselors*, is the only national credentialing organization for counselors. The Board also has established several specialty-area certifications requiring passage of the National Counselor Exam (NCE). A corporate partner the ACA, the CACREP, the *Council for Accreditation of Counseling and Related Educational Programs*, establishes state-of-the-art standards for counselor education programs that address curriculum, program objectives, program evaluation, faculty and staff criteria and other requirements.

Secret Key #1 - Time is Your Greatest Enemy

Pace Yourself

Wear a watch. At the beginning of the test, check the time (or start a chronometer on your watch to count the minutes), and check the time after every few questions to make sure you are "on schedule."

If you are forced to speed up, do it efficiently. Usually one or more answer choices can be eliminated without too much difficulty. Above all, don't panic. Don't speed up and just begin guessing at random choices. By pacing yourself, and continually monitoring your progress against your watch, you will always know exactly how far ahead or behind you are with your available time. If you find that you are one minute behind on the test, don't skip one question without spending any time on it, just to catch back up. Take 15 fewer seconds on the next four questions, and after four questions you'll have caught back up. Once you catch back up, you can continue working each problem at your normal pace.

Furthermore, don't dwell on the problems that you were rushed on. If a problem was taking up too much time and you made a hurried guess, it must be difficult. The difficult questions are the ones you are most likely to miss anyway, so it isn't a big loss. It is better to end with more time than you need than to run out of time.

Lastly, sometimes it is beneficial to slow down if you are constantly getting ahead of time. You are always more likely to catch a careless mistake by working more slowly than quickly, and among very high-scoring test takers (those who are likely to have lots of time left over), careless errors affect the score more than mastery of material.

Secret Key #2 - Guessing is not Guesswork

You probably know that guessing is a good idea - unlike other standardized tests, there is no penalty for getting a wrong answer. Even if you have no idea about a question, you still have a 20-25% chance of getting it right.

Most test takers do not understand the impact that proper guessing can have on their score. Unless you score extremely high, guessing will significantly contribute to your final score.

Monkeys Take the Test

What most test takers don't realize is that to insure that 20-25% chance, you have to guess randomly. If you put 20 monkeys in a room to take this test, assuming they answered once per question and behaved themselves, on average they would get 20-25% of the questions correct. Put 20 test takers in the room, and the average will be much lower among guessed questions. Why?

16. The test writers intentionally write deceptive answer choices that "look" right. A test taker has no idea about a question, so picks the "best looking" answer, which is often wrong. The monkey has no idea what looks good and what doesn't, so will consistently be lucky about 20-25% of the time.
17. Test takers will eliminate answer choices from the guessing pool based on a hunch or intuition. Simple but correct answers often get excluded, leaving a 0% chance of being correct. The monkey has no clue, and often gets lucky with the best choice.

This is why the process of elimination endorsed by most test courses is flawed and detrimental to your performance- test takers don't guess, they make an ignorant stab in the dark that is usually worse than random.

$5 Challenge

Let me introduce one of the most valuable ideas of this course- the $5 challenge:

You only mark your "best guess" if you are willing to bet $5 on it.

You only eliminate choices from guessing if you are willing to bet $5 on it.

Why $5? Five dollars is an amount of money that is small yet not insignificant, and can really add up fast (20 questions could cost you $100). Likewise, each answer choice on one question of the test will have a small impact on your overall score, but it can really add up to a lot of points in the end.

The process of elimination IS valuable. The following shows your chance of guessing it right:

If you eliminate wrong answer choices until only this many remain:	1	2	3
Chance of getting it correct:	100%	50%	33%

However, if you accidentally eliminate the right answer or go on a hunch for an incorrect answer, your chances drop dramatically: to 0%. By guessing among all the answer choices, you are GUARANTEED to have a shot at the right answer.

That's why the $5 test is so valuable- if you give up the advantage and safety of a pure guess, it had better be worth the risk.

What we still haven't covered is how to be sure that whatever guess you make is truly random. Here's the easiest way:

Always pick the first answer choice among those remaining.

Such a technique means that you have decided, **before you see a single test question**, exactly how you are going to guess- and since the order of choices tells you nothing about which one is correct, this guessing technique is perfectly random.

This section is not meant to scare you away from making educated guesses or eliminating choices- you just need to define when a choice is worth eliminating. The $5 test, along with a pre-defined random guessing strategy, is the best way to make sure you reap all of the benefits of guessing.

Secret Key #3 - Practice Smarter, Not Harder

Many test takers delay the test preparation process because they dread the awful amounts of practice time they think necessary to succeed on the test. We have refined an effective method that will take you only a fraction of the time.

There are a number of "obstacles" in your way to succeed. Among these are answering questions, finishing in time, and mastering test-taking strategies. All must be executed on the day of the test at peak performance, or your score will suffer. The test is a mental marathon that has a large impact on your future.

Just like a marathon runner, it is important to work your way up to the full challenge. So first you just worry about questions, and then time, and finally strategy:

Success Strategy

1. Find a good source for practice tests.
2. If you are willing to make a larger time investment, consider using more than one study guide- often the different approaches of multiple authors will help you "get" difficult concepts.
3. Take a practice test with no time constraints, with all study helps "open

book." Take your time with questions and focus on applying strategies.

4. Take a practice test with time constraints, with all guides "open book."

5. Take a final practice test with no open material and time limits

If you have time to take more practice tests, just repeat step 5. By gradually exposing yourself to the full rigors of the test environment, you will condition your mind to the stress of test day and maximize your success.

Secret Key #4 - Prepare, Don't Procrastinate

Let me state an obvious fact: if you take the test three times, you will get three different scores. This is due to the way you feel on test day, the level of preparedness you have, and, despite the test writers' claims to the contrary, some tests WILL be easier for you than others.

Since your future depends so much on your score, you should maximize your chances of success. In order to maximize the likelihood of success, you've got to prepare in advance. This means taking practice tests and spending time learning the information and test taking strategies you will need to succeed.

Never take the test as a "practice" test, expecting that you can just take it again if you need to. Feel free to take sample tests on your own, but when you go to take the official test, be prepared, be focused, and do your best the first time!

Secret Key #5 - Test Yourself

Everyone knows that time is money. There is no need to spend too much of your time or too little of your time preparing for the test. You should only spend as much of your

precious time preparing as is necessary for you to get the score you need.

Once you have taken a practice test under real conditions of time constraints, then you will know if you are ready for the test or not.

If you have scored extremely high the first time that you take the practice test, then there is not much point in spending countless hours studying. You are already there.

Benchmark your abilities by retaking practice tests and seeing how much you have improved. Once you score high enough to guarantee success, then you are ready. If you have scored well below where you need, then knuckle down and begin studying in earnest. Check your improvement regularly through the use of practice tests under real conditions. Above all, don't worry, panic, or give up. The key is perseverance!

Then, when you go to take the test, remain confident and remember how well you did on the practice tests. If you can score high enough on a practice test, then you can do the same on the real thing.

General Strategies

The most important thing you can do is to ignore your fears and jump into the test immediately—do not be overwhelmed by any strange-sounding terms. You have to jump into the test like jumping into a pool- all at once is the easiest way.

Make Predictions

As you read and understand the question, try to guess what the answer will be. Remember that several of the answer choices are wrong, and once you begin reading them, your mind will immediately become cluttered with answer choices designed to throw you off. Your mind is typically the most focused immediately after you have read the question and digested its contents. If you can, try to predict what the correct answer will be. You may be surprised at what you can predict.

Quickly scan the choices and see if your prediction is in the listed answer choices. If it is, then you can be quite confident that you have the right answer. It still won't hurt to check the other answer choices, but most of the time, you've got it!

Answer the Question

It may seem obvious to only pick answer choices that answer the question, but the test writers can create some excellent answer choices that are wrong. Don't pick an answer just because it sounds right, or you believe it to be true. It MUST answer the question. Once you've made your selection, always go back and check it against the question and make sure that you didn't misread the question, and the answer choice does answer the question posed.

Benchmark

After you read the first answer choice, decide if you think it sounds correct or not. If it doesn't, move on to the next answer choice. If it does, mentally mark that answer choice. This doesn't mean that you've definitely selected it as your answer choice, it just means that it's the best you've seen thus far. Go ahead and read the next choice. If the next choice is worse than the one you've already selected, keep going to the next answer choice. If the next choice is better than the choice you've already selected, mentally mark the new answer choice as your best guess. The first answer choice that you select becomes your standard. Every other answer choice must be benchmarked against that standard. That choice is correct until proven otherwise by another answer choice beating it out. Once you've decided that no other answer choice seems as good, do one final check to ensure that your answer choice answers the question posed.

Valid Information

Don't discount any of the information provided in the question. Every piece of information may be necessary to determine the correct answer. None of the information in the question is there to throw you off (while the answer choices will certainly have information to throw you off). If two seemingly unrelated topics are discussed, don't ignore either. You can be confident there is a relationship, or it wouldn't be included in the question, and you are probably going to have to determine what is that relationship to find the answer.

Avoid "Fact Traps"

Don't get distracted by a choice that is factually true. Your search is for the answer that answers the question. Stay focused and don't fall for an answer that is true but incorrect. Always go back to the question and make sure you're choosing an answer that actually answers the question and is not just a true statement. An answer can be factually correct, but it MUST answer the question asked. Additionally, two answers can both be seemingly correct, so be sure to read all of the answer choices, and make sure that you get the one that BEST answers the question.

Milk the Question

Some of the questions may throw you completely off. They might deal with a subject you have not been exposed to, or one that you haven't reviewed in years. While your lack of knowledge about the subject will be a hindrance, the question itself can give you many clues that will help you find the correct answer. Read the question carefully and look for clues. Watch particularly for adjectives and nouns describing difficult terms or words that you don't recognize. Regardless of if you completely understand a word or not, replacing it with a synonym either provided or one you more familiar with may help you to understand what the questions are asking. Rather than wracking your mind about specific detailed information concerning a difficult term or word, try to use mental substitutes that are easier to understand.

The Trap of Familiarity

Don't just choose a word because you recognize it. On difficult questions, you may not recognize a number of words in the answer choices. The test writers don't put "make-believe" words on the test; so don't think that just because you only recognize all the words in one answer choice means that answer choice must be correct. If you only recognize words in one answer choice, then focus on that one. Is it correct? Try your best to determine if it is correct. If it is, that is great, but if it doesn't, eliminate it. Each word and answer choice you eliminate increases your chances of getting the question correct, even if you then have to guess among the unfamiliar choices.

Eliminate Answers

Eliminate choices as soon as you realize they are wrong. But be careful! Make sure you consider all of the possible answer choices. Just because one appears right, doesn't mean that the next one won't be even better! The test writers will usually put more than one good answer choice for every question, so read all of them. Don't worry if you are stuck between two that seem right. By getting down to just two remaining possible choices, your odds are now 50/50. Rather than wasting too much time, play the odds. You are guessing, but guessing wisely, because you've been able to knock out some of the answer choices that you know are wrong. If you are eliminating choices and realize that the last answer choice you are left with is also obviously wrong, don't panic. Start over and consider each choice again. There may easily be something that you missed the first time and will realize on the second pass.

Tough Questions

If you are stumped on a problem or it appears too hard or too difficult, don't waste time. Move on! Remember though, if you can quickly check for obviously incorrect answer choices, your chances of guessing correctly are greatly improved. Before you completely give up, at least try to knock out a couple of possible answers. Eliminate what you can and then guess at the remaining answer choices before moving on.

Brainstorm

If you get stuck on a difficult question, spend a few seconds quickly brainstorming. Run through the complete list of possible answer choices. Look at each choice and ask yourself, "Could this answer the question satisfactorily?" Go through each answer choice and consider it independently of the other. By systematically going through all possibilities, you may find something that you would otherwise overlook. Remember that when you get stuck, it's important to try to keep moving.

Read Carefully

Understand the problem. Read the question and answer choices carefully. Don't miss the question because you misread the terms. You have plenty of time to read each question thoroughly and make sure you understand what is being asked. Yet a happy medium must be attained, so don't waste too much time. You must read carefully, but efficiently.

Face Value

When in doubt, use common sense. Always accept the situation in the problem at face value. Don't read too much into it. These problems will not require you to make huge leaps of logic. The test writers aren't trying to throw you off with a cheap trick. If you have to go beyond creativity and make a leap of logic in order to have an answer choice answer the question, then you should look at the other answer choices. Don't overcomplicate the problem by creating theoretical relationships or explanations that will warp time or space. These are normal problems rooted in reality. It's just that the applicable relationship or explanation may not be readily apparent and you have to figure things out. Use your common sense to interpret anything that isn't clear.

Prefixes

If you're having trouble with a word in the question or answer choices, try dissecting it. Take advantage of every clue that the word might include. Prefixes and suffixes can be a huge help. Usually they allow you to determine a basic meaning. Pre- means before, post- means after, pro - is positive, de- is negative. From these prefixes and suffixes, you can get an idea of the general meaning of the word and try to put it into context. Beware though of any traps. Just because con is the opposite of pro, doesn't necessarily mean congress is the opposite of progress!

Hedge Phrases

Watch out for critical "hedge" phrases, such as likely, may, can, will often, sometimes, often, almost, mostly, usually, generally, rarely, sometimes. Question writers insert these hedge phrases to cover every possibility. Often an answer choice will be wrong simply because it leaves no room for exception. Avoid answer choices that have definitive words like "exactly," and "always".

Switchback Words

Stay alert for "switchbacks". These are the words and phrases frequently used to alert you to shifts in thought. The most common switchback word is "but". Others include although, however, nevertheless, on the other hand, even though, while, in spite of, despite, regardless of.

New Information

Correct answer choices will rarely have completely new information included. Answer choices typically are straightforward reflections of the material asked about and will directly relate to the question. If a new piece of information is included in an answer choice that doesn't even seem to relate to the topic being asked about, then that answer choice is likely incorrect. All of the information needed to answer the question is usually provided for you, and so you should not have to make guesses that are unsupported or choose answer choices that require unknown information that cannot be reasoned on its own.

Time Management

On technical questions, don't get lost on the technical terms. Don't spend too much time on any one question. If you don't know what a term means, then since you don't have a dictionary, odds are you aren't going to get much further. You should immediately recognize terms as whether or not you know them. If you don't, work with the other clues that you have, the other answer choices and terms provided, but don't waste too much time trying to figure out a difficult term.

Contextual Clues

Look for contextual clues. An answer can be right but not correct. The contextual clues will help you find the answer that is most right and is correct. Understand the context in which a phrase or statement is made. This will help you make important distinctions.

Don't Panic

Panicking will not answer any questions for you. Therefore, it isn't helpful. When you first see the question, if your mind goes blank, take a deep breath. Force yourself to mechanically go through the steps of solving the problem and using the strategies you've learned.

Pace Yourself

Don't get clock fever. It's easy to be overwhelmed when you're looking at a page full of questions, your mind is full of random thoughts and feeling confused, and the clock is ticking down faster than you would like. Calm down and maintain the pace that you have set for yourself. As long as you are on track by monitoring your pace, you are guaranteed to have enough time for yourself. When you get to the last few minutes of the test, it may seem like you won't have enough time left, but if you only have as many questions as you should have left at that point, then you're right on track!

Answer Selection

The best way to pick an answer choice is to eliminate all of those that are wrong, until only one is left and confirm that is the correct answer. Sometimes though, an answer choice may immediately look right. Be careful! Take a second to make sure that the other choices are not equally obvious. Don't make a hasty mistake. There are only two times that you should stop before checking other answers. First is when you are positive that the answer choice you have selected is correct. Second is when time is almost out and you have to make a quick guess!

Check Your Work

Since you will probably not know every term listed and the answer to every question, it is important that you get credit for the ones that you do know. Don't miss any questions through careless mistakes. If at all possible, try to take a second to look back over your answer selection and make sure you've selected the correct answer choice and haven't made a costly careless mistake (such as marking an answer choice that you didn't mean to mark). This quick double check should more than pay for itself in caught mistakes for the time it costs.

Beware of Directly Quoted Answers

Sometimes an answer choice will repeat word for word a portion of the question or reference section. However, beware of such exact duplication – it may be a trap! More than likely, the correct choice will paraphrase or summarize a point, rather than being exactly the same wording.

Slang

Scientific sounding answers are better than slang ones. An answer choice that begins "To compare the outcomes…" is much more likely to be correct than one that begins "Because some people insisted…"

Extreme Statements

Avoid wild answers that throw out highly controversial ideas that are proclaimed as established fact. An answer choice that states the "process should be used in certain situations, if…" is much more likely to be correct than one that states the "process should be discontinued completely." The first is a calm rational statement and doesn't even make a definitive, uncompromising stance, using a hedge word "if" to provide wiggle room, whereas the second choice is a radical idea and far more extreme.

Answer Choice Families

When you have two or more answer choices that are direct opposites or parallels, one of them is usually the correct answer. For instance, if one answer choice states "x increases" and another answer choice states "x decreases" or "y increases," then those two or three answer choices are very similar in construction and fall into the same family of answer choices. A family of answer choices is when two or three answer choices are very similar in construction, and yet often have a directly opposite meaning. Usually the correct answer choice will be in that family of answer choices. The "odd man out" or answer choice that doesn't seem to fit the parallel construction of the other answer choices is more likely to be incorrect.

Special Report: Additional Bonus Material

Due to our efforts to try to keep this book to a manageable length, we've created a link that will give you access to all of your additional bonus material.

Please visit http://www.mometrix.com/bonus948/priiscguidcoun to access the information.